770.8

# MASTERS OF PHOTOGRAPHY

# Daniela Mrázková

Hamlyn
Books

# Masters of Photography

*Photographs on dust-jacket:*
Front cover: Henri Cartier-Bresson
Back cover: Bill Brandt

Designed and produced by Artia for The Hamlyn
Publishing Group Limited, Bridge House,
69 London Road, Twickenham, Middlesex
TW1 3SB, England, and distributed for them by
HDS, Rushden, Northants NN10 9RZ, England

Text by Daniela Mrázková
Translated by Šimon Pellar
Graphic design by Aleš Krejča
Reproductions of original photographs by Blanka
Lamrová

Copyright © 1987 Artia, Prague

ISBN 0-600-35191-2
Printed in Czechoslovakia
2/99/76/51—01

# Contents

# Introduction

'From today painting is dead!' exclaimed Hippolyte Delaroche, the French painter, when he first saw a daguerreotype, the original form of photograph. 'The times of philosophy are over, the age of photography has begun,' stated some time later Jules Vallès, a writer and journalist in the Paris Commune. In fact, neither was right, since then, painting has not died as worried artists of the 1850s thought it would — what has changed, though, is its status and function. Philosophy has also flourished and has since formulated ways of profound, sensitive analysis of the laws of existence and outlined man's place in the world.

From its very beginnings, photography asserted itself with great vitality and force. Once light had been persuaded to produce an exact image of reality, photography mercilessly swept away miniature painting and made portraiture available to all. Then photography ventured into other traditional domains of painting: the landscape, still life and genre painting. Moreover, once Eadweard Muybridge had adopted photography to study the essentials of motion, photography became an invaluable tool for the scientist. When it reached the battlefields of the Crimean War, it established itself as an ever-present witness of the dramatic developments of the modern world. Ever since Jacob August Riis took up photography as a tool of social criticism, the medium has been a judge of man's deeds and social ills, and with the allegorical portraits by Mrs. Cameron or tableaux vivants produced by Oscar Rejlander, photography became an expression of man's creative genius and imagination.

Photography, this child of the modern age, has become the most employed pictorial medium of our time; it is a document, an expression, a message, a confession. Thanks to photography we have the world before our eyes in the public image as well as private moments of statesmen, movie stars, pop music idols and heroes of the sports arenas; the tragic and joyful events taking place every minute in every corner of the globe; the dark side of the Moon; intimate insights into the depths of the human soul; the fascinating drama of the development of the embryo inside the womb; the confusing labyrinth of the brain or the enigma of atom nuclei — all this has become intimately familiar, something we are able to see with our own eyes. We are even able to see what photography has not captured, we are able to see beyond the mere image because photography is also a projection of our own experience and imagination. Herein lies the secret of photography's magic, power and appeal because as a substitute of reality photography may be more powerful and appealing than reality itself.

Photography has become a modern image, a contemporary language more persuasive, more graphic and more communicative than speech. The story of photography is the history of the modern world, a living pictorial chronicle of the last hundred and fifty years. It is a unique memory bank of mankind, a fascinating story of drama, dreams, disappointment, hope, faith, aspirations and frustrations, a story not unlike the unique life story of every individual human being. It is the aim of this book to tell the story. Yet it is not going to be a traditional history of photography because this book will tell the story of photography through the life stories of those who have contributed significantly to the development of photography as an art by lending it new inspirations, tastes, rhythms and meaning. Different story tellers might select different protagonists for their story of photography. They would probably offer different arguments, select different pictures which would reflect best their own taste and opinion. And they would be perfectly within their rights, because in doing so they would merely offer a different point of view to a subject which by its very nature solicits as many opinions as there are photographs to take and people to look at them.

# I

# THE BIRTH OF PHOTOGRAPHY

When the French painter Hippolyte (Paul) Delaroche first saw a daguerreotype image, he was convinced that the days of painting were over. His conviction was quite understandable because the image that he saw on the silver-covered surface of a copper plate was a shiningly clear reproduction of nature, true to the last minute detail. It was a perfect copy of reality which he believed to be the ultimate objective of painting.

Word of M. Daguerre's sensational invention spread rapidly. Just one hour after the famous French physicist, Dominique François Arago, had officially announced Daguerre's invention at a session of the French *Académie des Sciences* on January 7, 1839, Paris opticians were besieged by people wanting to buy, or at least place an order for, the miraculous mechanism which produced pictures.

From their inception, people were so awed by these 'photogenic drawings' that some people even thought they were produced by supernatural powers. Magazine and newspaper articles of the period accounted unique emotions experienced when viewing photographs, and miracles taking place in front of the observer's eyes. M. Daguerre himself offered the following more didactic comment: 'The invention will prove invaluable not only to science but will be also a fresh impulse for the arts; it will not damage the artist but will benefit him greatly.' At the same time that Daguerre was becoming famous the press remained silent about Daguerre's compatriot J. N. Niepce who, in his efforts to develop a new lithographic reproduction process, had struck upon the very essence of the modern photographic process, the negative. For the time being, however, the fame and honour went to the direct positive method — the daguerreotype.

During the first ten years, from 1839 to 1849, some two thousand cameras and over half a million plates were sold in Paris alone. Over this single decade the daguerreotype developed into what we today regard as photography. In fact the term photography had been coined immediately following the conception of the daguerreotype and seems to have been first used by the Berlin astronomer Johann Mädler who spoke of Daguerre's inventions as 'photography' and actually used the word in print on February 25, 1839.

Thus, in a very few years, photography, albeit at first only in the form of a daguerreotype original which could not be duplicated, started winning the world. The new process was available to everybody because it was not only fast and highly graphic, but also cheap. It became one of the essential inventions of the modern age and rapidly found use in many spheres of life.

Among those who welcomed the invention most eagerly were natural scientists because they understood that with photography they were gaining a great new tool for scholarly research. Many painters quickly switched trades and established themselves as photographers. Some made the transition to make more money more quickly than they could ever hope to earn from painting. Other painters merely used the process instead of a traditional sketch. There were also some who loudly attacked the new art as an attempt to destroy painting and those who made a living from it. In a certain sense they were right because the portrait, previously only available to the high society, now became widely available in the form of photographs. Photographers could make a portrait of the aristocrat and worker alike — at a low price — completely revolutionising the art of portraiture. In 1849 alone some one hundred thousand Parisians had their daguerreotype taken. 'As a Narcissus, our pitiful society rushes to stare at its trivial image captured on a piece of metal,' complained Charles Baudelaire, the poet. 'All admirers of the sun have been seized by madness and a peculiar form of fanaticism.' Yet Baudelaire himself was one of the first to have his likeness captured by the new process.

Although period speculations envisioned the use of the daguerreotype process as an imitation of art, the report in which Dominique François Arago explained to the French government the importance of the process, intending the daguerreotype mainly as a vehicle for natural studies. The great physicist stated that the utilization of the process in natural sciences would bring about its fast development. After all, this was precisely the reason why Arago had descended from the ivory tower of his Paris observatory and decided to use his influence to seek support for Daguerre.

Daguerre was a skilful artist with a good head for business who had used the photographic idea of a retired officer named Niepce to produce perfect illusionist sets for his own theatre, cityscapes and landscapes, still lifes, and portraits of well-known ladies and gentlemen. Arago's speculation went further than even this: he suggested that the daguerreotype process be used in what was later to become photometry, stating that the process would enable scientists to determine absolute intensities of light by comparing their relative effects.

Despite its initial enormous success the daguerreotype became technically obsolete almost as soon as it appeared. Just three weeks after the sensational announcement of Daguerre's invention in France, an aristocrat of diverse scholarly interests named William Henry Fox Talbot presented his invention to the English public. Talbot's method used plain paper to produce perfect images for which the daguerreotype process had to use copper plate. His process could even copy images in any number desired. Talbot had invented his process sometime earlier but had simply hesitated too long and thus made his own process public only after having read about Arago's announcement across the Channel. Experimenting with what he called calotype and what was later renamed Talbotype in his honour, Talbot from the very beginning strived to develop the negative-positive process which has since become an essential of modern photography. The greatest advantage of his process is that any number of positive copies can be printed from a single negative. However, like the original and unreproduceable daguerreotype, Talbot's calotype soon itself became obsolete.

It was in 1851 that another Englishman, Frederick Scott Archer, came up with the so-called collodion process. Scott used a glass plate covered with a viscous collodion solution of potassium and other iodides to which light-sensitive chemicals were then applied. The process was a wet one which means that the collodion film lost its sensitivity as it dried and therefore had to be applied to the plate just prior to exposure. The main advantage of the process — to produce a near perfect image — was greatly offset by the disadvantage of the need to have a laboratory near at hand to develop the image promptly.

Each of the men who helped to improve and develop the process of photography in these early years was both an inventor and an artist, for all were looking for both the technical and aesthetic potentials of the medium. The dominant feature of the mid 18th century was the need to learn, discover and invent, to push the wheel of history forward and to put the new inventions into the service of all mankind. Photography was to become one of the great tools and pastimes of the age. As time went by the inventor was replaced by the businessman as the *spiritus àgens* of further development of photography, for it was the businessman who excelled in the art of making practical use of photography and doing so at a profit. Photography also owes much to its inherent marketability because without a possibility of wide use it could have never become as universal as it has.

A long series of associated events led to the first image that can be termed a photograph as we know it. The names of inventors who helped photography become what it is today can be found in any basic encyclopedia while others have been long forgotten because the rewards for their particular contribution were reaped by those who were just plain lucky or had more business acumen. It is generally forgotten that the principle of the *camera obscura,* though developed by the Renaissance scholar and artist, Leonardo da Vinci, can be traced as far back as the 4th century BC, to Aristotle and before. Neither should we forget people like Sir Isaac Newton, who, in the 17th century, formulated his theories concerning the properties of optical glass. Nor should the contribution of Angelo Sala, the Italian, or the German physicist and chemist Johann Heinrich Schulze, who in the 17th century arrived independently at the discovery of sensitivity of silver salts to light.

It was these and countless other scholarly, inquisitive and practical minds who paved the way for the first photograph produced by J. N. Niepce, titled *View from the Window at Gras,* which was made in 1826, thirteen years before the official announcement of the discovery of the photographic process made almost simultaneously by Louis Daguerre and William Fox Talbot. The actual date of this first photograph, however, is quite inconsequential as its potential at that time was missed because what Niepce was after was not a photograph but an improvement of lithography. (Ironically it was lithography which was soon to be improved by photography.) Even the terms negative and positive were not coined by the inventor of the process, Talbot, but by another Englishman, Sir John Herschel, the eminent astronomer, in 1840.

It is beyond doubt that photography was born to become more than just an art. Just as the physicist Arago was primarily interested in using photography to map the surface of the Moon and the inventor Daguerre in producing life-like sets for his theatrical productions, so the entire development of the new art only proved the original promise of the invention. Over the past 150 years photography has become a powerful tool, a witness of the visible and invisible events of this world, a judge of human deeds, *plus* a means through which man can express his imagination, ideas and dreams.

# Joseph Nicéphore Niepce

/1765—1833/

Although a professional soldier, J. N. Niepce won much less fame in combat than so many of his contemporaries. When he fell ill with typhoid fever, he resigned his commission and left the army. And yet the name of a virtually unknown, prematurely pensioned officer entered encyclopedias side by side with Napoleon, four years his younger, for Niepce lived in an age that was bent on discovering and inventing things. He was one of the first to build a bicycle, however, his design of a marine engine fuelled by powdered club moss remained a mere fancy.

He was only one of many who tried to discover various substitutes for things. For Europe, shuddering under the marching step of Napoleon's troops, had no other alternative if she wanted to sweeten her tea or dye her fabrics despite the English blockade. Indigo and sugar cane from overseas had to be replaced by European substitutes. The possibilities excited his brother Claude but Joseph Nicéphore had a different dream. He was fascinated by lithography. The process developed by Aloys Senefelder was just becoming fashionable, opening new possibilities for reproduction techniques and Niepce tried to replace the Solenhofen limestone by a different material which was available in France.

At first he experimented with stone found in a nearby vicinity. The polished surface of the stone was coated with asphalt (bitumen), engraved and then etched. During his experimental work Niepce discovered that asphalt exposed to light hardened and could not be washed off by oil. He tried to coat the prepared surface with other substances and even attempted to copy a transparent drawing, what was later to become the negative, onto the sensitized surface of the plate. Since he was not an expert draughtsman, he relied on the *camera obscura*. In fact as early as 1793 or thereabout Niepce and his brother Claude had already tried to use this popular painters' and draughtsmen's aid to produce permanent images with light.

That had been in Sardinia. Two years later when Niepce, then thirty, retired from the army, he first settled in Nice, in 1801 moving permanently to Châlon-sur-Saône where his and Claude's father managed a princely estate. Here Niepce spent his time reading his favourite Latin classics, writing verse and inventing things practical and impractical. It was also here that he kept returning to his original idea of capturing permanently the fleeting images of reality produced by the *camera obscura*.

His first work on the subject was published in 1802. Ten years later he took up the experiments again but it took another decade before he was to obtain the first permanent images. In 1822, using a glass plate sensitized with a coating of the widely available asphalt, Niepce produced a copy of an engraving representing Pope Pius VII which he then 'developed' by washing with a mixture of

lavender oil and kerosene to remove the unhardened unexposed places. Unfortunately, the plate was broken and lost during Niepce's lifetime. Had it been preserved, it would have constituted the first photographic print in the world. Niepce continued experimenting and refining his technique and in 1826 his efforts were at last crowned with success: the first extant photograph from nature fixed on a pewter plate. The image is some $20 \times 16$ cm in size and shows a view from Niepce's window at Gras near Châlon-sur-Saône, France. The bitumen of Judea (asphalt) film took 8 hours to expose as attested by shadows seen falling on both sides of the backyard.

A success at last! The following year Niepce brought the picture to Kew, England, where it was lost, only to be discovered in 1952 by the English historian Gernsheim, who obtained it for his collection.

Heliography, as Niepce called his process of producing images by sunlight, was born. Searching for a new lithographic reproduction process, Niepce stumbled upon the essentials of photography. Having progressively replaced lithographic stone with other

materials, namely glass, copper, zinc and silver, he was now afraid that the results of his painstaking work would be stolen and thus he refused to respond to Daguerre's first attempts to establish a partnership. In 1827 he presented a report on his invention to the Royal Society but because he omitted vital details, the Society refused to recognize his discovery.

In the end Niepce made a deal with Daguerre whose own experiments in the field had so far amounted to nothing. Prior to the conclusion of the deals, Niepce made another picture representing a laid table, again using a glass plate sensitized with bitumen. For many years it was this picture which was thought to be the oldest extant photograph in the world.

When the inventor was dying, in 1833, he had no idea how revolutionary his invention was to become. Using light, he had managed to imprint a sensitized plate with a true image of reality and produce a negative as a positive print. Due to his own mistrust of people, he failed to win fame as the discoverer of photography although he had been the first to develop the process.

# Louis Jacques Mandé Daguerre

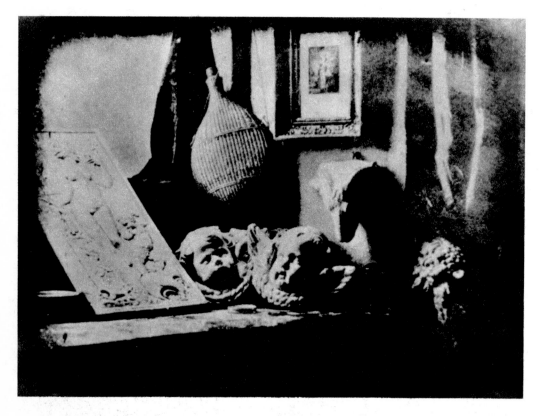

command; the dark ruins of an old abbey were haunted by realistic looking spirits. It was a spectacle that was never boring for the spectator because things were always happening.

The Diorama was a result of an ingenious lighting system with several translucent paintings placed one behind another and lit consecutively. To produce exact sketches of his huge sets and to produce them to scale quickly, Daguerre relied on the *camera obscura*. Daguerre heard about Niepce's experiments at Chevalier's, a popular Paris optician, in whose shop wealthy dilettante inventors congregated. Immediately his interest was so much aroused that he offered a partnership to Niepce.

At first Niepce would not even see Daguerre, only later when his brother Claude fell seriously ill, did Niepce decide to meet the then famous Daguerre. Niepce was immediately captivated by Dagurre: here was the right partner who could be trusted to develop his still unfinished process. In a contract which split any profits evenly between the two partners, the ageing Niepce thoughtfully provided for his son, Isidore.

Louis Jacques Mandé Daguerre was a theatre set painter by trade and talent. From 1807 to 1814 he was assistant to Pierre Prévost, a painter of panoramic set pictures in Paris, and spent the following four years, 1814—18, gathering invaluable experience as painter of sets for the *L'Ambigu-Comique* and the Opera. When working for Prévost's theatre of comical ambiguities, the play *Vampire* was staged using Daguerre's sets. The sets were so striking and ingenious, that Daguerre became famous almost overnight and was soon flooded with commissions he could never hope to fulfil. As time went by he gained the reputation as a stage designer whose sets could save even a potential outright flop. No wonder then that in 1820 Daguerre started thinking of establishing his own business. Two years later his spectacular 'Diorama' opened its doors for an eager Paris public. It was an immediate success and a sensation of the day. The painted landscapes were breathtakingly realistic: his Mount Vesuvius spouted smoke and fire on

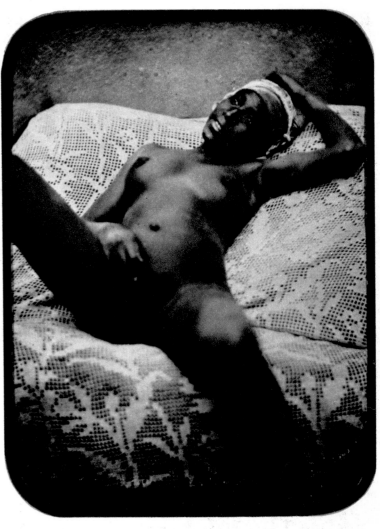

Then in 1835 working on his own, Daguerre arrived at the ingenious use of mercury vapours to develop a latent image. According to the Czech historian of photography, Rudolf Skopec, Daguerre had probably wanted to amalgamate his plates to improve the gloss and a previously exposed image was accidentally developed. Other sources quote different reasons, which make the discovery as accidental as Skopec's explanation. In fact, Daguerre had already experimented with iodine vapours forming a thin film of light-sensitive silver iodide as early as 1831. Adhering to their contract, he informed Niepce of the promising results, but it took him four more years to develop a good light-produced image on an iodized silver plate.

The improved sensitivity of the plate resulted in a considerable reduction of the exposure time — Niepce, for instance, had had to expose his plates for hours. But a new problem had to be solved with this iodized silver plate method: the images were not permanent and disappeared almost as soon as they were developed. It was only as late as 1837 that Daguerre finally discovered the second important part of the process, namely that the image could be partially fixed with a solution of common salt. The first fixative, a necessary prerequisite for the future practicability of the process, had been discovered. Daguerre thus found a practical procedure by which exposure, development and fixing produced an original positive image but which could not be copied. The inventor called his process daguerreotype but like Niepce before him, he ultimately failed to make the process a profitable venture.

Only when Daguerre asked the eminent physicist and astronomer Arago for help, did he finally became successful. On January 7, 1839, Arago informed the French *Académie des Sciences* about Daguerre's process. Although he mentioned no details, the news became a world-wide sensation. Six months later, on June 15, 1839, King Louis Philippe signed a statute entitling Daguerre to an annuity of 6,000 francs. Niepce's son, Isidore, received an annual fee of 4,000 francs and Daguerre himself was decorated with a Legion of Honour. On August 19, 1839, the process was made public at a ceremonial session of the *Académie*.

At the time this probably made the inventors somewhat unhappy because had they patented the process, they would have made enormous profits, but by making the process property of the state the French government made the daguerreotype available to everyone.

# William Henry Fox Talbot

/1800—1877/

William Henry Fox Talbot succeeded not only in developing but also fixing the latent image produced by the action of light. At the very moment of his breakthrough news from the other side of the Channel arrived about Daguerre's invention. All hopes that Talbot might have had during the long years of painstaking experiments of being first with a viable photographic process were suddenly thwarted. He did not give up his work, however, and continued developing his own process with a conviction that would make him, not Daguerre, recognized in time as the father of modern photography.

Like Niepce and Daguerre, Talbot wanted to make light 'draw pictures'. With no real talent for drawing, he longed to preserve a permanent image of what he saw during his travels in Italy. He used Wollaston's *camera lucida* only to be repeatedly disappointed when the 'treacherous pencil left on the paper traces that had nothing in common with the observed image'.

The situation repeated in early October 1833, when he tried to capture the beauty of the shores of Lake Como where he remembered that ten years earlier he had used the *camera obscura* to copy from and now he started thinking how to make the images become imprinted on paper so that he would not have to trace the contours with his untrained hand but could preserve the genuine image exactly. Immediately upon his return home in January 1834, Talbot started experimenting with light-sensitive chemicals, exposing tree leaves, flowers, lace and other flat objects of intricate shape, but the imprints produced were not the true, sharp image of reality he was looking for. Then he started experimenting with silver iodide and chanced upon a process which finally met his requirements. The paper was first treated with a solution of silver iodide and then potassium iodide, washed in distilled water and then dried. After exposure, the sensitized paper produced a latent image which was developed in a solution of silver

a report published on June 10, 1841.
In 1844, in an effort to 'document the early days of the new art', Talbot published a remarkable book titled *The Pencil of Nature,* the first book ever to be illustrated with original photographs. A year later he published another volume under the title *Sun Pictures of Scotland.*
Talbot remained obsessed with photographic inventions until his death. In 1849 he had a patent issued for his phototype on porcelain. He kept making photograms of plants and insects, experimented with macro- and infraphotography and even managed to win over the great French photographer Hippolyte Bayard to his calotype method and was named a honorary member of the Royal Photographic Society in 1873.

nitrate and gallic acid. This produced the negative which was subsequently fixed with a solution of sodium thiosulphate which had been discovered in 1819 to be a solvent of silver halides and recommended to him for this purpose by his friend J. F. W. Herschel, the astronomer.
All through 1835 Talbot continued his experiments, and managed to obtain papers of such high light sensitivity, that he was able to reduce the exposure time to only six minutes, under clear skies.
Until the announcement of the daguerreotype process he had not progress much with his experiments. However, a possibility of being able to fix the light-produced image by means of a direct positive method made him follow Daguerre's anouncement reporting the results of his work to the Royal Society in London and to the *Académie des Sciences* in Paris on January 31, 1839.
While Daguerre's process became an instant success and became widely adopted, Talbot's own method which established the basis of the modern negative-positive photographic process won no recognition at the time because no one realized its greatest advantage, that of the possibility of producing as many copies of the original image as desired. In spite of his considerable dismay at being pre-empted by Daguerre, Talbot had his own process patented, describing it in detail in

# II PHOTOGRAPHY IN SEARCH OF A ROLE

By the 1860s the mechanics of photography were more or less known and the new medium gradually started gaining ground in various fields of application.

Early on, photography made portraiture available to almost everyone. Although it had been the daguerreotype that had made portraits available to all, sitting for one remained tiresome. The sitter needed special head rests to keep immobilized for the required exposure time which ranged from five to forty minutes depending on the season and available light. Then the wet collodion process discovered in 1851 considerably reduced the exposure time and made the photographer free to take objects in motion. Three years later, in 1854, André Adolphe-Eugène Disdéri, a gifted entrepreneur, invented the photographic cartes-de-visite and started the real revolution in portraiture which was to mark the explosion in photograph's popularity. The picture was the size of a visiting card and no longer had a mere representative function but was a popular souvenir one could carry in the pocket. Disdéri even devised a camera with several lenses and a special device which advanced the negative. In this way, he was able to capture eight or ten different pictures on a single plate. The resulting contact print was then cut up into individual pictures. A new era of photography as a business was started, an era of mass-produced portraiture: everyone in the world it seemed longed to see their likeness in a photograph.

Yet among the flood of mechanically produced portraits, mere technical imprints of human likeness, there started appearing photographs that were consciously striving to express the character of the person. Among the first photographers in France who trained their cameras on the important personalities of the period with this in mind were Nadar and Etienne Carjat. In England at the same time Julia Margaret Cameron was showing the importance of close-ups in the characterization of the model. Besides producing expressive photographic portraits, Mrs Cameron became famous also for her allegoric scenes which so appealed to the romantic Victorian sentiment.

At approximately the same time photography moved into the field of journalism. In 1855 the Crimean War broke out. This 'modern' war for the first time employed the railway, the steamship, the telegraph and photography. A man named Carol Popp de Szathmari, a photographer and painter who normally worked at the court of a Romanian magnate, appeared on the battlefields of Crimea with a makeshift wet collodion laboratory installed in a carriage. When the famous English photographer Roger Fenton, who had been commissioned by a newspaper to cover the war, finally arrived to Crimea, Szathmari was already reaping fame for his war pictures. His photographs, however, have not survived and thus the credit for the first war photographs has gone to Fenton.

The next major armed conflict which captured the interest of photographers was the American Civil War. When hostilities broke out in 1861, many portrait photographers left their plush studios and followed the troops into the smoke and din of battle. Among the best known Civil War photographers was Matthew B. Brady with his team of fifteen assistants, which included his first assistant and thereafter eternal rival, Alexander Gardner. Although the period photographic equipment did not make it possible to take dynamic pictures of combat action, both Brady and Gardner learned how to use photography to show the real consequences of war. Gone was the idyll of dignified postures and freshly pressed uniforms which prevailed in Fenton's photography. The gallantry was replaced by horrible images of dead and wounded, the slaughter of battle, the cruelty of retaliatory executions, the abominable inhumanity. One of Brady's assistants, Timothy H. O'Sullivan, went behind the combat action to capture the horrors which accompany any war: the maimed bodies, the torn landscape, the smoldering ruins of civilian houses. Photojournalism, albeit still unknown as a term, had been born. The desire to use photography to investigate phenomena and things invisible to the naked eye is as old as photography itself but in the early years scientists had to wait for mechanisms to be developed which would let them use photography as a scientific tool. A typical example in this respect are studies of motion. For a long time, moving objects had to be photographed from a considerable distance so that the motion disturbed the image as little as possible. Then, in 1872, Muybridge decided to study motion by photographing its individual phases. His successful studies of locomotion led the physiologist Etienne Jules Marey to replace several cameras with a single piece of equipment featuring a disc-shutter which enabled him to capture a number of phases of a single motion onto a single plate. This meant not only an advance in the study of natural sciences but the equipment constituted the birth of cinematography because when in 1888 Marey used roll film in his improved 'photographic gun', he had built what was in fact the first motion picture camera. Marey's pioneering idea, however, remained overshadowed by a much better apparatus invented by the brothers Lumière, the pioneers of movie pictures.

A similar approach to capturing motion on film was adopted by the US painter Thomas Eakins. Eakins wanted to base his paintings on scientific principles and so he studied anatomy and motion using a home-built camera featuring two shutters which doubled the number of motion phases captured. Eakins paved the way to our understanding of fast motion because he developed the principles of slow motion photography.

From the beginning photography made a very different mark on art from that made on science. It was quite clear that photography could replace painting, graphics and sculpture in their role as means of straight reproduction but it took many years for photography itself to develop into a genuine art form. At first painters used photographs as substitutes for sketches. Alphonse Mucha for instance created a photographic sketchbook which ultimately grew into genuine photographic art work. Similarly, Edgar Degas, who hated painting outdoors, depended on photography to make cartoons for his canvasses. Photography was also utilized by a number of other Impressionist painters to capture the fleeting moment and its unique atmosphere. Photographers themselves were eager to 'make art', but since they could think of photography only within the framework of the criteria of period painting, their highest objective was nothing but the imitation of the artists' sentimental scenes, bucolic idylls,

mythical allegories or folk legends which were dictated by period taste. The pictorialists, as these photographers called themselves, disregarded the reality of life to create an artificial world in their photographic studios. Their ideal was photography which looked just like painting. Since, unlike painters, they in fact depended on reality and since to stage genuine monumental tableaux in the studio was just impossible, they were forced to resort to various forms of montage. Sometimes these montages would require as many as thirty different photographs which were then carefully assembled. The resulting composite picture was then mounted in a heavy gilt frame and exhibited as 'art' in social salons. Such was the method of O. G. Rejlander who used his combination prints to persuade the public that the artistic potential of photography equalled that of painting.
A similar approach was adopted by H. P. Robinson, the uncrowned king of pictorial photography, who first meticulously sketched his intended picture and then, using these cartoons, arranged the scene and photographed it. Robinson's book *Picture Making by Photography* was a manifesto and instruction manual which influenced photographers and photographic aestheticism so much that it became a synonym for this sort of artificially produced painting-like montage. This artificial pictorialism is seen for example in the work of David Octavius Hill and Robert Adamson whose pictures captured scores of their friends and acquaintances costumed as angels or monks, or posing for historical pageants. The annual exhibitions of London's Photographic Society became a grandiose display of these artistic efforts whose aura of respectability was only heightened by the gilt frames and the refined atmosphere of the salons. Photographers spent months preparing for these gala occasions, dreaming of becoming famous, viewing their rivals' successes with a jaundiced eye, trying to outdo the competitors and capture the interest of the public and the press. Period art critics accustomed to reviewing painting were not at all sure whether photography was an art or a science or perhaps both and in their reviews they judged photography by the traditional yardsticks used to evaluate painting. All this only contributed to the fact that in the public

mind photography was, among other things, just another painting technique.
It was only thanks to the photographic industry which flooded the market with hand cameras and dry plates in the 1880s that a fresh breeze disturbed the stale waters of official red-plush-and-gilt 'art' photography. Suddenly, photography became an 'art' for all because all one needed was to trigger the shutter release to capture a piece of reality. Amateur photography boomed, becoming a highly popular hobby for the middle and upper classes. While some amateurs remained happy with their snaps of everyday life, others attempted to use the medium to pursue their artistic inclinations. By the end of the 19th century there existed no less than 256 photographic clubs in Britain alone, 23 on the Continent and 99 in the United States. Aesthetically, however, all developed more or less along the lines of the Robinsonian pictorialism.
At the end of the 1880s a new phenomenon appeared on the photographic scene. Peter Henry Emerson was a physician whose rational, realistic mind made him reject Robinson's artificial, staged photographs and turn to nature for his source of inspiration. His book *Naturalistic Photography* caused heated discussions especially in England where the Robinsonian pictorialist tradition had become deeply rooted as the only concept of photography as an art. Now Emerson shocked everybody with his heretical statements that photography need not imitate painting and that it could be art even when a 'mere representation of reality'.
This fresh breeze as well as the first exhibition of French Impressionist painters held in England in 1889 resulted in the establishment of the Linked Ring Brotherhood lead by A. Morsley-Minton, a society of photographers which in 1892 became a platform for independent 'art photography'. The Linked Ring was quickly joined by French, Austrian and American photographers of similar aesthetic views and annual international salons were used to exhibit the so-called 'new photography'.
It was this trend which ultimately led to the establishment of the 'Photo-Secession' group by Alfred Stieglitz which played an important role, with the Linked Ring, in raising the

popularity of natural photography. Moreover, the group had a direct influence on the coming of age of various national photographies. For example, Czech photography was freed after the disintegration of the Austro-Hungarian Empire of its former dependence on German culture, by the patronage of one of the spokesmen of the US Photo-Secessionists, D. J. Růžička, an American of Czech origin. Photo-Secessionism was different pictorialism from that of the Robinsonian and Rejlanderian school because it sought its ideal in reality. It gave the photograph a discipline and order with laws of composition, in terms of points and lines, which emphasized the photogenic and solved for photography the relationship between form and content.
With Emerson, photography asserted itself as an art and started searching for its own, specific expression.

# Nadar /1820–1910/

'The love of life is the gift of a poet ... and Nadar is gifted more than anyone else,' so said one of Nadar's contemporaries. For ninety years Nadar lived a life full of activity: he studied medicine but never practiced it; he was a journalist, writer, playwright, caricaturist, painter, publisher, inventor, a convinced democrat and during the Paris Commune he was even a revolutionary. Yet his main achievements were in the fields of photography and aviation.

Nadar was one of the most popular figures of his period. He was one of the first people to make money out of photography, earning enough not only to live a comfortable life but even to be able to satisfy his thirst for knowledge and to pursue his daring, often even crazy projects.

Born Gaspard Félix Tournachon, he came to Paris in 1842, full of ideas how to popularize Daguerre's invention. Eager to make his mark, he began styling himself as an 'Artiste en daguerreotypie' and soon acquired a great skill in the process.

His interest in photography started when somebody gave him a camera in lieu of a loan.

This gave Nadar the idea of opening a daguerreotypic photographic studio, which he did in 1852, with his brother Adrien. Before long they switched to the new wet collodion process when it became clear that the popularity of the daguerreotype was fading. The plush furnishings of the studio and craze for visiting card portraits which his friend Disdéri had just started, soon enabled Nadar to expand his business. During this period, Nadar was somewhat derisively called the Barnum of photography because the public were drawn to his salon as much by his

11    Chemist Michel-Eugène Chevreul, 1886
12    George Sand, 1866
13    Sarah Bernhardt, 1859
14    Franz Liszt, 1886

flamboyant character as his photography. In fact Nadar skilfully managed to advance the new medium with progressive technology as well as novel ideas. He was among the first photographers to equip his studio with the dazzling novelty of electric arc lamps, and when he ventured to photograph the underground catacombs and sewers of Paris, he used magnesium lights of his own design. He achieved several other photographic firsts: in 1858 he made the first aerial photograph from an anchored balloon and immediately afterwards started gathering financial backing for his project of aerial topography. His imagination never ran dry. Just as in Jules Verne's works which merely anticipated the potentials of modern technology, Nadar's own projects were an embodiment of the enterprise of the latter half of the 19th century. He quickly grasped the vast possibilities of a close association of the retail trade and industrial manufacture and soon after the establishment of the Kodak Company, he became its chief representative in France.

His son Paul soon proved to be his father's equal as a photographer, inventor and businessman.

In spite of these impressive achievements, the greatest contribution of Nadar senior to photography is to be seen in his portraiture work which is distinctly different from the work of other portraitists of the day due to the originality of his concepts and consistent efforts to capture the character of the sitter. From the very beginning, Nadar's studio was a meeting place of Parisian writers, artists and scholars. He wrote at the time: 'The instinctive understanding of your subject: it is this immediate contact which can put you in sympathy with the sitter ... and enables you to

make not just a chancy, dreary, cardboard copy ... but a likeness of the most intimate and happy kind — a speaking likeness.' Portraits of some of his sitters including Dumas, Sand, Baudelaire, Rossini, Doré, Chopin, Liszt, Delacroix and others, all of whom were Nadar's friends, were published in book form as *Le Panthéon Nadar* in 1854 and *Galerie Contemporaine* in 1876.

Today, Nadar is rightfully regarded as the founder of portrait photography although his skilful use of technology and modern methods laid also the foundations of photojournalism.

# Roger Fenton

/1819—1869/

'I take mostly officers,' Fenton wrote home, 'or I could not move from place to place.' His job was not easy because the unbearable heat permitted him to work only from five to ten in the morning and his two assistants — a cook named William and a driver called Sparling — were constantly drunk. The wooden van he used was not merely a means of conveyance but served also as a kitchen, bedroom, laboratory and stockroom on wheels. The thirty-six pieces of luggage Fenton took with him contained five cameras working with different plate formats and seven hundred glass plates. When Fenton wanted to take a picture, he had to perform a number of complicated operations: first, the plates were cleaned, coated with collodion containing potassium bromide or potassium iodide until a homogeneous film developed on the surface; then the plates were sensitized in a bath of silver nitrate and the plates, still wet, placed in lightproof cassettes. Only then could Fenton embark on a photographic expedition. Once he exposed his plates he had to hurry back to the van to develop, fix and dry them over a flame, and then polish them. During all

Roger Fenton was the perfect English gentleman: a barrister, a member of a very old and very rich family, photographer of fashionable portraits, romantic landscapes and still lifes. He was the founder of the Royal Photographic Society, court photographer to Queen Victoria, Prince Albert and their numerous children. Yet it was Roger Fenton who in February 1855 left England for the battlefields of Crimea where some sixty thousand English, Turkish and French troops were besieging Sevastopol. Here camps sank in deep mud, field hospitals were hopelessly crowded and ravaged by cholera, and everything was shrouded in the overpowering stench of death. At the time this aspect of the war was not the concern of Victorian England because what the newspapers printed was news of heroic deeds performed by dapper young officers for the greater glory of Britannia. The Crimea, however, was the first war which was not only conveyed by telegraph and mail ship alone. It was also reported with photographs reproduced in newspapers by lithography or woodcuts.

this he could only pray that no stray bullet pierced the van and let light in at a wrong moment. Luckily, such an accident happened only once.

Thus it is not only period taste and the author's priggishness but also the primitive equipment and Fenton's position of an official court photographer that these first war photographs seem so static, arranged and ceremonial. Fenton's 360 Crimean War photographs more than anything else resemble romantic, unreal playing at soldiers. However, Queen Victoria was enchanted and personally made a selection of photographs which she proudly showed to Napoleon III. Before the Crimean War Roger Fenton had

been a well-known photographer but now he was famous.

In the spring of 1856 peace was concluded and the fickle society soon forgot there ever had been a Crimean War. As a result, Fenton's negatives fetched only a few shillings at an auction and Fenton himself took to photographing castles and country halls and in the end quit photography altogether. The times had changed and so had the public taste and the press now required not ceremonial pictures but pictures which conveyed information. Thus ten years after Fenton, photographers of the American Civil War, Matthew Brady, Alexander and James Gardner and Timothy O'Sullivan returned

from the battlefield with an appalling testimony of human cruelty and suffering. Nevertheless, Szathmari, a Romanian count, and Fenton, an English gentleman, remain the first true war photographers.

# Eadweard Muybridge

/1830—1904/

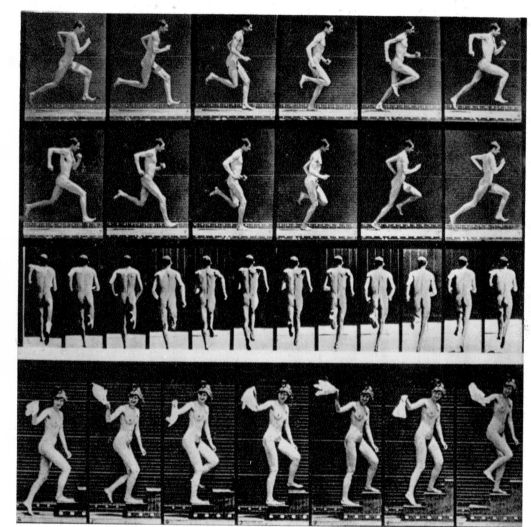

foot apart were progressively triggered by threads tied to the shutter releases. As the trotting animal snapped the threads, the shutters clicked and the cameras took pictures against a background wall bearing a distance scale which permitted measurement. Later Muybridge received a grant from the University of Pennsylvania and made some one hundred thousand negatives of tigers, horses, monkeys, ostriches and people in motion. In 1887, more than 20,000 of his images making up 781 series were published in a book called *Animal Locomotion*. Many of Muybridge's locomotion studies also captured the nude male and female body which not only provided new physical and anatomical information but oriented the popular interest to yet another emerging genre of photography, 'the nude'.

Muybridge came to the United States in 1852 and four years later he owned a bookstore in San Francisco. Where he learned to make

The first series of photographs which show animals and humans in motion owe their existence to a whim of the American multimillionaire, railway magnate, one-time governor of California and founder of the Stanford University, Leland Stanford. He was a great lover of horses and once made a bet of twenty-five thousand dollars with another rich sportsman named McCrelish that in one phase of the trot a horse had all four hooves off the ground. The dispute was decided by a man named Muggeridge who had emmigrated to the United States some 20 years earlier from England, changing his name to Muybridge. He photographed Stanford's horse Occident, using the exposure of one twelfth of a second but the image was just a blurred blotch. Only when Muybridge improved the camera shutter, was he able to obtain better photographic evidence and win Stanford's bet for him. In exchange, Stanford offered him unlimited financial support to continue with his locomotion studies. Muybridge accepted the money and in 1872—8 he spent over forty thousand dollars on equipment which would capture automatically the individual phases of a horse's movement. Originally twenty-four, later twelve cameras spaced one

photographs remains obscure but by 1860 he was photographing the landscape and people of the Pacific coast and also working on commission for the War Department. In 1877 he started using stereoscopic cameras and ultimately designed his own Zoöpraxiscope, equipment which permitted projection of phased pictures which resembled the later movie picture.

The Zoöpraxiscope was taken up by the French physiologist Marey who for twenty years had been making graphical studies of moving animals and birds in flight. After meeting Muybridge, he decided to use photography in his experiments. He designed a special photographic gun, an improvement of the earlier photographic revolver invented by the astronomist Jansen, and using Kodak roll film he was ultimately able to present the French Academy of Sciences in October 1888 the first continuous recording of motion. Although his primary interest lay in

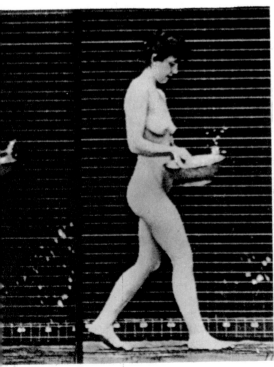

locomotion studies, he had in fact made the first practical movie camera and even came with the concept of the 'shot' or 'take'. Indirectly, Muybridge thus became one of the forerunners of cinematography.

Muybridge's locomotion studies showed that photography could be used whenever time needed to be stopped to investigate phenomena otherwise indiscernible to the naked eye. They also showed that the possibility of producing moving pictures was not out of the question. At that moment in time, however, the wet collodion process which reduced the exposure to a few seconds could not produce ten images in a second as required if the recording of motion was to be continuous. This was still beyond the

possibilities of the extant technology but cinematography was waiting in the wings ready to appear on the stage.

The future utilization of film had been already anticipated and scientists had envisioned both slow and fast motion recording for scientific research, e.g. in astronomy as Arago had once dreamed. However, until cinematography appeared, all who wanted to record motion photographically had to make do with the method of progressive takes — Muybridge's phase pictures.

# Julia Margaret Cameron

/1815—1879/

Julia Margaret Cameron was temperamental, whimsical and unconventional. She dressed with great taste and all men who met her adored her. Until the age of forty-eight, Mrs. Cameron's life was typical of an affluent Victorian middle class housewife. Born one of the seven daughters of a British colonial civil servant stationed in Calcutta, she received her education in India where she also married her husband who was twenty years her elder. On returning to England the Camerons bought a house on The Isle of Wight and Mrs. Cameron spent her days taking care of her six children and several orphaned relatives as well as entertaining guests and running the household. She would probably have

continued this existence had she not suddenly found an entirely new and totally unexpected purpose in life: her daughter gave her a camera and Mrs. Cameron became fascinated with photography.

With characteristic enthusiasm and zeal she turned the coal-house into a darkroom and a chicken-house into a studio and started photographing people using relatives, friends, neighbours and servants as models. After a short while the whole house showed permanent marks of her passionate pastime, clothes, carpets, everything bore the stains made by the wet collodion. 'I began with no knowledge of the art. I did not know where to place my dark box or how to focus my sitter,

and I defaced my first picture by rubbing my hands across the glass ... My husband has seen every picture with delight from first to last, and it is my daily delight to run to him with every glass newly stamped with a fresh glory and listen to his enthusiastic applause. This habit of running into the dining room with my wet pictures has stained so much table linen that I should have been banished from any less indulgent household,' she admitted once.

In her enthusiasm technical things meant little and her soft, slightly blurred, romantically delicate pictures were often a product of chance. 'When focusing and coming to something which was, to my mind, very

beautiful, I stopped there instead of screwing the lens to a more definite focus which all other photographers insist upon.' However, what her pictures lacked in skill, they gained in her perfect arrangement of models. Mrs. Cameron photographed men and women, although mostly young girls or children, alone or in groups, dressed them up and arranged them in poses expressing despair, joy, anxiety or tenderness; more often than not her models represented famous historical, literary or mythological figures.

Sometimes these allegorical scenes made her life quite complicated. Not only did she require several models at a time, and more than natural light, focusing was more difficult and there was always the danger of one of the models in the group moving during the long exposure and thus spoiling the plate. 'Mrs. Cameron and her entire household took no notice of the time. Upstairs, girls were being dressed in airy dresses, arranged in groups and photographed and Mrs. Cameron appeared with glass plates in her wet hands . . .' remembered one of her guests who had to wait till dusk before the mistress of the house

realized that lunch should have been served. Despite her problems with technology, Mrs. Cameron understood the human character as few photographers of the time did and she was one of the first to find how to capture character with different lighting or detail. One of her close friends was her neighbour Alfred Tennyson, who was visited by many famous men of letters, artists and members of the high society, and Mrs. Cameron waylaid them to sit for her including people like Carlyle, Browning, Longfellow and Darwin as well as Tennyson himself. Mrs. Cameron's perseverance and sensitivity to peoples' feelings backed up by her uncommon talent for producing portraits, led her to be rightfully

recognized as a genius of 19th century portrait photography. Perhaps most photographed of all her subjects it was Mrs. Cameron's maid, Mary Hillier, who became a symbol of virginal purity for the age. Dressed in a loose, much folded robe, with a spirited expression in her face and with her hair fluttering against a dark background, she was photographed as the Virgin Mary so often that after some time people started calling her the Lady Madonna. Those few years spent in England as a photographer won Julia Margaret Cameron an everlasting fame. After 1875 she followed her husband to Ceylon where this gifted lady took to being a housewife again and took very few photographs thereafter.

# Alphonse Mucha

/1860—1939/

The artist Alphonse Mucha never really regarded himself as a photographer and yet his work constitutes an important part of the history of photography. Although a photograph was for him little more than a cartoon or sketch for the final rendition of a painting, he left behind a unique catalogue of photographic work. The chief representative of the Art Nouveau style, the Bohemian-born Alphonse Mucha first took up photography with the enthusiasm of an amateur snapping pictures of everything he was fond of, first in Vienna in the streets of which he started working in 1880, later in Munich where he came to study. He photographed his friends and family as well as anything else that caught his fancy. Throughout the years he produced a remarkable photographic sketchbook. By 1903 Mucha had married and already stopped using photography as a mere sketchbook and like other painters at the turn of the century he discovered that it could be used to advantage for the study of the model and the milieu. He started producing photographic sketches or cartoons which he used for his paintings. The final versions often showed the models in different poses and frequently even in a different dress but sometimes the photographic models were already arranged according to his idea of the final painting. In such a case Mucha overlaid the photographic study with the age-old painter's grid system facilitating the transfer of the study onto the canvas in perfect proportion and exact detail.

His purposeful utilization of photography for drawing and painting can be traced back to 1894 when Mucha started poster work in his studio in Rue de la Grande Chaumière which he shared for a time with Paul Gauguin. Mucha painted the posters, on commission, for Sarah Bernhardt's *Théâtre de la Renaissance* in Paris. It remains unclear whether it was Mucha who helped promote the fame of the 'Divine Sarah' with his posters or whether it was Mlle. Bernhardt who helped Mucha become famous as a painter. In any case, the association proved fruitful for both artists. Mucha's photography from this period is as attractive, alluring, fanciful and exciting as his drawings. Unfortunately, Mucha the painter never cared much for his photographs and once the plates had fulfilled their purely utilitarian function, he laid them aside. (In fact, he even did not know how to stabilize and store the negatives and prints.) Although the famous painter never intended, many of his photographs have become unique

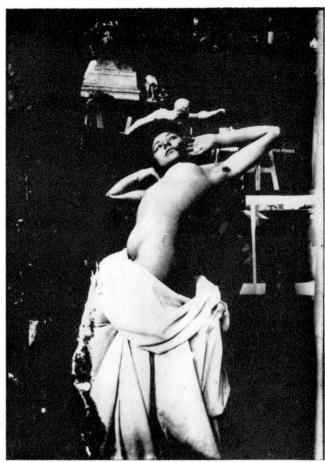

examples of photographic art. They are
characterized by the same richness of
ornament as his paintings and graphics, yet
they possess an authenticity and appeal
unique to photography. Thus Mucha's female
symbols of Life, Desire, Good, Evil, Birth and
Destruction are often more expressive in their
nudity than their elegantly, seductively
dressed painted counterparts.

Alphonse Mucha was lucky enough to achieve
what only a few artists have achieved: he
became famous during his lifetime and his
work sold well and he became rich. He was
a great success, was a man of society; he had
one-man shows in Paris, Vienna and Prague,
and designed the decorations for the pavilion
of Bosnia and Hercegovina at the 1900 Paris
World Exhibition. In 1904 he even started
teaching at art academies in New York,
Chicago and Philadelphia.

Born in Ivančice near Brno, Moravia, Mucha
decided in 1910 to return to his native country.
He settled in Prague and started working on
a large cycle of monumental paintings titled
*The Slavic Epopee.* Even for this grand-scale
work he used photographic sketches some of
which constitute a unique chapter in his
photographic heritage. The pictures date from
1913 when he visited Russia to collect
material. Since he worked mainly outdoors
and was unable to arrange reality as he could
in his studios in France, America or Bohemia,
he produced a unique, acute, profound and
candid social document on the life of the
Russian people some four years before the
Revolution. This work alone proves that had
not Mucha become a famous painter, he
would have been a remarkable photographer
despite the many technical shortcomings of
his photographic work.

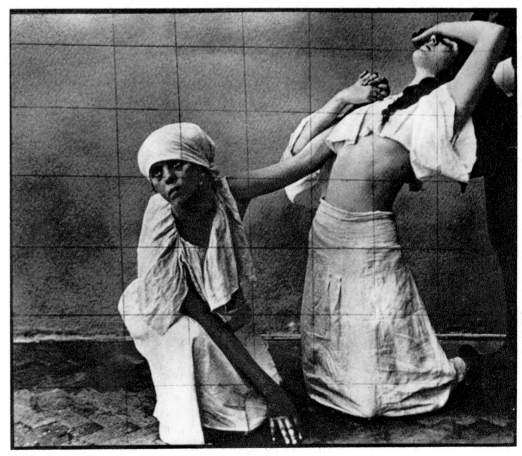

# Oscar Gustave Rejlander

/1813—1875/

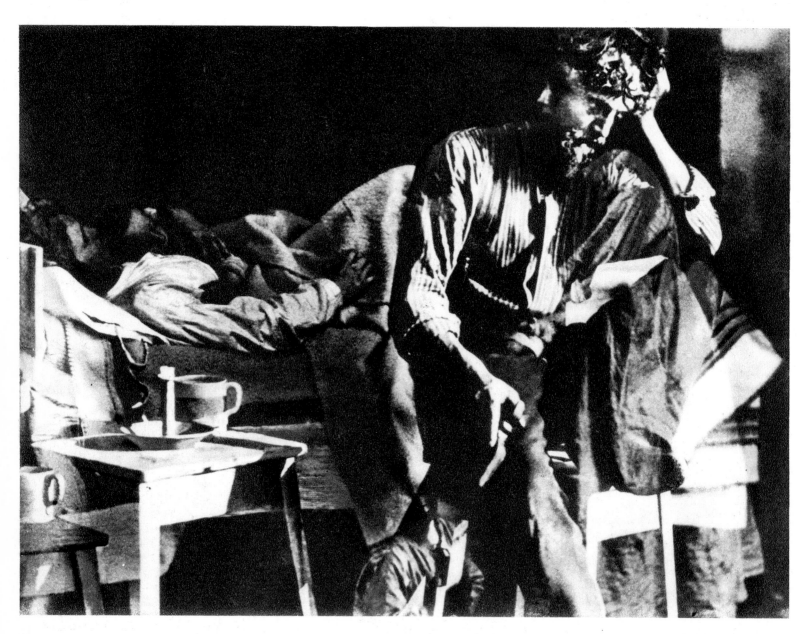

In 1857, at the Manchester *Art Treasures Exhibition*, photographs were displayed side-by-side with paintings and sculpture for the first time. Among the exhibits was an allegorical large size 40 × 80 cm composition entitled *Two Ways of Life*, by Oscar Gustave Rejlander, depicting twenty-five figures representing a scene whose right side symbolized labour, piety and charity while the left side showed drinking, gambling and other forms of frivolity and debauchery. To stage the scene and to capture it on a single negative, the author would have needed a huge studio. Instead, he hired itinerant actors to pose for him for the individual groups which were photographed and then the individual negatives combined to produce the final print of the tableau.

*Two Ways of Life*, which was composed of no less than thirty separate photographs, had been intended to prove that photography was capable of producing the same effect as painting. In fact, Queen Victoria so admired the moral and educational message of the combination picture that she purchased it as a present for her consort, Prince Albert, who had it hung in a prominent place in his study.

Other people, however, were much less enthusiastic about the work and Rejlander was even accused of being indelicate because photography rendered the nude and semi-nude figures too realistically and they were deemed obscene by period taste and morals. In Scotland the picture was even banned from being exhibited as a whole and visitors were allowed to see only its right, i.e. modest, half. However, the royal approval and the opinion of the artistic circles who regarded the work as the ultimate achievement in photography encourage Rejlander to continue experimenting with such combination prints, or montages.

Among other things, Rejlander considered his allegoric compositions a perfect example of how the camera could serve the artist for sketching individual parts of a painting. He even stated that he did not know of a better way to render the beauty of the human body. He spoke sharply against those who criticized photography for being a product of technology rather than the human spirit and imagination and vilified those who held that photography could never become an art. 'We photographers have a good ground for complaint against your art critics for the sneering and overbearing manner in which you assign limits to our powers ... Who disputes that photography is not engraving or

29  Hard Times. Spiritualistic photograph made from several negatives, 1860
30  Two Ways of Life. A composite picture made from thirty negatives, 1857
31  The Dream, 1860

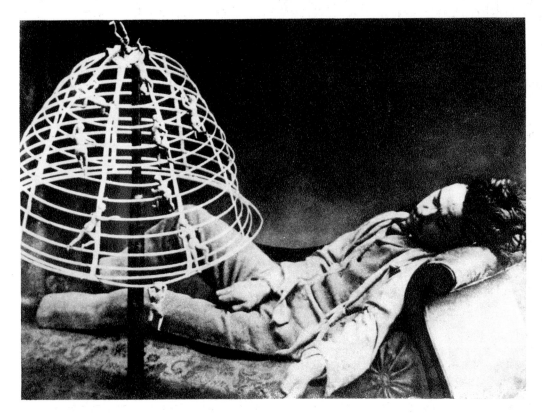

lithography, wood engraving or etching? We are satisfied that it is an art in itself, only guided by the general canons of art for successful combination to produce an art-looking result ...'

Born in Sweden, Rejlander had studied painting and worked as portrait and copy painter in Rome before settling permanently in England in the early 1840s. He took up photography as a sketching tool but instead of devoting his life to painting he opened a photographic studio. He lived mainly from portraiture and although a number of his combination prints were bought by Prince Albert, he remained in extreme poverty. The montages were very laborious to arrange and the staging of scenes to be photographed tiring. In 1859 he wrote: 'I am tired of photography-for-the-public, particularly composite photographs, for there can be no gain and there is no honour, only cavil and misrepresentation.' Disillusioned, Rejlander later tried to re-establish himself as a portrait painter but amounted to nothing. He died totally impoverished, leaving behind a small but remarkable work, a testimony to the great imagination of a man who gave photography what it perhaps needed most at the time: a proof that it need not be a mere recording of fact but that it could also be capable of artistic composition.

31

# Henry Peach Robinson

/1830 — 1901/

From the mid 1850s, the most successful photographs were those which most resembled paintings, and the grand master of this art of photographic copying was Henry Peach Robinson. He was called the 'king of photographic picture-making' and ranked among the most prominent photographers of the Victorian period, and wrote extensively on painting-like photography in his books *Pictorial Effect in Photography* and *Picture Making by Photography*, which saw many editions in various languages.

The vogue of the period was pictorial painting with diverse, mostly sentimental subjects and Robinson was adroit at telling a story or painting a scene, be it pastoral, full of the domestic bliss of childhood, or moral. His most famous photograph is titled *Fading Away*. This composition of five different negatives dates from 1858 and represents a dying young girl surrounded by the bereaved family. 'It was calculated to excite painful emotions.' Robinson was forced to admit. The public was shocked because the pathetic scene, so much catering to the current taste, had a much more powerful effect when expressed photographically than when painted. The problem was that the viewer took the photograph as fact rather than fiction and was scandalized because such

a scene offended rather than entertained him. However, it is often the end that justifies the means and Henry Peach Robinson was willing to resort to anything to produce the desired effect. Not only did he make composite pictures from a number of negatives but, when he thought necessary, he would even go so far as transform the drain of his darkroom into a country brook complete with shrubbery and with painted clouds in the background. 'Any dodge, trick, and conjuration of any kind is open to the photographer's use . . .' he maintained. 'It is his imperative duty to avoid the mean, the bare and the ugly, and to aim to elevate his subject, to avoid awkward form, and to correct the unpicturesque.' Without a qualm, Robinson blended the real with the artificial in a single scene or combined elements of several different negatives into a single print. He maintained that if photography was to be an art, it should not be a mere record of reality. 'No possible amount of scientific truth will in itself make a picture. Something more is required. The truth that is wanted is artistic truth — quite a different thing.'

Robinson was originally a bookshop assistant and painter. At the age of twenty-two he exhibited his paintings in the Royal Academy. Then in 1850 he became acquainted with the daguerreotype and photography became his destiny. He started making photographs and in 1857 opened a portrait studio, became a member of the Royal Photographic Society and a few years later its vice-president. Each year for almost three decades Robinson prepared one of his famous pictorial compositions for the annual exhibiton of the Society, pictures which helped coin the notion of 'pictorial photography'. His compositions were skilfully arranged stage scenes which were first sketched by hand, then photographed part by part, cut out and pasted onto a separately photographed background and foreground. When the picture was assembled and the splices carefully retouched, the whole was re-photographed and printed. Robinson's entire life was devoted by his desire to equal painting with photography. Since he considered painters his rivals, he wrote about them quite scornfully: 'I don't know that there is anything more exasperating for a painter than to take it for granted that it is a photographer's business to play jackal to his lion, and hunt up food for him . . . Painters ought to be more grateful to us than they are. Besides providing some of them with subjects, we have taught them what to avoid . . . Art has vastly improved during the half-century of our existence. We have made the column and the curtain background absurd. When our art was born painters thought nothing of violating perspective by placing the horizon as low as the feet of their portraits, and made no difficulties about hanging heavy curtains from the sky . . . A painter should never use photography until he is capable of getting on without it, and then he should make his own photographs.'

# Peter Henry Emerson

/1856 — 1936/

rational argument, irony, sarcasm and malice managed to thwart the vitriolic attacks of the opposition.

He was exceptionally fond of nature, especially coastal fogs, biting winds and the simple grace of the picturesque Norfolk Broads where he photographed the landscape as well as the life of the villagers, fishermen and shepherds and their ways and customs. His work resulted in a number of portfolios which were astute ethnological studies of the region. His ideas were summarized in his *Naturalistic Photography,* published in 1889. The book argued that photography must be a vociferous image of reality and that the photographer had no right to interfere with this image. 'Can photography which is but a picture of nature be a work of art, or is art only such a photograph which resembles painting?' was the much discussed question of the period. Emerson's book was said to be a 'bomb dropped amongst a tea party' by Emerson's advocates. The book even rejected retouching as a process, turning bad photography, or average or even good photography for that matter, into bad drawing or bad painting. 'The photographic technique is perfect and needs no such bungling,' Emerson wrote.

Peter Henry Emerson was a staunch opponent of the artificial, sentimental arranged scenes so popular in the photography of his time. His opposition was so vehement that in the end he shook the very basis of period aesthetic thought. His arguments were obvious in his photographs, articles, lectures and books and in a speech presented in 1886 to the London Camera Club he sharply rejected the work of H. P. Robinson and his disciples as artistic anachronism and photographic folly and came forward with his own theory of art based on the scientific understanding of nature.

He held that the artist's holiest objective is not to sentimentalize the world through tricks and deception but rather to render it in the way it is viewed by the eye, and argued his case citing the sculpture of the ancient Greeks, Leonardo da Vinci's *Last Supper* and the paintings of the 'Naturalist' school — Constable, Corot — and the Barbizon masters,

as examples of the ultimate in art achievement. In photography he similarly regarded the spontaneity of expression and natural environment to be of basic value, and opposed in principle anything artificial, including arranged compositions.

Originally a physician, Emerson had been fascinated with Hermann von Helmholtz's book *Physiological Optics* and capitalized on this theoretical knowledge in his own approach to photography. His pictures were sharply defined in the centre of the image and slightly out-of-focus in the margins because he held this was precisely the way the eye saw things, i.e. with different definition throughout the field of vision, and demanded that photography be a copy of the eye's image. He also maintained that it was due to this very ability to reproduce exactly what the eye saw why photography had no equal. Although his opinion met with violent criticism, his gift for

However, within less than two years Emerson renounced all his previous views. In a book titled *Death of Naturalistic Photography* he proclaimed naturalistic photography worthless because it did not allow for any personal expression. Alas, it was too late. The opinion that photography was a unique, specific means of representation totally independent of other arts had already taken root. In fact, Emerson's original ideas which so rejuvenated photography have survived to the present. Indeed, without Emerson's ideal of a return to nature the modern ideal of photography may not have been born. Even after his proclamation against everything for which he had stood, Emerson continued making pictures and even complimented photographers, dead and living, whom he admired: Julia Margaret Cameron, Nadar, Stieglitz, Brassaï. A few years before his death he finished a book devoted to the history of pictorial photography. However, his last manuscript never saw print.

# III PHOTOGRAPHY AS AN ART FORM

If practically anybody can release the shutter of a camera, what will happen to photography as an art? This was the burning question in photographic circles at the turn of the 20th century — it was a question that made many photographers uneasy.

Ever since the start photography had been trying to overcome its inferiority complex — a suspicion that it was not a bona fide art but merely a copy of traditional art forms. In the early stages of its development it did not have to try too hard because a simple reproduction was considered a work of art in its own right, but as the initial enthusiasm wore off, the situation rapidly changed and after a short while painters curtailed their earlier attempts to paint like photographs. In fact, the very term 'photography' started having a pejorative overtone in the vocabulary of period aesthetics because it became to signify something which merely copied, which was not transcended by the creative genius of an artist. Small wonder then that photography with artistic aspirations wanted to look different from 'photography'.

After the previous era of artificially arranged 'reality' and elaborated montages, photographers started feeling the same desire as painters to use their art to convey emotion and feeling. In order to achieve the picturesque effect of Impressionist painters, they started interfering with both the negative and the positive in various ways, resorting to fine printing techniques to produce, for example, oil, bromoil, charcoal and gum prints which suppressed the essential qualities of photographs and changed things like the clarity and form of the print so that the finished product was not a pure reflection of reality. A new period began in which photographers searched for new ways how to render reality more artistically, how to produce photographs which would be as aesthetically valid as art.

The most typical representatives of the photographers who were in search of these new photographic ideals were two prominent French photographers, Robert Demachy, a rich amateur, and Constant Puyo, an officer. Both produced emotionally effective Impressionistic pictures quite unintentionally, guided just by intuition.

Among other photographers of the period who were guided by the new pictorialist tendencies was František Drtikol, a Czech, whose work is a shining example of the emerging relation between the 'painterist' approach and the specifics of photography. Although he used various transfer processes and observed the laws of classical pictorial composition, he nevertheless developed a spontaneous, purely photographic vision depending on light as the basic means of expression. Together with another Czech, Jaromír Funke, he even formulated a manifesto in the 1920s in which he wrote: 'A camera ... is for us what the brush is to the painter, or the pen to the poet ... We do not compete with painters because we are no painters, just as we are no graphic artists, for our position is diametrically different from theirs, yet we stand on the same line. Our relation to painting is based on our desire for independence of both media ...' Unlike his French peers, Drtikol consciously and programmatically attempted to free photographic expression from its dependence on painting.

By the turn of the century, the battle between the pictorialists and the purists had reached a most vicious stage. The pictorialists, especially those in Europe, held that any means, even non-photographic ones, could be used to produce an aesthetically valid picture. The purists, mainly in the United States, were against not only the use of fine print or transfer techniques which they considered non-photographic, but even opposed any, however minute, interference with the negative and the positive, emphasizing a formal order of the image. They waged a fight for 'pure photography', i.e. photography that would be capable of achieving the same effect as the transfer processes but would do so in a purely photographic manner, for example by using soft lenses, rather than by manipulation of the negative. The chief spokesmen for this pure or straight photography, as it is sometimes called, were members of the Photo-Secession Group founded in the United States in 1902. These photographers, e.g. Alfred Stieglitz, Edward Steichen, Clarence White, Gertrude Käsebier and others, were among the first to grasp the great transformation of modern art, that is a transition from a representative to a cognitive or intellectual function. In their own way, they helped photography to rid itself of its inferiority complex with respect to painting.

The *spiritus agens* of the Photo-Secession Group, its brain and soul, was Alfred Stieglitz. His thorough knowledge of photographic chemistry, his personal acquaintance with Emerson, the great British photographer, and his book *Naturalistic Photography,* and, last but not least, his sensitive understanding of the revolutionary changes affecting modern art, resulted in his profound grasp and practical utilization of the specifics of photography. Stieglitz realized that the magic of photography stemmed from its intimate bond with reality. Therefore Stieglitz chose only the most ordinary of subjects and never resorted to interfering with reality.

At the start of his career he produced moody, Impressionistic pictures, although he never resorted to artificial aids or soft lenses, achieving the desired effect by employing natural phenomena like rain of fog. 'My picture *Fifth Avenue* is the result of a three hours stand during a fierce snow-storm ... awaiting the proper moment,' he wrote. Later, however, he abandoned even these effects and became an advocate of the sharp image, emphasizing the realistic vision of photography. Alfred Stieglitz's work represents a historical milestone and the work of his disciples made photography respected as a a bona fide art in its own right with its own unique mechanisms. In fact, Stieglitz's struggle to see photography recognized as an art was a struggle waged for modern art in general. With the help of his friend Edward Steichen, his '291' Gallery exhibited artists such as Rodin, Matisse and Picasso, who were still largely ignored by the old artistic world which did not understand them. Using their example, Stieglitz showed how difficult it was for painting and sculpture to do what was better achieved by photography and vice versa.

A genuine torchbearer of the realistic line adopted by Stieglitz and his followers from the Photo-Secession Group was a Czech physician naturalized in the United States, Drahomír Josef Růžička. Dr. Růžička was an enthusiastic amateur photographer whose profession gave him an innate respect for nature and natural things. Like his English colleague, Emerson, Dr. Růžička primarily saw photography as a unique medium which permitted a true reflection of reality. Dr. Růžička eagerly sought and studied opinion on the aesthetic foundations of photography inviting photographer friends to his house, including Clarence White, a member of the Photo-Secession. In this role as herald of the new aesthetics for photography he became famous in his native Bohemia where he sent his pictures and later visited. It was here, in the heart of Europe, where the seed of the American Photo-Secession found the most fertile soil which ultimately gave point to a generation of outstanding art photographers such as Josef Sudek and Jaromír Funke.

The historic milestone in the development of photography was World War I because by the time the war broke out, modern photography had emerged. Attuned to the new imagination and scientific and technological development, photography found its main objective: to show truth rather than embellishing reality or emphasizing beauty. 'The search for truth is my obsession,' stated Alfred Stieglitz, voicing the aesthetics of the photographic image. In 1917, of the eleven hundred photographs submitted to the Philadelphia International Exhibition, Stieglitz selected only fifty-five pictures giving priority to those which revealed the new approach to photography as an art. Interestingly, the main prize went to Paul Strand who himself thoroughly radicalized the realistic line of the Stieglitzian straight photography. In 1917, Strand's photographs were the first examples of what was to become called New Objectivity photography and anticipated the typical subjects of the future New Objectivity. He found the significance of a detailed representation of the surface structure of the subject.

Strand inspired an interest in the qualities of the objective world which was developed to absolute mastery in America by Edward Weston. Weston's style is based on absolute verism, on the greatest possible transcription of reality, albeit a transcription much more perfect than that to which the eye is accustomed, so that the resulting image is in fact an 'abstraction'. In his best work Weston's desire to let nature speak for itself produces a unique blend of objectivity and intellectual abstraction. His acute sense for photography and his extremely sophisticated vision made the public see his pictures as profound symbols of nature and civilization.

Weston's influence became especially marked when the 'f/64' Group was established in 1932. As the name implies, the members of the group followed Weston's example by using maximum aperture setting and like him, they saw nature as an ideal of purity of form with which they wanted to become spiritually a part. Apart from Weston, the best-known members of the group were Ansel Adams, Imogen Cunningham, Henry Swift, and the movie maker Willard van Dyke.

It was probably the traditional American realism, a lack of burdensome art traditions that were the reasons why photography found its specific expression, independence, aesthetic validity and even social recognition more rapidly and easily in the United States than in Europe. Yet there was a European who based his photographic vision on this realism, who felt that everything which surrounds us is sheer poetry. He was no American and neither rational pragmatist nor technically minded. On the contrary, he worked his whole life guided only by his mood and feeling, holding heretically that beauty lay in the ambiguous and mysterious. This peer of Weston, Strand and Adams was the Czech photographer Josef Sudek.

The main features of Sudek's best work are a provocative magic, dream-like haze, mysteriousness and an intimate emotional message. Having no personal needs to speak of, this strange yet life-loving ascetic used his unique encounters with objects and people to express a great variety of emotions, forming a unique personal vision. Sudek's photographs represent a fulfilment of the ideal of existential harmony and a challenge to the dulled sensibility of modern man. They are a culmination of photography's effort to achieve its own, aesthetically valid expression. Photography's quest for independence, however, did not take place only along the line of art photography. As early as the beginning of the 20th century Lewis Hine in the United States, and Eugène Atget in France had started working in documentary photography: Hine to correct what he saw as gross social injustice, Atget to capture the inner drama of people in their milieu. Both, in their own way, produced a testimony about the world they lived in.

While art photography wanted to become an aesthetically valid expression and documentary photography wanted to produce a document, the result of these efforts was that by the beginning of this century photography in its bi-polarity had been constituted as an art whose unique position was to be proven by its later development.

# Robert Demachy

/1859 — 1936/

Like so many of his contemporaries, Robert Demachy believed that photography could be an art only if it resembled painting or drawing, and he absolutely refused to recognize that photography as a copy of reality could be art. 'Do not say that Nature being beautiful, and photography being able to reproduce its beauty, therefore photography is Art ...' he wrote in one of his numerous articles on the subject. 'Nature is often beautiful, of course, but never artistic "per se", for there can be no art without the intervention of the artist in the making of the picture. Nature is but a theme for the artist to play upon. Straight photography

registers the theme, that is all ...'
The conflict between the pictorialists and the purists was a furious battle of two radically different aesthetic opinions. Does the photographer have the right to modify the image registered by the camera? 'Of course', was the cry of the pictorialists headed by Robert Demachy and his friend Puyo who were eagerly experimenting with the possibilities of various transfer processes which made photography resemble painting or drawing. 'Where will this swindle lead?' queried the Englishman Emerson only to be answered to by the Frenchman Demachy:

'Wherever we want it to ... It makes no difference to me if the amateur uses oil and eraser or platinum ... so long as he offers me a picture interpreting his feelings.'

A son of a rich Paris banker, Robert Demachy had ample financial means at his disposal and even though the family bank bore also his name, he was never involved in its operations, devoting all his time to his hobbies of music, painting and photography. He was an accomplished violinist and reasonably skilled in painting but first he was a photographer and it was this passion which was to make him the best-known French photographer of the early 1900s.

As the spokesman for the new concept of French pictorialist photography he knew many young painters with whom he used to spend long hours in small cafés and bistros of the Montmartre district of Paris. His photographs bear the traces of these friendships, their intimate feelings and the atmosphere of the moment making them

exhibit the novel and even revolutionary elements of the Impressionist style, not those of classical oil paintings. In order to produce these effects, Demachy used the gum bichromate or pigment processes because of their soft rendition of tone. Despite the fact that his pictures were the result of much 'interference', he still respected — though perhaps only intuitively — the naturalism of the camera view, for example, he was especially brilliant at capturing the texture of a sitter's dress, the character of the fabric, its folding, the lace and frills. More often than not he became more interested in these details than in the face of his model. Likewise, his nude studies reveal a natural sense for the fleeting moment.

Despite the aristocratic friends of his family, Robert Demachy liked simple things and felt most at ease with simple people. This was also one of the reasons why he divorced his socialite wife and why after his mother's death he left the family residence to settle where he

always felt most at home, among the penniless artists, vagrants, streetwalkers and other down and outs of the Montmartre.

In 1914, at the height of his popularity and fame, Demachy suddenly and unexpectedly left photography forever, refusing even to take pictures of his grandchildren for the family album. The reasons for his decision were subject to wild rumours and speculation but the most probable explanation seems to be that after having written hundreds of articles defending photography as an art compatible with painting, Demachy slowly and quietly resigned to the arguments of his opponents. Regardless of the reason, the fact remains that he never took a picture again, spending the rest of his life in the quiet seclusion of his country retreat near Trouville, a place so unlike Montmartre which teemed with life.

Only occasionally did Demachy go to the local beach where he drew caricature portraits of the holiday makers.

# František Drtikol

/1883—1961/

rejecting the painters' techniques of composition and drapery, replacing them with arranged geometrical shapes, liberating the form from the yoke of decorativism and concentrating instead on the utilization of light to give expression and composition to his pictures. In accordance with the movie picture aesthetics he became fascinated with the possibilities of close-up and motion. He was a child of the style of his period, Art Nouveau,

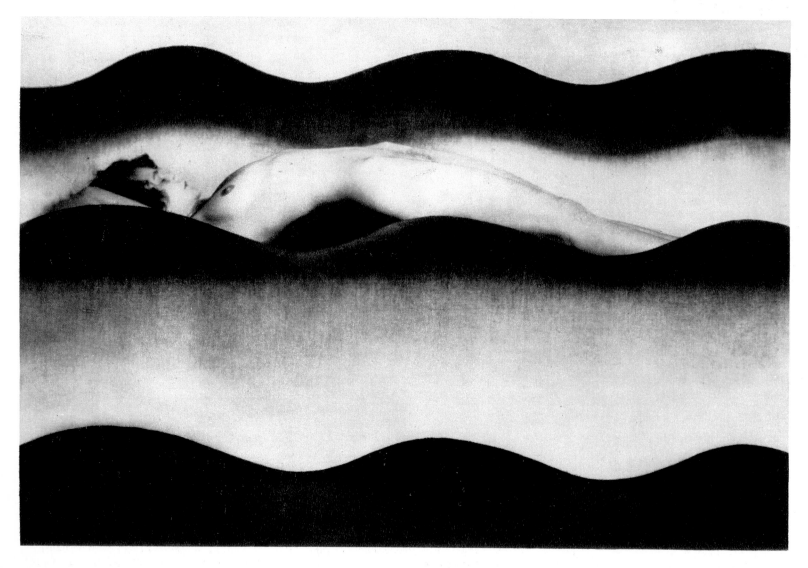

'Ars una, species mille — there is but one art with a thousand likenesses. And thus I view photography as but one of the many expressions of artistic feeling,' wrote František Drtikol, the first man in Bohemia to raise photography to the status of a creative art and whose work substantially helped to shape the art of the period.
František Drikol entered the field of photography in 1901. It was time when commercial photography was booming in his native Bohemia, amateur photographic clubs were springing up everywhere and Bohemian photographers were regularly exhibiting at

various national and international exhibitions, although nothing that Bohemian photography had produced at that time had exceeded in quality the usual run-of-the-mill standard. In the beginning, even Drtikol bowed to the period pictorialist taste, employing various pigment transfer techniques to make his photographs resemble painting or graphics. He even followed the practice of commercial photographers by painting over the photograph or supplementing a photographed figure with a painted background. Gradually, however, he started searching for novel, specifically photographic methods by

and he absorbed its artistic, literary and philosophical stimuli, transforming them in his own unique way just as later in his life he drew on other trends of modernistic art, including Cubism.
Like many of his photographic peers, Drtikol started his career as a photographer's apprentice because his father, a grocer, wanted him eventually to have a business of his own. During his apprenticeship he learned at a two-year vocational school for photographers, the *Lehr- und Versuchsanstalt für Photographie* in Munich, and in 1901, on completing his apprenticeship, he immediately

left his native country to enrol.

In Munich Drtikol became acquainted with the works of the great painters of the past — Lucas Cranach, Rembrandt, Dürer, van Dyck, Velazquez and others — and under this influence he started thinking of photography as an art in its own right. In later life, his ideas consolidated, he placed the beginning of his career as an artist in 1910 when after years of wandering around Europe, he returned to Prague where he opened a portrait studio with a partner.

The Drtikol and Škarda Studio quickly became popular among Prague's celebrities. Drtikol himself became a well-known figure and to have one's portrait taken by him was a status symbol. It was during this period when he had to exert an almost superhuman effort to handle the ever-growing business, that he produced his finest work on the subject of the woman.

The woman was his obsession, a symbol of both good and the evil, a saint as well as a *femme fatale*. The eroticism of the woman and the feminine mystique in fact remained the unifying feature of Drtikol's work from the early 20th century up to the 1930s when

Drtikol unexpectedly retired never to take up photography again.

Drtikol's creativity and fame reached its peak in the 1920s when his work was regularly exhibited at major international exhibitions and a de luxe portfolio of his nudes was published in Paris when he was living among the avant-garde community.

Then came the 1930s which represented a great change in his work. Drtikol stopped working with live models and started using cut-out paper which he arranged in his compositions. The reason was quite prosaic. Years later Drtikol wrote about this particular period in his life and work: 'My name was known all over the world. I guess you could

say I was famous but in fact I hardly managed. The business was slack . . . and I had to get by on what I made as instructor in amateur photography courses . . .' Drtikol's last pictures date from 1935. Soon after this he sold his stylishly decorated studio and took up philosophy, studying Hatha Yoga and oriental philosophy and trying to live according their principles. His photographic work remained forgotten for many years so that at the time of his death in 1961, a short obituary which appeared in the press called him 'a long-dead photographer'. However, Drtikol's work ranks among the best produced during the period when photography was comming of age.

# Alfred Stieglitz

'Photographers must learn not to be ashamed to have their photographs look like photographs,' Stieglitz wrote in 1913. It is somewhat paradoxical, yet perhaps only logical, that Stieglitz's campaign for the recognition of photography as an independent art ultimately transcended into one for the recognition of modern art as a whole. Edward Steichen wrote to Stieglitz from Paris at a time when Stieglitz managed a small Photo-Secession Group gallery which was located in New York's Fifth Avenue and later became known after the street number as the '291' Gallery, and asked him if he wanted an exhibition of selected Rodin's drawings.

Stieglitz replied by telegraph accepting, and soon after his friend Steichen brought to New York a number of Rodin's exquisite drawings as well as a portfolio of an artist whose name still meant nothing in America. His name was Henri Matisse. In a similar manner, Stieglitz introduced America to the work of Cézanne, Toulouse-Lautrec, Picasso, Braque and Brancusi. The legendary Armory Show, a project which was largely Stieglitz's conception, held in 1913, presented to America modern art which was obstinately rejected by the Old World. Stieglitz, however, was not content with co-organizing the Armory Show and concurrently exhibited his recent photographic work at the '291' because he felt it was an excellent opportunity to show the public what was photography and what was not painting just as at the Armory Show what was painting and what was not photography.

Stieglitz had brought his undying faith in photography as an art from the country of his ancestors, Germany, where he went to study engineering and photographic chemistry. Upon his return to America in 1890 he spent several years as a commercial photographer,

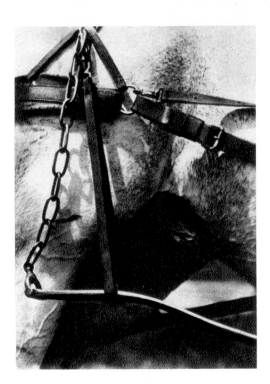

45 Portrait, 1918
46 Portrait, 1918
47 America, 1923
48 Dorothy's Truth, 1919

experience. 'I have to have experienced something that moves me ... before I can see what are called shapes. Shapes, as such, mean nothing to me, unless I happen to be feeling something within, of which an equivalent appears in outer form ... My cloud photographs, my "Songs of the Sky", are equivalents of my basic philosophy of life.' Indeed, Stieglitz called a number of his images 'equivalents', asserting his ideal that straight, i.e. unretouched, photography, could be a medium of expressing the author's personal experience. In fact, after Stieglitz the question whether photography was or was not an art became irrelevant.

Stieglitz had a great gift for finding new talents in photography and engaging them in his struggle for a new concept of photography. Together with these photographers, he founded, in 1902, a group called the Photo-Secession which quickly won international recognition for American art photography. The platform of the Photo-Secessionists, the *Camera Work* quarterly magazine, was considered the most radical of art magazines.
In the catalogue to his one-man show held in New York in 1921, Stieglitz admitted: 'Photography is my passion. The search for Truth my obsession.'

moving on to edit various magazines, including the influential *Camera Work*, manage galleries, organize exhibitions, work as an art photographer, all in an effort to prove that photography could have an aesthetic validity without imitating painting. His own pictures were the result of his extreme patience, for he never interfered with reality and was content to spend hours on end waiting for the right moment when 'everything was in balance', when reality itself acquired the qualities of composition and atmosphere which reflected his own ideas and mental state.
One of Stieglitz's best-known pictures was taken in the summer of 1907 when he and his wife sailed for Europe. 'There were men and women and children on the lower deck of the steerage ... I longed to escape from my surroundings and join these people. A round straw hat, the funnel leaning left, the stairway leaning right ... white suspenders crossing on the back of a man in the steerage below, round shapes of iron machinery ... I saw a picture of shapes and underlying that the feeling I had about life.' Acting on an impulse, Stieglitz rushed to his cabin, grabbed his Graflex camera and ran breathlessly back. Everything was as he had left it but he had only a single unexposed plate left. When he later developed it, he found that the image captured exactly what he had seen and felt at that moment.
Stieglitz believed that photography could be a metaphoric expression of the author's inner

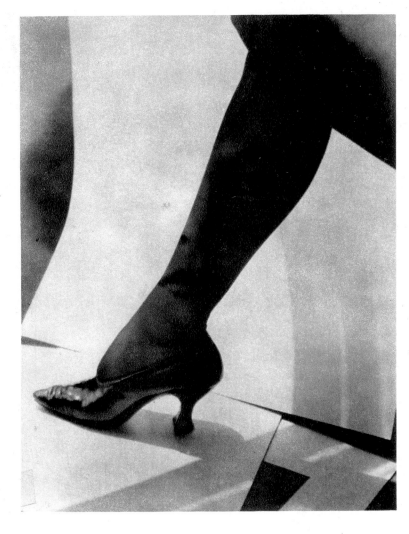

# Drahomír Josef Růžička

These young people had a different life experience and different views from those older photographers who ran the photographic clubs. For them, photography was not a mere hobby to idle leisure time away. Nor did they want to use photography as a mere gratification of their creative urge. What they wanted was to speak to the public and they wanted to do so through straight photography rather than by imitating photographically other arts. In this situation Dr. Růžička materialized as a proverbial deus-ex-machina to show the young a new way; to reveal to them that photography could be a unique, independent medium of expression.

Růžička was a staunch advocate of the

In 1921, Drahomír Růžička, a popular physician to New York's Czech community and an ardent promoter of American straight Photo-Secessionist photography, came for an extended visit to the country of his ancestors, Bohemia. His arrival was to actively influence the further development of Czech photography which was then experiencing a generation gap. The period saw the emergence of a young generation of photographers who had just recently returned home from the battlefields of World War I.

Photo-Secessionist principles and had even helped Clarence White to establish the association of Pictorial Photographers of America. He was strongly against decorativism and symbolism because he deeply revered objective reality, albeit a reality grasped subjectively with the camera. Růžička flatly rejected all fine print, transfer and pigment processes, regarding them as non-photographic. He advocated the use of light as a means of modelling and emphasizing the rendition of the surface texture of the photographed object. Above all Růžička's concern was that the negative should remain untouched. His credo 'A perfect negative produces a perfect enlargement' included any interference with the image, with the exception of the mask. Through this philosophy Růžička discovered for Czech photographers the world of ordinary things as photographic subjects.

Růžička visited his old country several times. Whereas during his first stay in Bohemia he still used the soft lens technique, during subsequent visits he strongly advocated sharply focused images. No longer content with exhibiting together with other photographers, holding discussions and showing his work only to friends, in 1925 he held a one-man show in Prague. For Prague, the show was a revelation of straight photography. Růžička was originally a landscape photographer but later started making monumental pictures of urban architecture. In both fields his work dealt a great blow to the then still prevailing concept in which photographers were still trying to copy genre painting. In the 1930s Růžička threw his lot in with the young generation of photographers and, influenced by the New Objectivity trend, he took up objective photography.

D. J. Růžička was born in Trhová Kamenice near Chrudim, Bohemia, in the family of a pharmacist. When he was six his family emigrated to America where his father hoped to find a better existence which would enable him take better care of his five children. Růžička studied medicine in the US and in Vienna and in 1894 opened his private practice in New York. He was one of the pioneers of radiology but a lack of knowledge concerning necessary precautions against the dangerous radiation impaired his health for the rest of his life.

In 1904 Růžička started photographing as an amateur and from 1911 on he exhibited all over the world. At the age of fifty he retired from practical medicine and devoted his time solely to photography. His influence on modern Czech photography is a unique example of the importance of a single personality on the photographic art of a nation.

# Edward Steichen

/1879—1973/

Edward Steichen lived a long and fruitful life during which he always had his finger on the pulse of the times. Steichen never thought of photography as an isolated medium but as integral part of his art and his entire life style. This is perhaps why his name appeared prominently in all major stages of development of art from the early 20th century up to the 1970s when he died.

Born Édouard Jean Steichen, he emigrated to America with his parents from his native Luxembourg. He studied at an art school and designed posters for a lithographic company. In 1900, when he was 21, he met Alfred Stieglitz and together with other photographers they formed the Photo-Secession. From then on Steichen's name was associated with all the innovations in American photography up to his death. He helped Stieglitz with the management of the '291' Gallery, discovering new talents not only among photographers but also painters. In addition, he designed covers for the Photo-Secessionist quarterly, *Camera Work.* However, his own photographic work long remained in the style of pictorialism and the canon of soft lens usage. Then came World War I and Steichen as the commanding officer of an aerial photography unit was forced to make sharp, clear pictures from the badly vibrating aircraft. He began to appreciate the appeal and impact of straight, unstylized photography, its emotionally charged detail and wide tone scale. 'Now I wanted to know all that could be expected from photography,' he said about this time, some years later. After his discharge from the airforce, he destroyed his previous Impressionist and aestheticizing work, swearing to devote his time only to 'straight', or 'pure' photography. This was precisely the time when the traditional concepts of attractiveness and beauty were rapidly losing value while the new tendencies were oriented towards showing the world as it is.

Thus, Steichen radically changed his approach to photography and his style. He began experimenting, trying to understand and utilize all aspects of photographic expression. He even went so far as to make over one thousand studies of a single white cup and saucer against a grey background.

Everything that Steichen undertook was an

instant success. He worked as chief photographer for the prestigious Condé Nast publishing firm, became famous as fashion photographer for *Vogue* and as a portrait photographer of *Vanity Fair*. He provided large format wall photographs for *A Century of Progress International Exhibition* in Chicago. When World War II broke out Steichen became the commanding officer of the aerial photography unit for the US Navy.

It was roughly at this time that he started thinking about using photography in a new way: an entirely new type of a photographic exhibition where the individual pictures would not speak just for themselves but would be carefully arranged in a composition which would convey a new message.

The first of such shows opened in 1942 in the Museum of Modern Art in New York. Five years later Steichen became Director of Photography of the Museum of Modern Art. In this capacity, Steichen organized forty-four other exhibitions of this kind. The critic J. Deschine wrote that 'these expositions have given the word "exhibition" a new meaning'. The most famous exhibition of all, the legendary *Family of Man*, is still considered a milestone in photographic history, the beginning of a new stage of development of photography — photography concerned with the fate of the human race, the meaning of life and the moral responsibility of mankind for humanity. With Steichen's *Family of Man*, humanist photography emerged as a concept. When Edward Steichen died, he left behind the fruits of almost a century of life; a life of constant growth and learning: 'When I first became interested in photography ... my idea was to have it recognized as one of the fine arts. Today I don't give a host in hell about that. The mission of photography is to explain man to man and each man to himself.'

# Paul Strand

/1890 — 1976/

encounters. During his studies at the Ethical Culture School in New York, he was influenced by a member of the faculty, the sociologist and photographer Lewis Hine who taught him to respect fact and reality. A few years later Strand met Alfred Stieglitz and it was at his '291' Gallery that Strand first realized that the unique aesthetic power of photography stemmed from its ability to reveal the true nature of things, their true character hidden under the visible surface. Absorbing Hine's and Stieglitz's powerful stimuli and influenced by modern trends in painting, Strand transformed the traditional concepts of reality into a new vision which

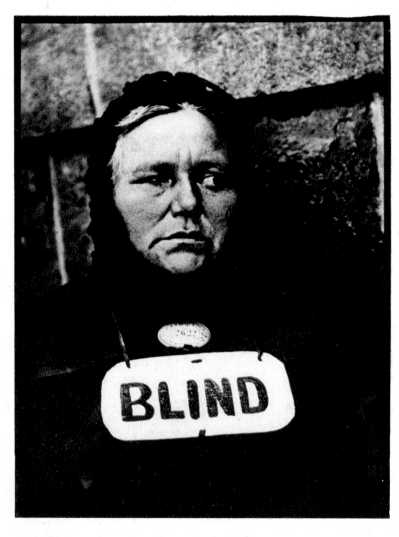

The last two issues of the *Camera Work* magazine from 1916 and 1917 presented the work of a young photographer which years later Alfred Stieglitz characterized as 'brutally direct, pure and devoid of trickery'. The name of the photographer was Paul Strand and his work represented the final break with the traditional concepts of photographic subject matter and conformity of expression, and constituted a pure example of straight photography which ultimately became the basis of the traditions of modern American photography.
Strand's role in the development of photography as an art was determined by two

fused together two seemingly contradictory approaches: documentarism and abstraction. He was attracted to documentarism because he was interested in the qualities of ordinary objects, their shape and the texture of their surface, while abstraction appealed to him because he hoped to photograph real forms which would be an expression of ideal experience. The ideas of documentarism and abstraction made him place the camera as close to the subject as possible, to observe it

57  Blind, 1916
58  Men from Santa Anna, Lake Pátzcuaro, 1933
59  Church, Chimayo, 1931
60  Graveyard, Vermont, 1946

copies as direct contact printing. His interest in the expressive potential of the camera ultimately made him experiment with movie pictures. In 1920—1 he worked as a cameraman, collaborating on the production of a poetic movie called *Manahatta*, a joint project with Charles Sheeler the photographer and painter. In the early 1930s Strand was appointed chief of photography and cinematography at the Department of Fine Arts of Mexico's Secretariat of Education, and worked as a film documentarist. 'I think it's very important for the photographer to realize that his art ... is related to all the other arts ... He doesn't have

at a close distance from various angles and to capture as sharp an image as possible. In this way Strand made his famous pictures of shadows cast by a picket fence, of kitchen bowls, telegraph poles, trees, leaves, rocks, landscapes and people. The pictures were taken on a large format camera, the negatives or prints being totally untouched, their strength being in their perfect rendition and objectivity.

'Objectivity is of the very essence of photography, its contribution and at the same time its limitation ...' thus he formulated his concept of photography in 1917. 'Honesty no less than intensity of vision is the prerequisite of a living expression. This means a real respect for the thing in front of ... the photographer ... The fullest realization of this is accomplished without tricks of process or manipulation through the use of straight photographic methods.' Later, when he was

teaching photography, Strand was fond of adding to this credo that the camera had its own aesthetics and that, unless this was generally accepted, photography could never free itself from the bondage of painting. What Strand also had in mind was the need to master perfectly photographic techniques because he was one of the first to emphasize the basic use of the camera and laboratory processing in the final aesthetic quality of the image.

Strand's most frequent studies were people and nature. Wherever he took pictures, be it in Mexico, France, Italy, Egypt, the Hebrides or Morocco, Strand always attempted to capture the fragrance and taste of the place, the landscape and the local way of life. For years, he produced only contact prints of his negatives, usually 20 × 25 cm in size. Strand adopted enlargement only when he became satisfied that it could produce as perfect

to know about it in detail, but it's very important to know what they did and for the photographer to relate himself to the vision of mankind that has taken form in all the arts.' This statement showed that Paul Strand fully realized the need for a comparative view which would help the photographer understand his own medium better. In this respect, his interest in photography and film was not a mere fancy.

49

# Edward Weston

/1886—1958/

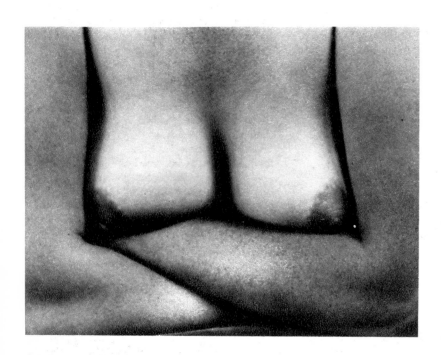

life, for rendering the very substance and quintessence of the thing itself ... [and that] the very approach to photography is through realism.' Destroying practically all his previous work, he started anew.

He started studying the forms of the simplest of natural objects as well as items of everyday use produced by man. He studied the role of light, trying to express as truly as possible the structure, texture and facture of the subject. He became obsessed with nature, left the studio forever and following the example of his close friend, the poet Robinson Jeffers, he settled near Carmel, California, amidst unspoilt coastal landscape where he found what he was searching for: sand dunes untouched by human feet, quiet lacustrine waters, picturesquely shaped rocks and trees. His ideas were transformed into a unique personal style. He strived for a perfect rendition of reality and his images showed an absolutely sharp definition throughout the entire field, creating a perfect effect of plasticity and light. The pictures are

'Dear Papa, received camera in good shape. It's a dandy ... I think I can make it work all right,' wrote Edward Weston at the age of sixteen after his father had finally given it to his pleading and bought him a camera. By the time he reached nineteen, Weston was making a living as a door-to-door photographer, snapping pictures of people's children, family reunions, weddings and funerals, a dozen prints for a dollar each. At thirty-one he was known internationally. Working in his California studio, he employed soft lenses to produce romantic pictures of primaballerinas and Hollywood stars, sending his prints to photographic *salons* everywhere from New York to London. Then, in 1915, he first encountered modern painting, music and literature at the San Francisco Panama-Pacific International Exhibition which emphasized culture rather than achievements of industry and technology. Weston was deeply impressed by what he saw and in time he became acquainted with the work of Stieglitz, Strand and Sheeler, and discovered the poetic beauty of industrial structures in Ohio, and in Mexico where he met artists such as Diego Rivera, José Clemente Orozco and David Alfaro Siqueiros. He came to the conclusion that 'the camera must be used for recording

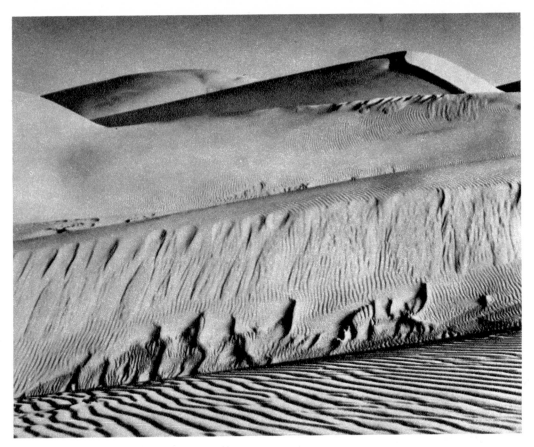

a reproduction of nature. I wonder why it should affect one emotionally — and I wonder what prompted me to record it. Many photographs might have taken this palm, and they would be just photographs of a palm. Yet this is a photograph of a palm, plus something — something — and I cannot quite say what that something is . . .' he commented on one of his pictures in his *Mexican Daybook.* To photograph a palm tree, a rock or a piece of wood to make them look just what they are and yet something more, this was the eternal objective of Weston's work.

Edward Weston married four times, had four sons and when he died on New Year's Day 1958, in his house on the Wild Cat Hill near Carmel, California, he had not taken a picture in ten years because of a serious nervous disorder. Throughout his career he never retouched his pictures, nor did he use masks, he never enlarged his pictures, he always used a large format camera and all his pictures are contact prints of his negatives. Between 1923 and 1943 he made it his custom to record his experience, thoughts and ideas in writing. Published much later, these *Daybooks* remain a unique document of the creative and emotional life of a man who has become a father figure of the American vision in photography.

dominated by simple, abstracted shapes and by light radiated by the rendered objects. He tried to 'see more than the human eye' and indeed, compared to Weston's imagery, human vision seems imperfect. His greatest desire was to let nature speak for itself, to make it reveal its inner meaning. 'The photographer's power lies in his ability to re-create his subject in terms of its basic reality, and present this re-creation in such a form that the spectator feels that he is seeing not just a symbol for the object, but the thing itself revealed for the first time.' Weston's philosophy and his approach to art gave birth, in 1932, to an association of young photographers known as 'f/64' Group. The name was derived from the maximum aperture setting of the large format camera from which the group members required maximum definition in accordance with the aesthetics of straight photography which Weston brought to an unprecedented peak, especially in his pictures from Point Lobos which are thought to be the peak of perfection for this type of photography. Here, Weston's effort to let the object speak for itself is overwhelmed by the intensity of his emotion. It is as if in these photographs the object fused with the subject. Light becomes the essential carrier of meaning, emanating from objects, infusing them with life, creating an unseverable bond between man and nature. 'Just the trunk of a palm tree towering up to the sky; not even a real one — a palm on a piece of paper,

# Ansel Adams

/1902 — 1984/

coloured and modulated by the great earth gesture of the Sierra.' He continued to study music but continually interrupted his studies regularly to make trips to the Sierra Nevada, eventually becoming totally obsorbed by photography and mountain climbing. Only as late as 1930 did he finally decide to make photography his career. The decision came at the time when he first met Paul Strand whose pictures revealed to him the potentials of straight photography. At last he found a means of expressing what he experienced in nature, and from then he devoted his time fully to precise, sharply focused, realistic photography. Six years later he received wide publicity when Alfred Stieglitz organized Adams' first independent show.

Originally, Adams wanted to be a concert pianist but he became a poet of visual imagery instead. His pictures are such masterful renditions of reality that in their time they were considered to *be* reality rather than its image. However, technique in

Ansel Adams has been called a 'poet of the American West'. Indeed, his pictures, full of dramatic moods and emotion, constitute a lyrical confession, a celebration and even a mystic idolatry of the natural beauty of this landscape. He was just fourteen when he first visited the Yosemite Valley and spent the rest of his life celebrating its breathtaking beauty. He went with a Kodak Brownie and expected to spend more time sporting than taking pictures, but the beauty of the landscape he found was, as he has called it, 'a culmination of experience so intense as to be almost painful. From that day in 1916 my life has been

photography, as in other arts, is but a vehicle for expressing one's feelings and what Ansel Adams tried to discover was that which would best convey his own mood and emotion. He would spend long hours waiting patiently for the right play of light during sunrise or sunset, for dramatic clusters of clouds penetrated by sun rays, for the shadows of the evening to start falling. For him, the landscape was never a static, unchangeable subject but rather an ever-changing image as fleeting as the light which constantly re-defined it, permitting him to make an unending series of variations of the same theme. It was his sensitive understanding of the specific quality of light falling on a specific place at a specific moment which allowed him to perfect his legendary technique. Thanks to this technique, the photographed objects seem as if they are freed from their natural environment, becoming exact, yet unreal reflections of reality. 'A great photograph is a full expression of what one feels about what is being photographed in the deepest sense, and is, thereby, a true expression of what one feels about life in its entirety. And the expression of what one feels should be set forth in terms of simple devotion to the medium — a statement of the utmost clarity and perfection possible under the conditions of creation and production.' Thus Ansel Adams has formulated his creative credo. Aware of the great importance of technical aspects of photography for the result of the photographer's work, he systematically studied photographic techniques and even published several books on the methods of the exact determination of the correct exposure and on the use of laboratory processes. Although an ardent admirer of Weston's 'large

format classicism', his technique differs considerably from this. Whereas Weston was largely interested in natural detail and surface structure, Adams remains predominantly a landscapist; he is even more subjective and lyrical in his approach than Weston. Ansel Adams has left his personal mark on photography not only with his pictures but also his publications and his untiring organization works — he is a co-founder of the Photographic Collections of the Museum of Modern Art and the San Francisco Art Institute. First and formost he has been an enthusiastic and dedicated promoter of

straight photography. At the age of seventy-two he went to Europe for the first time in his life to attend a festival of photography and photographers at Arles, France. In an interview he aptly compared American and European photography: 'I'm quite impressed by the symbolization of the subject I saw here. To me, this seems to be a venture beyond reality, as compared to American photography which investigates reality for reality's sake . . .' For this matter-of-fact, sober approach to photography, American photography is indeed greatly indebted to Ansel Adams.

# Josef Sudek

/1896—1976/

Josef Sudek did not have an easy life. Member of a one parent family, his father was a house-painter, and immediately upon finishing his apprenticeship as a bookbinder he was drafted to fight in World War I. He lost his right arm and spent three long years in various army hospitals, especially in Prague's Disabled Veterans' Home. Obviously as an invalid he could not return to bookbinding but the clerical jobs that were offered to him did not appeal either, as he used to say: 'It was springtime and the streets of Prague were full of sparrows' song.' Then, at the age of 24, he enrolled in a school of graphic arts and started a long, insecure career as a photographer. From the beginning he took an active part in the struggle for the assertion of modern Czech photography, rebelling with his friends Funke and Schneeberger against the decorativism and lack of real message of club photography. In 1924 he founded an independent Czech Photographic Society as a platform for modern photography. His nature and his desire to be free to create soon forced him to resolve once and for all the conflict between commercialism and creative freedom and the responsibility of a creative artist, problems essential for the growth of a creative personality: he never succumbed to the lure of style or money, always obstinately remaining true to his ideals. His aesthetic obstinacy marked all his work from commissions, commercial reproduction, advertising and portrait photography, to his work for various publishers and particularly his own commercial studio work.

In the 1940s Sudek decided to devote his time solely to free photography and was never to work commercially again. Embittered and dejected by the Nazi occupation of his country, he started living in isolation and poverty, subsisting often on dry bread and onions. His work acquired a more intimate character. In his studio — a wooden shack in the middle of Prague's Old Town tenement houses district — he became totally absorbed in 'the poetry of everyday objects'. Living with his ideas, dreams and music, he observed the everchanging windows of his studio: dewed with myriads of tiny rainbow-coloured droplets on balmy summer dawns; washed and blurred by rainy days like painter's

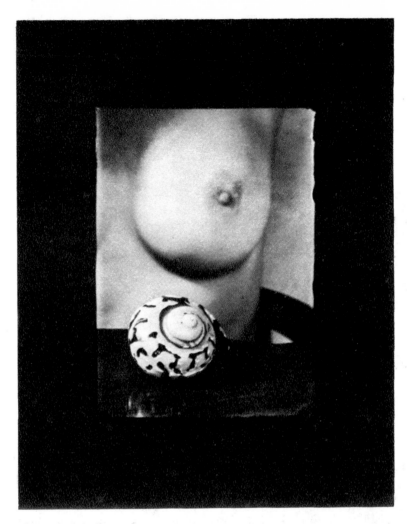

watercolours; embellished by surreal sculptures of frost. Outside, he sensed the external world: the silhouette of a bare tree skeleton; a fence post capped with snow. Thus, his *Windows* series of photographs was born, revealing Sudek's fascination with the poetry of the mysterious, ambiguous and indefinite. 'The beauty of all things lies in the mysterious . . .' he was fond of saying. At this time he also started working on his photographic series *Still Lifes*. He loved the world of ordinary things and had a unique talent for discovering in it a supreme beauty. He photographed everything around him which was a part of his day-to-day existence: a glass, an egg, bread, onions, an apple, a vase with flowers.

World War II was a turning point in Sudek's art not only in terms of it becoming more intimate but also because Sudek made a discovery which was to be of essential importance to his understanding of photographic quality. In 1940 he chanced to come across an old photograph of a statue in Chartres. The picture was 30 × 40 cm in size but as Sudek found out to his astonishment it was not an enlargement but a contact print of the negative. He was thrilled to notice the perfect rendition of the character of the stone and the pictorial quality of the image. From that time he never made an enlargement again and thus all his photographs produced after 1940 are contact prints of large format negatives. As in Weston's work, using large format became one of the style-forming elements of Sudek's work after 1940. In the contact print Sudek found what he was looking for since he never saw the quality of a photograph in its reproducibility but in a repeated rendition of the author's original. Sudek's photographs stem from his soul. He was fond of illusive lighting transforming real objects so that they tune in with the photographer's emotion and mood, making objects sometimes appear surreal. In Sudek's imagery it often seems as if the light is the main object and symbolic content of his message. It gleams, flashes, shimmers, infuses the objects with a soul of their own, takes up the entire space of the picture. Sudek's photography is an expression of an ideal experience, a culmination of photography's efforts to become true art.

# IV

# PHOTOGRAPHY AS WITNESS

From the beginning photography has been undergoing continual, rapid development. Regardless of transitory bias and orientation along the way photography has always been concerned with a single grand subject: man. The new medium soon became dissatisfied with the mere rendition of the human face or scenes of family life. Photography was eager to do more than just capture a face or a scene, it wanted to convey a message, to offer a commentary, to penetrate the surface and come up with the quintessence of life. Thus towards the end of the 19th century photography became the conscience of society, a critic, public attorney and judge. In this capacity, photography had a great psychological advantage because faith in photography as a reflection of reality produced a firm conviction that whereas painting or literature might be a fabrication, the camera, being bound by reality, must tell the truth.

It was no accident that the first attempts to use the camera for social commentary took place in England. In the early 1850s, at the time when Karl Marx was studying the increasing antagonisms of capitalism in England formulating his political ideas, a large sociological study was published in London under the title *London Labour and London Poor*. It was illustrated by woodcuts made from daguerreotypes by Richard Beard. Once the daguerreotypes had been rendered graphically, the pictures lost their original character but that this work was the conception of photography as a socially concerned document is beyond any doubt. It is tragic that the original daguerreotypes have not survived. At the end of the 1850s another book was published in London. This predominantly pictorial publication was titled *Street Life in London* and its author, the photographer John Thomson, put it together from his photographs of the life and work of the poorest urban class. At the same time, Frank Meadow Sutcliffe was photographing rural life in Yorkshire, training his lens on fishermen, market vendors, shopping housewives, children at play, itinerant musicians and farmhands at their back-breaking labour in the fields. However, Sutcliffe's pictures long remained unfamiliar to the general public and became widely

known only a century after they had been taken.

These, as well as many other works of this type, were still far from offering a critical view of reality, but they did constitute a sort of genre photography or photographic evidence to back up scholarly work. Nevertheless, even at this time, photography attempted to become more than a tool for social analysis — attempting to serve as social commentary in itself. In this way photography acquired the basic character of what was later to be called photodocumentarism. The places where this newly discovered ability of photography could be utilized fully were those countries which at the end of the last century were experiencing the the the worst social turmoil: the United States of America and Czarist Russia.

By 1900 photography had also become a plaything, especially in the hands of the affluent. The upper and middle classes started using the camera to capture memorable events in their lives, to record family history and to make pictures of their loved ones. This snapshot photography soon became a vogue. Cameras were owned by the aesthetically sensitive and insensitive alike. It was up to a French boy named Jacques-Henri Lartigue, however, to turn his family album — which he had started making at the age of six and to which he continued to add for the rest of his life — into a chronicle of his time, a chronicle composed entirely of amateur snapshots yet infused with the taste, fragrance and spirit of the period and its upheavals, changes, paradoxes and peripeties. It was another Frenchman, from a different social background from Lartigue, who recorded Paris with its multitude of images from historical palaces and gardens to boulevards teeming with life and deserted streetcorners; merchandise on display on the pavement in shop-fronts, the ethereal reflections in shop windows. His name was Eugène Atget and his camera went everywhere with him, capturing all he saw. Atget became an encyclopedist of the city yet his greatness lay in something totally different, for through photography Atget discovered a world of the most simple things, making the spectator look at them with new eyes. He did not snap the external appearance of reality; his pictures seem as if they had been created from within, as if the

artist had looked at things through the prism of his own emotion and experience, as if his emotional involvement had given the photograph an extra dimension. The results of this approach were not pictures intended originally as *documents pour artistes* but rather masterpieces of documentary photography. It was Atget who made a technical device, the camera, produce a deep, emotional testimony about our world. It was he who showed in his pictures a reality that was different from ordinary vision: a reality that was deeper and more profound. Among the first men who proved how powerful a weapon the camera could be in fighting social evil were Jacob A. Riis in the United States and Maxim Dmitriev in Russia. Riis employed the camera to show Americans the inhuman conditions of New York slum tenements overcrowded with thousands of immigrants from all over the world. In the end his photographs turned out to be more powerful than the journalistic articles they accompanied. Maxim Dmitriev did practically the same in the early 1890s and did so out of sheer desperation because as a dedicated revolutionary he realized that the only thing that would appeal to the conscience of the public and make people help the famine-stricken Volga basin was an authentic picture of what was taking place. As in the case of Riis, the pictures aroused public indignation and the Czarist government had to provide assistance. Of course, Dmitriev was not the only Russian artist to concentrate on the social conditions of the people for there were writers and painters of the same persuasion, and even photographers such as S. A. Lobovikov, N. A. Petrov, W. Carrick and others, but none went so far as to use photography as quite such a persuasive campaign tool.

Then on the scene came one of the greatest documentarists in the entire history of photography, Lewis Wickes Hine, a sociologist who included photography in his scholarly apparatus as a reliable source of case data concerning social conditions. A passionate loathing for social ills took Hine to mines, mills and sweatshops where he recorded the brutal exploitation of child labour, and to crowded tenement houses full of the human misery of those who had come to the New World seeking hope and finding only hunger, poverty and destitution. Hine always regarded photography as a social tool rather than an art. Yet like Atget he not only recorded social ills but became deeply involved in the events he recorded and this gives his pictures impact and strength. Thanks to Hine, we have today an authentic, emotionally involved pictorial testimony of the rise of capitalism in America.

In the years that followed photography began to play an increasingly important social role, becoming the stentorian voice raised in the defence of the insulted, injured and unfortunate. Then came the Great Depression and in 1933 some 16 million unemployed were registered in the US alone. The Roosevelt administration organized relief on large scale and recruited photographers to gather evidence which would help the government to push through the New Deal legislation in Congress. The team of photographers began working for the Farm Security Administration headed by Roy E. Stryker, a professor of economics. This was the first photographic team in history to work on an assignment from a government body to record living conditions for sociologic purposes. During the latter half of the 1930s these photographers took more than a quarter of a million pictures, mapping in detail the suffering of thousands of Americans. These documentarists made the notion of documentary photography part of the history of photography. Their collective work constitutes one of the best ever produced in photography because Roy E. Stryker hired for the team a number of outstanding photographers whose names have since come to symbolize humanist photography: Dorothea Lange, Walker Evans, Arthur Rothstein, Russell Lee, Ben Shahn, Gordon Parks and others.

The Great Depression also uprooted the economic system of Central Europe. The crisis in Germany paved the way for the Nazis who were to make work impossible for two major German photographers: Erich Salomon, the father of emerging photojournalism, and August Sander, who was unable to finish his large project *People of the Twentieth Century*, a pictorial social document of the period which still has not been surpassed in its contribution to social typology.

From the late 19th century to the outbreak of World War II, photojournalists concentrated on capturing contemporary conditions of life. Wherever they trained their cameras, they saw human misery and suffering, but they also managed to capture man's inner strength, his human dignity, his faith. These photographers believed that if they showed people the ills of the world, remedies would be found. In this respect, unfortunately, they were just romantic idealists.

Starting in the 1920s, documentary photography also began to be used for purely political purposes, especially in those countries which had experienced severe political and economic crisis and social revolution after World War I. Germany saw thus the birth of an international, revolution-oriented mass movement of worker photographers known as *Arbeiter-Fotograf* which influenced the establishment of a similar movement, the so-called Photo-League, in the United States in the 1930s. A highly active group of photographers of a similar persuasion existed even in semi-fascist Hungary, known as *Szociofotó*. The same name, *Sociofoto*, was adopted by the Slovak Progressive Photographers' Group, whose Czech counterpart was the Film-Foto Group of the Left Front, a left-wing socio-political and cultural association.

In Soviet Russia, photography was likewise used as a political tool, although its objectives were pursued from the opposite bank, so to speak. In the USSR, photography became the chief promoter of the construction of a socialist society — propaganda.

Throughout its development, photography has been attuned to the spirit of social protest against oppression, inhumanity and human degradation, a spirit that has always remained photography's most valuable ethical and humanistic contribution to mankind.

# Frank Meadow Sutcliffe

/1853—1941/

The life and work of Frank Meadow Sutcliffe was intimately associated with the northeastern corner of England. It was in Whitby, Yorkshire, that Sutcliffe spent a happy childhood with his family. His father was a painter, writer and art critic, widely known and respected throughout the area, and it was perhaps this intellectual and creative background that made the young Sutcliffe open a photographic studio. However, he often left the business unattended because he preferred working outdoors in the salty air of this lovely coastal area.

English photography in the 1870s and 1880s was still heavily influenced by the romantic creations of Rejlander and Robinson and followers of these two strong personalities were rapidly slipping into producing pictures which oozed sentiment and even outright kitsch. The time was ripe for a new aesthetics and before Peter Henry Emerson formulated his ideas for a return to nature, a few other photographers, perhaps of lesser note, preceded him.

One of these men was Sutcliffe, a commercial photographer usually ranked by historians of photography among the pictorialists enraptured by soft tones, and picturesque scenes. His outdoor work, however, reveals quite different qualities. Sutcliffe was one of the first pioneers of a new vision which fifty years later was to be called documentary photography. Naturally, Sutcliffe did not acquire this new vision overnight. His photograph *Water Rats,* showing a group of small boys in a rowing boat, is still largely marked by the pictorialist approach. The picture has an interesting history. It was taken in 1886 and since Sutcliffe was a regular contributor to exhibitions of all kinds, he entered *Water Rats* in the annual show of the Royal Photographic Society in London. The Prince of Wales, later King Edward VII, liked the picture so much that he purchased it. This provided great satisfaction to Sutcliffe who had been excommunicated by the prudish Whitby clergy on the grounds that his picture had a depraving effect.

What is valuable in Sutcliffe's work is not his genre pictures but rather his pictorial documents of the period and the people. These pictures, which show fishermen, itinerant musicians, smiling country women and small town matrons, comedians, draymen, firemen, farmers or women collecting

driftwood, are simple, unpretentious and earthy. They document the hard life but also produce a nostalgia for the 'good old days' when these fishing villages lived a hard existence but people remained close to nature and to each other. The dry development process discovered at about this time made Sutcliffe's work much easier but the long exposures remained a limitation and the photographer therefore had to pose his models. Still, Sutcliffe succeeded in giving his images such a natural, light and good-hearted character that they have become an outstanding document of the time.

At seventy, Sutcliffe retired from photography. Twelve years later he was honoured for his work with Honorary Membership of the Royal Photographic Society of Great Britain. By this time documentary photography had been long established but Sutcliffe's contribution

remained unrecognized in the shadow of the work of John Thomson, photographer of London street life. It was only as late as in

1974 that a book of Sutcliffe's work established his credit as one of the pioneers of documentary photography.

# Maxim Petrovich Dmitriev

/1858—1948/

Throughout history, the Upper Volga basin has often been ravaged by famine, drought and epidemics but never so hard as in 1891. The crops were a total failure and people and cattle had nothing to live on. The Czarist government remained largely uninterested in the fate of the *muzhik* peoples (peasants) of the area because, after all, they maintained, the country had too many people to feed, anyway. This time, however, the powerful were forced to act. In the centre of the stricken region, in the town of Nizhni Novgorod (now Gorki), a large group of intelligentsia gathered around the writer Vladimir Korolenko and used all means at their disposal to persuade the public to provide relief. Korolenko himself had spent five years of imprisonment and exile in Siberia but did not hesitate to publish a caustic sketch entitled *The Year of Famine,* in which he accused the government of the crime of fighting the hungry rather than hunger.

One of these men was a photographer named Maxim Petrovich Dmitriev. He abandoned his Novgorod studio and travelled in the most heavily stricken areas, photographing the emaciated bodies of peasants, cattle half mad with hunger, entire villages devastated by typhoid fever and cholera. Defying censorship, his friends helped him to publish his pictures in magazines as a document of social injustice. Like the work of his contemporaries such as Riis and Hine, working on the other side of the world, his pictures aroused public interest and indicted the powerful. As a strong voice condemning the Czarist autocracy the pictures helped to initiate the flow of relief to the stricken area. In the end they even appeared in book form when Dmitriev printed them in the autotype business which he had opened next door to his studio in the early 1890s. The portfolio was titled *The Cropless Year 1891—92 in the Province of Nizhni Novgorod: Photographs from Nature by M. Dmitriev.* In the means employed and objectives foreseen, this relief project was practically identical to the famous New Deal policies of the US Farm Security Administration during the Great Depression forty years later.

In his early years as a photographer Dmitriev had been apprenticed to the portraitist and landscapist Andrei Karelin, but had always been more interested in capturing the raw beauty of life. He found ample opportunity in Nizhni Novgorod, an urban centre with developing trade and industry where hungry, poverty-stricken peasants came looking for work. It was in this milieu that the young photographer found lasting inspiration. Although he knew only too well that he could

not count on receiving much publicity, he sent his pictures to every Russian photographic exhibition as well as to Paris, Antwerp and Chicago. Contemporary critics had always denied him the right to exhibit but now his Upper Volga photographs were likened to the critically acclaimed style of the 'red landscapist', Gustave Courbet, the artist of the 1871 *Paris Commune*.

Perhaps it was Dmitriev's life-long friendship with Maxim Gorki which made him concentrate on social motifs. The great Russian writer often sought inspiration in Dmitriev's photographs and in 1902 even asked him to take pictures of Russia's social down-and-outs for the actors of the Moscow Art Theatre who were rehearsing Gorki's play *Lower Depths* under Stanislavski.

Since the beginning of his career as a photographer, Dmitriev had been attracted by the power of photography as document. In the late 1880s he undertook a most difficult project, attempting to record the landscape and people of the Volga River. For nine consecutive summers he travelled the river from the source to the estuary, taking several thousand pictures. Although no sociologist, his photography involved him in a systematic analysis of society.

# Jacques-Henri Lartigue

/1894—1986/

Jacques-Henri Lartigue had no ambition to be a photographer and in spite of his achievements in this field has never regarded himself as one. It was only for fun that he started snapping pictures of his relatives, friends and acquaintances, anything that took his fancy. *Mon Papa et Maman, Mon frère Zissou deguisé en fantome, Ma cousine Simone dans la plage, Ma nounou Dudu, Lilian au volant de ma voiture Pic-Pic, Mon jardin secret, Bibi à Nice,* such are the captions of his purely personal, totally unpretentious pictures, full of the charming naiveté characteristic of almost all amateur snapshots. He grew up in *la belle époque,* the happy times, those few short years which shone

brightly at the turn of the century, and were extinguished forever in the trenches of World War I. Yet in spite of its short duration it was a grand era of industrial boom and technological advancement revolutionizing labour, leisure and life style, the time of the first automobiles and motorcycles and those daring young men and their flying machines. Paris was the meeting place and playground for socialites and bohemians, a metropolis of fashion and art. The promenade in the Bois de Boulogne was frequented by rich aristocrats and industrialists, theatre stars, fashion trend-setting ladies and cocottes, for it was a place to be seen in.

Jacques-Henri Lartigue, the son of an affluent

family, was only five when he discovered modern photography. First he tried to photograph with his eyes, opening and closing them again to capture in his mind's eye the scenes and views which appealed to him. When he was unable to recollect them later, he was so unhappy and dejected that Père Lartigue finally consented to buy him a camera. Little Jacques took his first picture when he was six but he had to stand on a stool to be able to see onto the ground glass viewfinder of his tripod-mounted camera. The next year he was given for his birthday a hand-held plate camera, with relatively high-speed-shutter and short exposure time. This was the real 'picture trap' he longed for.

overnight transformed Lartigue into one of the best known photographers of all time. Lartigue was soon called a child genius because it seemed quite improbable that a six-year-old boy could have consciously started photographing systematically in a manner as spontaneous, direct and fresh as the style of the generation of photographers which followed his, facilitated among other things also by light and easy to handle reportage cameras. Whatever the reason, Lartigue's photography is the work of an exceptionally sensitive person unfettered by traditions, prejudices or the experience of others. It was probably artistic intuition which produced these private snapshots that have since become a living chronicle of the times.

He started recording virtually everything around him. As he grew older, he pointed his camera at airplanes and automobiles and, later, fashionable women in their romantic lacy dresses and magnificent hats with bird-of-paradise plumes.

This passion for photographing people and things around him never left him, not even when he started studying painting or when he was a relatively well-known painter living alternately in Paris and on the French Riviera whose name appeared more often in social than art columns of the French press.

As a photographer he remained virtually unknown until 1963 when the press hailed him as the 'discovery of the century'. By this time he was sixty-seven and had won high appraisal with his exhibition in the Museum of Modern Art in New York which presented pictures from his album for the first time. Then in 1970 Richard Avedon published a selection of Lartigue's snapshots in book form. The content as well as the presentation resembled a diary and the English language edition of the book was aptly titled *Diary of the Century*. Indeed, the book, which recorded the life of a man in pictures snapped between the age of six and almost eighty, buzzed with the atmosphere of the times and became a record of the changing life style of the 20th century. The exhibition and the book almost

# Eugène Atget

/1857 — 1927/

At about the time Jacques-Henri Lartigue started recording the happy life of his family, Eugène Atget began laying the first stones of his monumental mosaic — a photographic documentary of his beloved Paris. His pictures were often called naive and haphazard because at a time when other photographers were possessed by a desire to outdo painters and were willing to try anything to make their photographs not look like photographs, Atget was photographing 'vulgar' subjects such as street vendors, market stalls and prostitutes on street corners. Atget disparaged the grand ambitions of the new art and offering his small pictures on Paris boulevards to passers-by, he would say: 'They are mere documents, I have thousands of them.'

He took up photography relatively late in his life, at the age of forty-one, for no other reason than to make a living. He was an orphan and his uncle sent him to an orphanage but he spent his time dreaming of wide horizons and a life other than the clergy, a career which had been decided for him by his guardian. He ran away from school and got himself hired as deckhand on a ship leaving for Uruguay. It is uncertain how long he worked as a ship's steward but by 1881 he was back in Paris working as an actor in a travelling company. Not a handsome, masculine-looking man, he never played the leading characters and after eighteen years he left theatre to take up painting. The few paintings that survive testify to a talent that could have grown into a real creative personality. But because he was virtually penniless, he soon took to the more lucrative occupation of photography and each day took a heavy stand-camera and large format plates, and trundled them to churches, parks and lower class residential districts.

His pictures were not a success, for Atget, wrapped closely in this threadbare coat, did not stroll through the haze of early mornings to seek beauty; he did not want to produce art but rather to give expression to the feelings invoked by the place and the atmosphere of the moment.

It is unlikely that Atget realized that his purely
documentary approach was discovering for
future generations of photographers that the
medium was not only able to register reality
but also express feelings, provoke thought and
convey ideas in the mind of the photographer
and that under the surface of reality he was
delving into the soul of things, lending a visual
form to the invisible. He photographed what
he felt he had to, what attracted him
irresistibly. He did not spend long hours like

his contemporary Alfred Stieglitz waiting for
the right moment when everything in front of
the camera was in perfect balance and
composition because what Atget did was to
express his immediate experience of the world
surrounding him.

For twenty years he subsisted on milk, bread
and lumps of sugar. Although his pictures are
priceless now, he used to sell them for 25
centimes each and more often than not merely
loaned them to painters, sculptors, architects
and journalists as study material. The list of
people who borrowed his pictures reads today

like a who's who in art: Vlaminck, Utrillo,
Braque, Kisling, Duchamp, Picasso and Man
Ray. One encounter proved to be a turning
point in Atget's life. A young American
photographer, Berenice Abbott, saw his
pictures in Man Ray's studio and was
fascinated by them. 'Their impact was
immediate and tremendous. There was
a sudden flash of recognition — the shock of
realism unadorned. The subjects were not
sensational, but nevertheless shocking in their
very familiarity. The real world, seen with
wonderment and surprise, was mirrored in

each print.' Thanks to Berenice Abbott his
pictures have been saved for future
generations, for she studied and classified
them and in the end purchased the entire
collection of first prints including the plates.
'Documents for Artists,' stated a plate on the
door of Atget's small apartment at 17 Rue
Campagne Première in the Montparnasse
district. The modest sign was indeed highly
symbolic because Atget's genius lay in letting
his photography use its own language and be
an authentic document of the intense
experience of its maker.

Atget always lived isolated from the
mainstream of photography and its objectives,
and the aims of his photographic
contemporaries were foreign to him. He
became reconciled to not being understood
and even to being ridiculed. Then in 1926 his
luck finally turned and the review *La
Révolution Surréaliste* printed four of his
pictures. It was too late, however, because,
devastated by the death of his wife, Atget died
soon afterwards.

# Jacob August Riis

/1849—1914/

One day in 1886 the New York *Evening Sun* reported that the previous night a strange group of people had been illuminating the city streets, with explosions disrupting the peace and rousing people from sleep. The group that the paper wrote about was composed of a reporter named Riis, two photographers and a public health officer, and the explosions had been caused by ignited magnesium powder, a recent invention which made it possible to take photographs even in the dimmest light. These dim corners were the infamous slums of New York's Lower East Side where three-quarters of the entire population of the largest American city lived cramped in foul-smelling tenements. On a single acre of land there were no less than five hundred and twenty-two houses ravaged by typhoid fever and a steadily climbing suicide rate.

Riis, a daily news police reporter for the *Tribune*, was convinced that the main cause of the crime and mortality rate in this area was the inhuman living conditions. He wrote scores of articles about the festering conditions in the slums, gave lectures, published exposées calling for immediate social reform, all with little result. Then he realized that artificial light photography could be used to advantage to argue his case by providing pictorial evidence which would dramatically highlight his articles. If one half of the country tried to pretend not to see 'how the other half lived', let them try to ignore documentary photographs, he reasoned.

At first he did not know how to take photographs and had to hire a photographer to help. He was not satisfied with the pictures, however, and set about learning photography for himself. It was not easy, for the highly inflammable magnesium was quite dangerous and Riis twice nearly caused major fires and once almost blinded himself. However, his results were astonishing and in 1890 he published a book *How the Other Half Lives,* which was devoted to the conditions of life in New York tenements and was accompanied by photographic evidence that as many as fifteen people were forced to live in a single tiny room; that small children had to sleep on bare floors amidst rubbish; that hygiene was badly lacking. The book, and especially the photographs, caused an uproar and Theodore Roosevelt, then a New York Republican

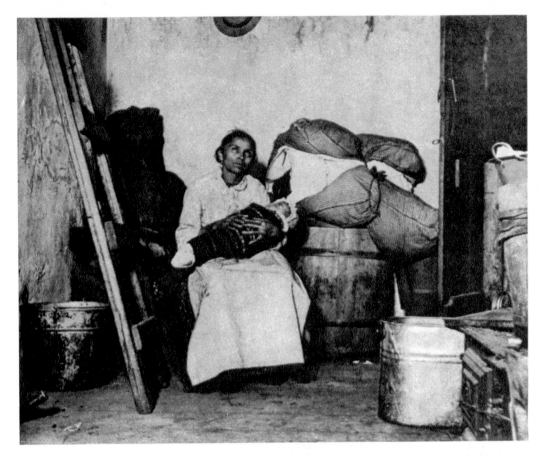

unemployed, hungry and with no place to call his own he lived in desperation and several times was on the verge of committing suicide. He spent many nights in a shelter provided for the homeless by the police. Only after several years of futile searching for a permanent job was he finally hired as a reporter.

As a journalist, Riis gave photography a social assignment which has remained relevant to this day. He was one of the first to show how photography could become a critic, public prosecutor and judge of social ills, a critic more powerful than the written word. His photographs became the conscience of society but their value lies not only in their documentary character but also in their emotional involvement.

politician, later the head of the New York Police Department and ultimately the 26th president of the United States, called at Riis' office one morning while he was out and left a card with this message: 'I have read your book and I have come to help.' The book led to the first New York legislation designed to curb the worst evils of tenement housing. The foul, decrepit houses were torn down and the central part of the former slum area was rebuilt as the Mulberry Street Park with the J. A. Riis Community House.

The fast economic growth of America at that time had not only produced numerous rags-to-riches miracles but also countless impoverished people, their numbers swelled by the influx of immigrants from virtually all corners of the globe: during the first decade of this century some ten million people arrived at America's shores to seek a new life where they could feed and clothe their families, have a place to live, and find desperately needed jobs.

Riis himself knew what it was to be an immigrant. Born in Denmark where he had been a carpenter, he left for the United States at the age of twenty-one. It is not known what compelled him to leave his native country — a better chance of finding a job or a dream of becoming rich quickly, perhaps. Initially

# Lewis Wickes Hine

/1874—1940/

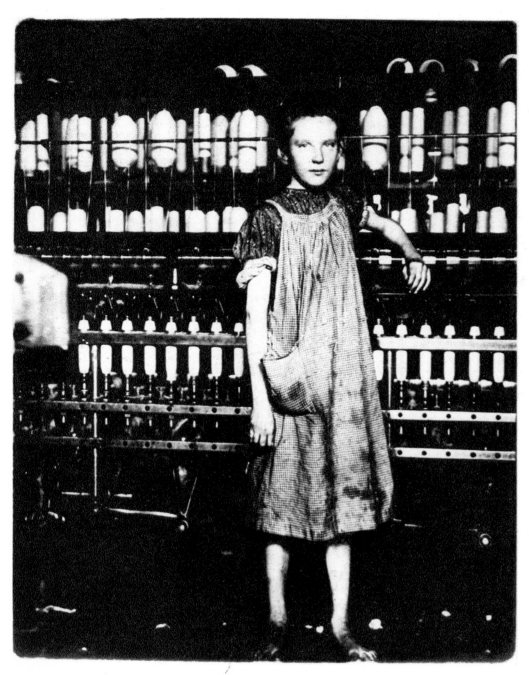

'I wanted to show things that had to be corrected,' was the credo of Lewis Wickes Hine's work. Like Riis, Hine put his faith in photography's ability to mirror society and to arouse its conscience. Unlike his reporter predecessor, however, who had merely used photographs to document what he had been writing about, Hine relied on photography alone to convey his message. As a sociologist, he put photography to the service of social research.

Hine was given his first camera by a friend to use as a teaching aid because he was then earning his living as a teacher of natural sciences. Every day Hine visited New York's Ellis Island, the immigration point for the largest migration into any country in modern history. Daily, ships landed thousands of people here, mostly those on whom Europe had turned her back. It was here that Hine realized that this human suffering and emotion defied words and that only with photographs could the situation be conveyed. In 1908 he was hired by the National Child Labour Committee as official photographer, and spent the next thirteen years travelling all over the country, photographing West Virginian mines, South Carolina cotton mills, Indiana glass factories, the cotton fields of the South and the sugar beet belt of the Midwest, in urban streets and on fishing boats, in rich households — wherever children were forced to work as many as twelve hours a day to make a living. On the back of his prints, Hine made notes: Sadie Fiefer, 10; South Carolina; Mart Payne, 5, picks 20 lbs cotton a day; newspaper vendor, 9, Washington, D. C. Although the country had already adopted legislation curbing child labour, the laws were frequently broken because children could be paid less than adult workers. The thin, tireless and compassionate sociologist with a camera, Hine, gathered evidence: five thousand pictures. His assignment was not easy because he was often banned from premises, or the youngest children were ordered to remain hidden while he was taken around; often he was expelled from factories by force. He had to pose as an insurance agent, fire inspector or legislator, taking his camera from under his coat on the sly, measuring the children's height by the buttons on their suit jackets, feverishly making a few notes on a scrap of paper to transfer later to the back of his

prints. His photographs of child slavery, however, aroused public indignation more effectively than the most eloquent article or most fiery speech.

His photographs lacked the then current standard features of a 'picture'. They were earthy, and unsophisticated. The subjects usually stared directly at the lens but these frontal shots have a remarkable 'eye-to-eye' communication quality, enhanced by the environment and characters: immigrants, child workers, breakerboys and newspaper vendors are presented in flop houses, streets and workshops. It is reality that does the talking here, the raw truth unadorned and unembellished. Thus Hine, the most modest of men, created new pictorial aesthetics for documentary photography which were subsequently to be used by the famous documentarists of the Great Depression. What Riis had done to help destroy the terrible tenements of New York's Lower East Side, Lewis Hine did to help abolish the most blatant cases of exploitation of child labour. The strength of his photography, however, cannot be explained only in terms of the indignation-arousing subject or unembellished reality. The appeal lies in the personal involvement of the photographer in his subject, in his showing things as he sees them, in expressing his concern. Small wonder then that Hine himself called his pictures 'interpretation photographs'.

# Dorothea Lange

/1895—1965/

'She was never after the beautiful things which are presumed to be the subject of photography, but she was warm-hearted and full of sympathy for people. When she photographed people, she talked to them and what she was told became an inseparable part of her pictures,' so wrote one of the contemporaries of Dorothea Lange. She was an unusual woman. She was never very interested in the affluent existence that was hers by birthright and did not hesitate to exchange security for the life of a hobo; the comfort of a studio for nights without shelter; financial profit for an uncertain career as a travelling photographer.

She started life as many other people of her background. After graduation from university, she opened a portrait studio but soon grew less and less interested in the people who came to her to have their portrait taken. So she decided to leave the glamour, fame and money of her clientele behind and went in search of places where *life* was to be found. One day she looked from the window of her San Francisco apartment, saw a long breadqueue and went down to photograph it. She never worked in the studio again. The year was 1932 and the Great Depression was at its bleakest.

The first picture which made her famous was totally unlike anything she had done before: an old man leaning heavily against a railing, his back turned to the people, his wrinkled hat low on his forehead, his lips bitterly pressed together holding a tin cup in his gnarled hands.

Dorothea Lange's photographs were completely different from the studio portraits of her day. She concentrated on people's faces, noticing how they lived, recording the emotion revealed by their eyes, their clenched fists, bent necks or raised chins. In other words, Miss Lange started photographing the human condition.

Paul Taylor, professor of economics at the University of California, was so impressed by these documents of the period that he asked Miss Lange to work with him on a report on seasonal farm labour. Theirs was the first

Among the quarter million pictures taken by the FSA photographers, Dorothea Lange's photographs are distinguished by their strong emotional charge, by their tangible love for humanity. John Steinbeck who was inspired by the FSA photographs to write his *Grapes of Wrath* actually included in his novel scenes, people and places captured by the camera of Dorothea Lange, a woman who gave the lens, a dead mechanism, unparalleled passion and humanity because she wanted to help alleviate the cruelty of the world.

research teams composed of a sociologist and a photographer, the blueprint for sociological research teams today. The Taylor—Lange report on the despair and hunger of migrant farm workers and their families without permanent shelter led to the establishment of camps and provision of food relief. 'Two and a half thousand famished, ragged and sick men, women and children saved after weeks of suffering thanks to lady photographer,' ran the headline of the March 10, 1936, issue of *San Francisco News.* The picture which precipitated relief to one of the stricken areas was the now legendary *Migrant Mother* which has since become a permanent symbol of the Depression years. By the time this photograph was published Miss Lange had already joined other photographers working for the newly established Farm Security Administration gathering evidence for New Deal legislation. Dorothea Lange became a famous photographer. Perhaps she remains the most famous of all women who have ever worked with the camera. She took pictures in Georgia, Louisiana, Mississippi, Alabama, Texas, California, showing the sad eyes of children, the drawn, exhausted faces of their mothers, the raw hands of cotton pickers. 'How much do you make? Where do you come from? How many children do you have?' she kept asking again and again. The migrants liked her and were astonished that she was interested, that she cared.

# Walker Evans

/1903 — 1975/

become a symbol of an era, earning a permanent place in the photographic hall of fame.

Walker Evans differed from other FSA photographers. His pictures were among the first to shatter the American Dream by ridiculing it. He juxtaposed the promises of glossy advertisements with the bleak reality of life. His pictures contrast the rainbow colours of the billboards and the rose-tinted daydreams of Hollywood with the grey drabness of city streets. A sign on the corner advertising *Love Before Breakfast* in bold letters and next to it a pair of anonymous hands clutching a bowl in the hope of something to eat. Evans' work is devoid of pathos or moralizing. It is detached, characterized by an acute sense of irony. How had it happened that a bohemian with literary interests that had taken him to several universities had decided to take up photography? In 1928 when he was twenty-four, Walker Evans became fascinated by postcard and newspaper photography. He was so thrilled by the terseness, authenticity and seeming impersonality of the pictorial message that he decided to produce photographs in the same style himself, seeking

Walker Evans was never as popular as Dorothea Lange, perhaps because his pictures were not as emotional as hers. Yet his work was essential for the development of modern documentary photography, for Evans was a philosopher penetrating deeply under the surface, a philosopher in the Atgetian or Whitmanian vein, seeking truth and beauty in ordinary reality.

His name usually appears side-by-side his FSA colleagues Dorothea Lange, Ben Shahn, Russell Lee, Arthur Rothstein and others. Like them, he recorded the desperate Okie migrants forced to leave their dust bowl farms in dilapidated jalopies, people looking in vain for any job; camps teeming with the dispossessed waiting patiently for their daily relief rations. The economic crisis was over when he was working but the Depression continued and the suffering of some fifteen million white and black unemployed was not over. At the time nobody could know that the FSA and its photographers were destined to

beauty in the ordinary, attractiveness in detachment, tension in the static.
Some critics hold that Evans is a direct follower of Atget, others argue that he follows the Hinean vein. Undoubtedly both are right, for Evans respects the former with his ability to reveal the inner worlds of ordinary things but uses the terse, precise expression so characteristic of Hine. However, his work built upon the expressive style of both, with an absolute simplicity and directness such that *his* style ultimately influenced the other FSA photographers. Like Hine, Evans uses the milieu, the environment, for characterization and his subjects stare at the camera just as they do in Hine's work. His scenes are so rigid as to suggest still lifes. His effects — the astonishing simplicity of the subject and the composition, the perfect texture of his pictures, the feeling of reality beyond any doubt — are achieved on one hand by strictly frontal shots resembling snapshots from old family albums, on the other hand by the clarity of photographs produced by a large 8 × 10 cm camera.
Walker Evans was not merely a famous photographer who used the camera to confront society with reality and to help alleviate social injustice, but with his terseness, his interest in the hidden, inner and invisible world of man and his society, he anticipated today's sensibility and expression in photography. He knew that photography would always be better at raising questions than providing answers.

# August Sander

/1876—1964/

analysis of man within his social context. He photographed thousands of social types: shop assistants, masons, farmers, cooks, house painters, circus hands, students, coaliers, people without jobs. As a rule he photographed people where they lived or worked since he noticed that the poses subjects will invariably and involuntarily assume in front of the camera reflect their social type and environment. In this way,

'Let me speak truthfully about our times and its people,' said August Sander, a German who in the 1920s started pursuing a hitherto unprecedented project: to publish forty-five different portfolios with a total of two and a half thousand pictures which were to be a social document of the period. The series was to be called *People of the Twentieth Century.*

He had been working as a portrait photographer in a commercial studio, like others using the transfer and oil processes and soft lenses 'turning maids into elegant ladies

and batmen into generals'. He decided he was tired of the artificiality of it all and started going out from the studio, photographing in city streets and in small villages in the German countryside, recording things as they were. In time he became convinced that one's profession and social status were encoded in one's physiognomy and that the most truthful picture of the make-up of society would be photographs of people bearing the typical signs of their profession and class.

Considering photography to be an essentially documentary medium, he began a systematic

Sander's individuals lost their individuality, becoming credible representatives of various social groups and social strata.

Sander's method was very simple. His pictures were usually static, with an exposure of two or three seconds, and his subjects always knew they were being portrayed and were aware of the seriousness of the moment so to speak. However, for Sander a portrait was not merely a head or bust but rather the entire figure. In this way Sander produced a series of pictorial documents in which the individual pictures had no aesthetic or documentary

value on their own but acquired it in the context of the whole work, which grew into a picture of the social composition of Germany between the two world wars.

In 1929, Sander published the first portfolio of his planned series. It was titled *Das Antlitz der Zeit (Face of Our Time)*. The introduction was written by the writer Alfred Döblin who considered Sander's method a pioneering feat, calling it 'comparative photography ... approximating the scholarly approach and surpassing the scope of ordinary photography'. After Hitler's rise to power, however, Sander was forced to abandon his project because his social analysis was a direct contradiction of the Nazi myth of a special, superior, healthy, blond race. Unsold copies of Sander's book were confiscated and the author was even forbidden to publish his portrait photography. In vain, Sander tried to defend his work: 'People in my pictures are as they are in reality. One's photograph in one's mirror, it is one's self!'

Born in the mining country east of Cologne, Sander started life as a miner like most of the men of the area. After his military service, however, he worked as an assistant in a photographic studio. Later he gathered professional experience in studios in Magdeburg, Leipzig, Halle, Berlin and Dresden. In Dresden he eventually started studying painting at an art academy. This experience influenced his early photography because he consciously tried to have his photography resemble the work of his favourite painters. In 1910 he opened his own

photographic studio. His concept of photography then started to change because he was aware of reality and the documentary prospects of the medium.

Sander's objectivism set him apart from other documentarists for he remained uninvolved; restrained from showing any bias, he merely stated things as they were, leaving photography a legacy that was to be appreciated only by later generations: a systematic pictorial analysis and a comparative method.

# V
# PHOTOGRAPHY IN SEARCH OF A NEW VISION

From the turn of the century, millions of pictures produced daily by professional and amateur photographers were building up a composite picture of a decadent society. Then World War I broke out and this glittering world was submerged in the mud of trench warfare. The social and political revolutions that followed the Great War further shattered any remaining illusions. Rejection of traditional values led not only to social upheavals but also to a revolution against old conventions in art.

'In the new world, art has a new function. Art need not be an ornament and decoration of life any more because the powerful, naked beauty of life need not be veiled by decorative pendants,' exclaimed the prophet of the brave new world of post-war Europe in 1922, Czech architect and art theorist Karel Teige. Artists all over Europe were now aware that a new era was coming. They were no longer content to produce art in the traditional sense of the word but wanted to shape life itself — to create a new life style. Their aim was to bring art down from the Olympian heights to the common people, to make art an integral part of everyday life. They sought new values, new ideals, new ways of expression — a new imagination.

It was Karel Teige who came up with a rousing slogan which was to make Prague one of the major centres of an integrated, pan-European culture: 'The beauty of photography is akin to the beauty of an aeroplane or a transatlantic cruiser or an electric lightbulb.' The startling obviousness of the statement is illustrative because it reflects the new social status of photography in the early days of the century of science and technology. It reveals the confidence a technical civilization had in the power of photography, a product of physics and chemistry, to possess a dynamic authenticity and become a medium capable of expressing appropriately the changing character of life. For the same reason cinematography with its fascinating ability to record motion, or architecture as the dominant feature of the modern environment, were also admired. One of the most marked features of the post-World War I years was the interest shown by modern artists in photography. Photography transformed painting and

rejuvenated book illustration and graphic design. It became an appropriate and apt medium for the expression of a new life style, an integral part of avant-garde concepts of modern art. Photography became a unique tool in the hands of the Dadaists who set out to shock bourgeois morals and give art a playfulness as well as a sense of life's comedy and absurdity. Photography was creatively used by the Functionalists who asserted the principles of technical beauty and utility. It was an ideal vehicle for Surrealism and its principle of chance encounters and meanings. Besides, photography was deemed as an ideal social critic and a powerful clarion voice of new social ideals.

It was primarily painters with their radical diatribes against traditional art who were the first in Europe to consider photography in a new way. In 1918, Christian Schad, a member of the Zurich Dada group, created abstract pictures by placing strips of paper and pieces of string on sensitized paper. The pictures were rather like Talbot's photographic drawings but Monsieur Dada, as Tristan Tzara called himself, called them schadographs. Two years after Schad, Man Ray, an American expatriate and Dadaist painter living in Paris, used just light rather than the camera to produce his rayograms. Unlike schadographs, rayograms were produced by modulated light. Two years after this, László Moholy-Nagy, a Hungarian-born abstract painter living in Berlin, produced his photograms. All these experiments had but a single aim: to open new vistas for the imagination and produce images with a beauty analogous to that of the developing age of technology.

Another way of expressing the new ideals of the Dadaists was the photomontage with its fantastic melange of meanings — a total abnegation of traditional art. George Grosz, Hannah Höch, Raoul Hausmann, John Heartfield, Max Ernst and others composed these montages from fragments of photographs in order to ridicule academism and artistic snobery. 'It is machine and rotary print painting,' wrote Karel Teige about the photomontage. The montagists regarded themselves as 'engineers and technicians', a term coined by Raoul Hausmann once when he explained the notion of Dada photo-montage.

The new aesthetics of art in which photography — as well as architecture — was to be the most immediate expression of life style was then shaped further by the efforts of the Bauhaus School of Design and by a wide international movement of New Objectivity. In 1923 László Moholy-Nagy started teaching at a new, avant-garde school of design known as the Bauhaus, utilizing new techniques for photographic production of images, and investigating the application of photography to painting, typography, textile and furniture design, design of exhibitions, advertising, promotion techniques, stagecraft and other fields. Even prior to his coming to the Bauhaus, Moholy-Nagy published in 1922 in *Sturm* magazine his constructivist study titled *The Dynamic-Constructive System of Forces,* in which he rejected the traditional visual representation, refuted normal photographic viewpoints and proposed a new concept of composition based on shifting view angles. Then came the movement of *Neue Sachlichkeit* (New Objectivity). Its manifestos were two 1928 publications: *Die Welt is schön (The World Is Beautiful)* by Albert Renger-Patzsch and *Urformen der Kunst (Archetypal Forms of Art)* by Karl Blossfeldt. Renger-Patzsch was inspired by the aesthetic beauty and appreciation of both natural and man-made objects while Blossfeldt recognized nature as the only source of inspiration. In a novel way both concepts focused on reality in close-up detail, as if under a microscope, revealing the structure of animate and inanimate organisms; they made possible a close study of the texture, facture and structure of such reality. In the interest of better understanding the material essence of the objective world, both men emphasized clarity, matter-of-factness, precision and objectivity of representation. Once again, photography fully put to use its unique acuity of representation. It must be admitted, however, that independently of their European cousins and in a somewhat more straightforward manner, American advocates of straight photography were evolving a very similar concept. This is quite understandable because America, not burdened by centuries of art traditions, had from the very beginning accepted photography as a unique means of expression.

*Es Kommt der neue Fotograf!* *(Emergence of the new Photographer)* was the apt title of a book by Werner Gräff, member of the avant-garde German *Novembergruppe* and Dutch *De Stijl* groups, and one of the first students at the Bauhaus. The book appeared in 1929 and codified in an illustrative manner the new photographic expression and, what is most remarkable, evaluated the psychological significance of the idea of unusual views, the play of shadows and highlights and the even purely technical aspects of pictorial rendition. This evaluation was only one step removed from the ideological concepts of the new means of expression elaborated in the young Soviet state. Russian avant-garde art which had placed itself in the service of the new order regarded itself an integral part of the Revolution, for in Russia revolution in art was considered identical with that in politics and the economy because their common objective was a brave new world.

The spirit of the period slogan 'Revolution to Art and Art to Revolution' symbolized a symbiosis of the two, and with the dictum 'A New Life Requires a New Expression', Soviet poetry, painting, film, architecture, photography and other arts became fascinated with experiment. It was the time when Vladimir Mayakovski wrote his fiery futuristic poetry which endorsed the new world and scorched bourgeois ideals, and when Kazimir Malevich emphasized the conceptual character of the graphic arts, and laid the ground for the de-materialization which became one of the most distinct features of modern art. Around this time Vladimir Tatlin was stressing utility as the chief value of a work of art, Sergei Eizenshtein discovered the emotionally effective film montage and Dziga Vertov experimented with the dynamism of the film document message while Alexander Rodchenko and El Lisitzki adopted photography as a tool of propaganda and agitation.

Soviet experimental photography of the period was heavily influenced by Russian and Soviet modernist trends in art, such as Constructivism, a universal concept uniting artists from various fields. It was a trend which was conceptually close to the creative endeavours of the Bauhaus School. In fact a similar art institution was established in Russia under the name VKHUTEMAS where avant-garde artists taught. At the VKHUTEMAS school, photography was applied experimentally to various disciplines, new concepts of reality were formulated and a new programme for photography originated here. It was a programme which gave the new elements of style and principles of composition a new content: an intoxication with revolution and a passionate endorsement of the great changes taking place in the life of the country. Soviet Constructivists called for artistic creativity to be replaced by 'intellectual' production and art by 'constructive' creative work. Just as in the manifestos of their Western counterparts, Soviet artists were to be technicians and builders helping the emerging new social and political patterns and bringing new faith to millions. What was then called the 'art of propaganda' was unthinkable without photography, for propaganda was thought to depend on political slogan, colour and — photography.

The main trends of European art between the two World Wars were then Constructivism, Functionalism, Surrealism and social involvement. It is no mere chance that all these trends marked photography which — like architecture — contributed essentially to the formation of a new life style. In this respect, a close association between photography and architecture must be mentioned here. A major manifestation of this association was the so-called 'picture poems', examples of the process of visualization of poetry, of fusing verse and picture into a new whole. These pictorial poems were the product of that typically Czech offspring of Dadaism, Poetism, marked by a strong lyricism which was conceived as the essential feature of humanity and elevated to be the central principle of an art thoroughly democratized and fully committed to improving of the human condition. Among the first to produce these pictorial poems in Czechoslovakia were architects who were among the leaders of the pan-European programme for the destruction of bourgeois art.

The intellectual association of the cultural and the sociopolitical avant-garde trends in Europe between the two World Wars wrote one of the most important chapters in the history of the development of photography and modern art in general. It was a wide international movement whose manifesto was the international *Film und Foto* exhibition in Stuttgart in 1929, where progressive photographers, film-makers, journalists and avant-garde artists of the West and the East met to promulgate a new vision and new aesthetics of photography.

# Karl Blossfeldt

/1865—1932/

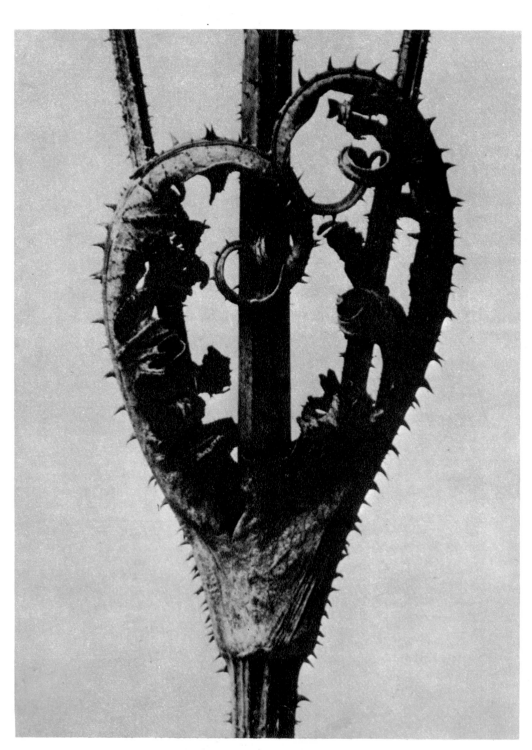

In 1928 a book containing over one hundred and twenty macrophotographs of leaves, blossoms, fruit and other parts of vegetation, entitled *Urformen der Kunst,* was published in Berlin. The author of the book was no professional photographer but a sculptor and modeller, professor of the art academy in Berlin; his name was Karl Blossfeldt. Blossfeldt's intention was to show the beauty of the plant kingdom as a source of artistic expression and to provide a teaching and comparative aid for his students. Quite unintentionally, Blossfeldt stumbled upon a purely photographic means of expression and his documentary pictures opened new vistas for photography.

Whether it was just a coincidence that Blossfeldt's book was published at a time when photographers had just started speculating about the specifics of photography or whether the publisher merely catered to the emerging interest in objectivity is hard to tell today, but the fact remains that Blossfeldt's photographs of plants, greatly enlarged and expressively presented, reflected precisely the endeavours of New Objectivity which had just formulated realism as abolishing the distortions of previous styles, emphasizing the utilitarian character of depiction. Its aesthetic programme stressed lucidity, objectivity and acuity of representation and considered nature to be the chief source of inspiration and, at the same time, a new subject for creative work.

'Even the most impassive observer would be thrilled to see that the enlargement of parts of plants visible to the eye could be as extraordinary as plant cells glimpsed through a microscope,' wrote Walter Benjamin, the eminent art historian, in his review of Blossefeldt's book. Paul Nash, another critic, offered his opinion: 'This is where the camera's eye proves its incalculable power, but not as an archeological, botanical or merely curious discoverer of "interesting" comparisons between art and nature; its importance lies, surely, in the wealth of matter it places at the disposal of the modern sculptor or painter which may prove stimulating to what Professor Blossfeldt calls

a sound expansion in the realm of art.' Thus Blossfeldt's documentary photographs acquired an unexpected and novel meaning and were accepted as works of art. Originally, Karl Blossfeldt had felt no urge to become an artist. He learned the modelling trade in the foundry in Mägdesorung, a place famous for metal artwork. He was able to appreciate this practical background fully only when he started studying sculpture and painting at an art school associated with the Museum of Applied Arts in Berlin. His true calling, however, was the result of his diligence and obliging character, for as a protégé of Professor Meurer he accompanied his teacher in 1891 on a study trip to Italy, Greece and North Africa to help him draw plants. The trip took four years and Blossfeldt soon started relying on photography instead of drawing for documentation. After his return to Berlin he began teaching plant modelling and in 1893 was appointed professor of the Art Academy in Berlin where he passionately pursued his

subject — modelling, preparation and photography of plants — until his death in 1932.

Karl Blossfeldt did not lead an exciting existence. As a teacher he considered nature to be the best teacher of art and art technique. 'It is impossible to conceive art and nature separately,' he wrote. This in fact echoed the philosophy of one of the first modernists, Auguste Rodin, who firmly believed that if he followed nature he could achieve anything. Neither artist, however, considered art to be identical with nature but rather thought nature to be a phenomenon enhancing the potentials of human sensory perception and opening new aesthetic possibilities.

Blossfeldt never thought of his 'vegetable documents' as anything but biological study material but his photographic emphasis of plant forms and structures as inspiration for artistic and technical aspects of reproduction led him to produce photographs unprecedented in approach which provided a strong impulse for the further development of morphological photography.

# Man Ray

/1890—1976/

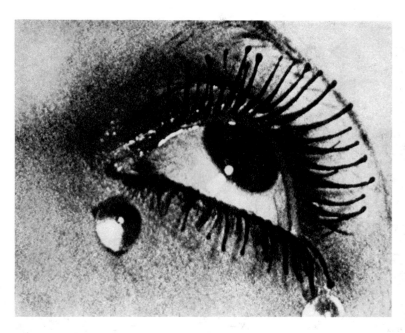

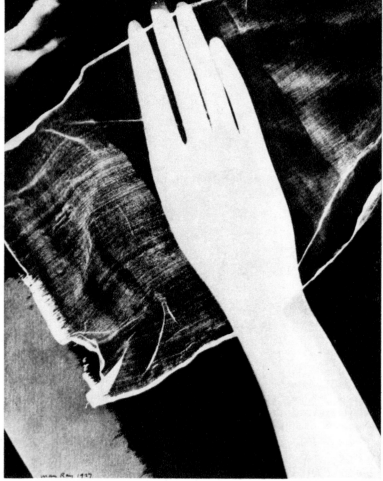

Man Ray spent the greater part of his life ridiculing everything that was conventional and, being conventional, therefore generally considered untouchable. Even as a student he stopped using his own name: 'My first name was Emmanuel and I changed it into Man ... My second name is nobody's business,' he once told an interviewer. There is some unsupported evidence that he may have been born as Emmanuel Rudnitzky. Before becoming a photographer he was a painter but he spent his whole life oscillating between painting, photography, sculpture, collage, construction of objects and film-making, tinkering with practically all modern art media.

He was born in Philadephia and at the tender age of seven was sure he wanted to be an artist. Whenever he was in New York he went to see exhibitions at Stieglitz's '291' Gallery and it was here that he was first exposed to modern art. He went to Paris where he associated with painters, poets and writers, especially the Dadaists and Surrealists, who lived in a happy-go-lucky community in the bohemian quarter. He was fascinated by these people who were resolved to give art a new order, a new vision and sensibility. To the circle of famous names like Marcel Duchamp, Tristan Tzara, Max Ernst, Francis Picabia,

André Breton was soon added the name of Man Ray. Then came World War I and Man Ray returned to the United States, living and working in Hollywood. He did not feel at home there, however, and soon returned to Paris which attracted him — as it did many other American expatriates — with its friendly, creative, international community of artists. Settling once again in Paris with his wife Juliet, he lived there until his death in 1976.

He is said to have taken up photography in order not to have reproductions of his works made but once he tried his hand with the camera he remained fascinated by photography for life. He was captivated by

people, or rather their faces, and so he started photographing faces and never painted a single portrait again. He came to the conclusion that painting and photography were two totally different media and that what could be photographed did not warrant painting. As a painter he felt that photography liberated him from the burden of reality. Now he was able to paint only his dreams or streams of consciousness.

His first photographs were realistic, quite unlike those which later earned him a permanent place in the history of photography. At this time Man Ray hoped that if he could not live from painting, he might make his living as a photographer.

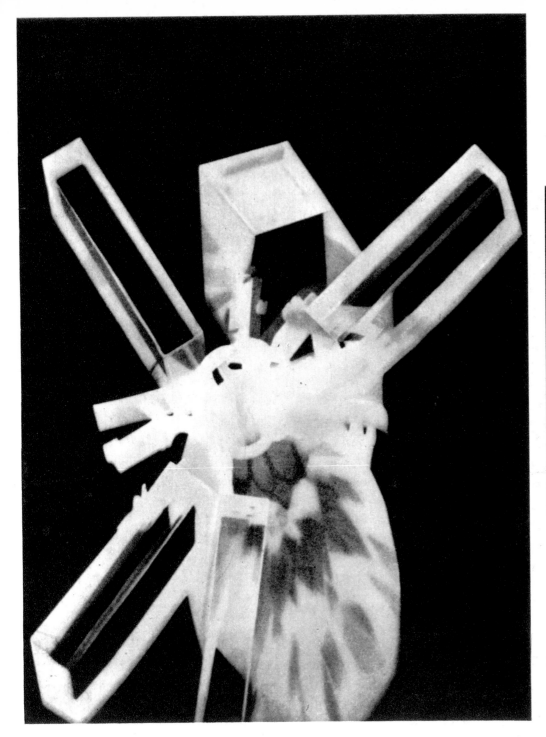

Soon, however, he rejected realism, or rather its descriptive method, and started experimenting, investigating the possibilities of a new imagery. About 1920 he stumbled upon the idea of the photogram, an image produced by direct exposure rather than using a camera. He started experimenting with this technique, placing three-dimensional objects directly on sensitized paper. Using shifting modulated light, he was able to produce most bizarre images which he called 'rayograms'. He published them in several portfolios under the title *Les champs délicieux*, with an introduction by Tristan Tzara.

What Man Ray did was to rejuvenate the principle of photogenic drawing invented by Talbot, although he gave it his own, unique meaning. His photographic work also involved other kinds of manipulation, utilizing, for example solarization, the Sabatier effect, montage, collage, multiple exposure, mirror effects. Together with László Moholy-Nagy, Man Ray was even called the father of photographic abstraction. However, he was never interested in technique for its own sake and always insisted that experimenting was for him but a means for expanding the possibilities of creative expression.

His manipulated imagery was sometimes rejected, especially by those who swore by straight photography. In Czechoslovakia, for example, he was called 'photogenic but not photographic' by the leader of the local photographic avant-garde, Jaromír Funke, while another Czechoslovak, the art theorist Karel Teige wrote about him in 1922: '...Man Ray's recent experiments reveal sheer photographic poetics, a magic befitting a magician... These "direct" images which Man Ray makes without using a plate or a lens constitute an artefact, a pictorial poem. Using a process utilized in scientific research, he produces aquatint-like values, subtle transitions which are practically impossible to produce by pure graphics. The effect is sometimes almost eerie...'

# Albert Renger-Patzsch

/1897—1966/

Although Albert Renger-Patzsch was no revolutionary, his photography nevertheless contributed considerably to the visual revolution. At the *Film und Foto* exhibition in Stuttgart in 1929, he exhibited fourteen pictures, all selections from his book *Die Welt ist schön*.

The book had been published a year before and turned out to be a bombshell. It was received so enthusiastically by the young generation that in December 1928, it was reviewed favourably in *Berliner Illustrierte Zeitung* by the formidable Thomas Mann. History has since fully vindicated Mann's judgement. Albert Renger-Patzsch's one hundred photographs of natural, industrial and utility objects, devoid of any manipulative interpretation, proved to be a lasting influence rather than a mere passing fad. Both the book

and the photographs exhibited in Stuttgart postulated the principles of New Objectivity in photography and confirmed that efforts at the establishment of a new style which reflected the ideals of a technologically oriented civilization had a general validity, proving that the beauty of technical design was not arbitrary but paralleled by natural objects.

The influence of these new stimuli has been aptly explained by Fritz Kempe, a contemporary German photographer and art theorist: 'The reason why Renger-Patzsch's photography had such an impact was among other things due also to the fact that his artistically interesting images of reality managed to captivate the aesthetic interest because the public was tired with soft, soapy pictures. And suddenly a man came who

proved that photography was an art in its own right rather than a mere vehicle for other media of artistic expression. This new, objective photography could be no longer called a pseudo-art, an imitation of painting. Albert Renger-Patzsch had been born into the family of a Würzburg musician and an enthusiastic amateur photographer. No wonder then that Albert himself started photography at twelve. He was interested in natural sciences and technology, although during his secondary school studies in Dresden he was more attracted by the humanities. He spent two years fighting in the Great War and after his demobilization he decided to study chemistry. After a few terms at the *Technische Hochschule* in Dresden, he dropped out, dabbling in photography in Berlin and Kronstadt, working as a salesman

and bookseller before opening his own photographic studio in the spa town of Harzburg. In 1925 he had his first show there. The show proved to be a success and Albert Renger-Patzsch was able to sell work for two thousand marks — an almost unheard of figure for the time. The same year he published his first two books of pictures on local subjects and started working on his opus *The World Is Beautiful* but included in it pictures dating from as early as 1922. The pictures represented details of natural and man-made objects which Renger-Patzsch, fascinated by their simplicity, presented isolated from their environment, emphasizing their material structure.

His imagery was sharp, capturing perfectly the surface texture of the represented objects. They were taken from unusual angles which made each image a fascinating maze of shapes that were highly bizarre yet intimately associated with reality. What Renger-Patzsch managed to prove with his imagery was that the aesthetic value of New Objectivity photography lay in its ability to discover beauty in our environment. This is why his book became the Bible of the new style. 'Let us leave art to the artists and let us try by means of photography to create photographs which can stand alone on account of their photographic quality without borrowing from art,' he said. The New Objectivity was a reaction to the sentimentality, picturesqueness and artificiality of pictorialism which was likened to the 19th century Romanticism. Photographers started re-discovering the unique quality of their medium and its particular possibilities for expression. In the words of William Blake, they were now once again able 'to see a World in a Grain of Sand and a Heaven in a Wild Flower'.

Ranger-Patzsch earned a permanent place in the annals of photography with work produced within a relatively short period between 1928 and 1930. His later books on a variety of local subjects met with no great acclaim. In 1944 his house in Essen including his large archive was destroyed and he moved to a village in Westphalia. After the war he took up photography again. The last project in which he was involved prior to his death was a photographic study of rock structure and forms.

# László
# Moholy-Nagy

/1895—1946/

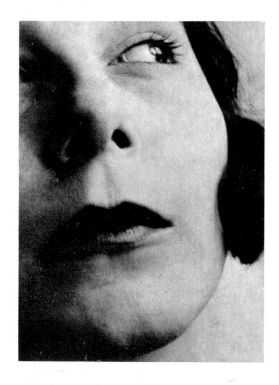

László Moholy-Nagy was a rebel of the
European artistic avant-garde. Born into
a world torn by conflict between rapidly
developing science and technology and man's
emotional world, he strove in his work to
bridge the gap and to create new symbols for
the representation of a new reality. A man of
exceptionally versatile talents, he was
a painter, sculptor, designer, film-maker,
teacher, photographer and art theorist who
was always able to back his experimental
work by theoretical ideas.

Born in Hungary, Moholy-Nagy studied law in
Budapest and wrote for various magazines
before the war broke out and he was sent to
the front. Totally unsuited for military life, he
could not shoot properly and probably did not
understand what happened when he was
wounded! After the war he thought of
finishing his studies, but Europe was in turmoil
and so many exciting things were happening
around him that reading law seemed boring. So
he left for Berlin where he started associating
with the Dadaists and Constructivists. He
liked their lampooning of traditional art and
their flirting with experiment. All of them
were young, unknown, bold and somewhat

113    Portrait of Ellen Frank, 1929
114    Penetrations. Photocollage, 1926
115    Poster for the Goerz Co. Positive and negative,
       1925

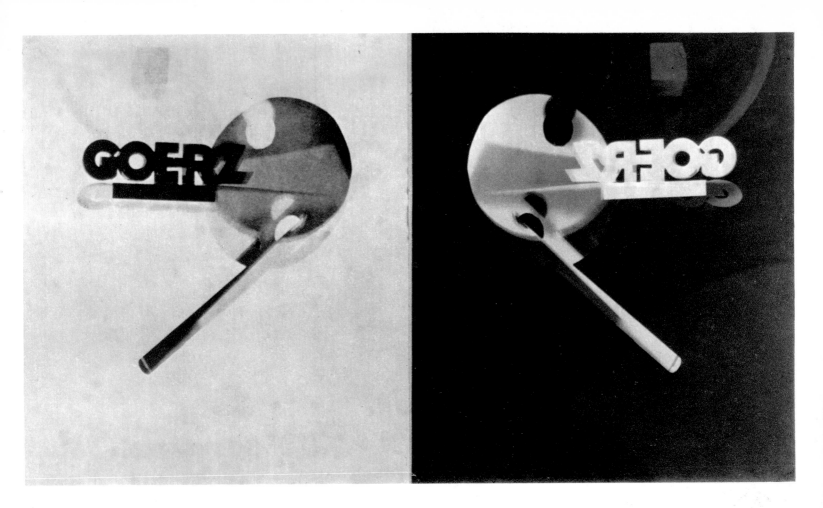

misunderstood: George Grosz, Hannah Höch, Viking Eggeling, El Lisitzki, all felt that traditional visual imagery had become obsolete and wanted to expand the limits of imagery.

By 1923 Moholy-Nagy was experimenting successfully with photograms and photomontage. Then he met Walter Gropius, who invited him to come to Weimar to teach at the Bauhaus, a school of design based on new aesthetics, new social thought and revolutionary practice which totally shattered old artistic values. It was here that Moholy-Nagy formulated the theory which ultimately became one of the most important impulses for creative endeavours at that time. He experimented with composition, light and colour, becoming involved in typography, advertising, light display and exhibition, stage and furniture design. Combining photography with print, he invented the so-called 'typophoto'. Striving to bring about the unity of technology and artistic expression, he threw open the doors of workshops and scientific laboratories, establishing a connection between applied arts and industrial manufacture.

Moholy-Nagy thought of photography as an 'objective form of a new vision', including in it not only reportage but also, for example, photomontage, photogram, microphotography, and radiography. He stressed that photography was not to be taken as 'imagery' in the sense of the usual aesthetics but rather as a vehicle of cognition. He put emphasis on the utilitarian, service character of photography, considering light to be its most valuable means of expression. Inventing shifting viewpoints he ignored the traditional terms of reference in representation. His pictures employed both ground and bird's eye views and tilting the camera transformed the familiar horizontal of the firm ground under one's feet into a dynamic diagonal. The public was shocked, but avant-garde artists received these experiments with enthusiasm. An expanded field of vision, objects seen in a new perspective and seeming to project from the plane of representation, everything set in motion: here was a principle worthy of the new age, an apt representation of the world of technology, hitherto presented in a manner totally alien to the new sensibility. 'The enemy of photography is the convention, the fixed

rules of "how-to-do" ... The salvation of photography comes from the experiment. The experimenter has no preconceived idea about photography ... He dares to call photography all the results which can be achieved by photographic means, with the camera or without it ...' Moholy-Nagy's fundamental ideas were summarized in his theoretical work *Malerei, Fotografie, Film*, which appeared in 1925.

After the Nazis' rise to power, Moholy-Nagy left Germany, moving to Amsterdam, Paris and London and travelling widely in Europe, for he had friends of kindred spirit and interest everywhere. In the end he emigrated to the United States and in 1937 became the first director of the New Bauhaus in Chicago. The former glories of the Bauhaus could not be repeated, but despite this, László Moholy-Nagy's sensitive and inquisitive intellect was a presage of the emerging audiovisual era; he accurately assessed the role photography was to play in modern aesthetic sensibility and life style.

# El Lisitzki

/1890 — 1941/

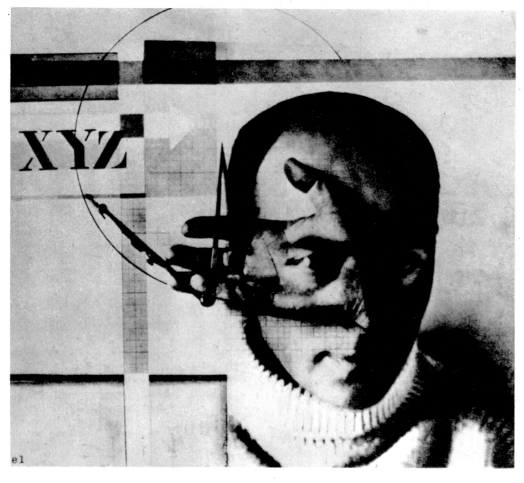

XYZ

el

Malevich's Vitebsk group called themselves. Like Alexander Rodchenko, Lisitzki also discovered photography in association with his own typographical work. After a year's study in Germany he was ready to return home but fell seriously ill and had to seek treatment in a sanatorium in Switzerland. He was rather short of money and accepted a commission for a series of advertising pictures for the Pelikan Co., an office supplies firm. This was when he first used a camera, an old $13 \times 18$ cm, loaned to him by his father-in-law. It was with this camera that his photomontages were made.

It was in Switzerland that he made in 1924 his best known photomontage, his own portrait. Two separate images, one of a hand wielding a pair of compasses, the other of his own face, are fused into a single image in which the eye peers through the palm, making the picture a powerful symbol of creativity. It is no mere chance that the self-portrait is titled *Constructor*. Lisitzki also employed

A brilliant phenomenon of Soviet avant-garde art, Lazar Markovich Lisitzki, who signed his work as El Lisitzki, left a deep mark on European architecture, typography, exhibition design and photography between the two World Wars.

He studied in Darmstadt, Germany, graduated as an architect and worked as a book illustrator. After the Russian Revolution he took up various forms of propaganda art. In 1919 he accepted an offer from Marc Chagall to teach at the Vitebsk art academy. This period in his development was marked by a search for identity and Chagall's influence was soon replaced by that of Kazimir Malevich, another teacher at the Vitebsk school. Malevich's manifesto of a new concept of art liberated from the burden of objective

representation made a deep impression on his own thinking and Lisitzki likewise rejected representational art, basing his imagery on elementary geometric forms: squares, circles and triangles. However, whereas Malevich's compositions were flat, Lisitzki's pictures revealed a distinctly constructivist approach. Lisitzki himself called his creations 'prouns'. These were compositions of stereometric forms which strove not for an arrangement of the area but rather for an organization and 'control of space' to use Lisitzki's own words. Indeed, his pictures look as though the geometric shapes projected into space constitute a structure which can be observed from all sides in one. This rejection of traditional concepts of art ranked El Lisitzki among the 'enforcers of new art', as members of

was to idealize rather than inspire, Lisitzki honestly tried to adapt to the trend but found it alien to his nature as an artist and failed to produce the desired effect.

Rather than a photographer, El Lisitzki was an artist who made use of photography to produce unique pictorial compositions. He remains admired as an architect of the image, a director of pictorial expression.

photography in a novel way in exhibition design and display. He was the first to use large format photomontages covering entire panels and even walls. As in the case of 'prouns' and his typographical work, he was guided by an effort to organize space. Perhaps his best work of this kind was his design for the Soviet pavilion at the International Typographical Exhibition in Cologne, 1928. Lisitzki and his co-autor S. Senkin produced a huge photographic frieze composed of scores of photographs forming a rhythmic arrangement of images with a dynamism approaching the effect of documentary film. In 1929 Lisitzki and his wife were appointed commissioners of the Soviet exhibit at the historic *Film und Foto* exhibition in Stuttgart.

Lisitzki's photomontages were simple and unpretentious yet metaphorical, a feature which also characterized his posters, billboards and book dust-jackets as well as the layouts for his own pictorial albums in which individual pictures were integrated by subject into a whole, taking on a new meaning. Starting in 1932, Lisitzki was also the layout artist for several issues of the Soviet magazine *SSSR na stroike (USSR in Construction)*, using principles of film montage to give each issue the character of a single comprehensive pictorial story.

When the dynamism of metaphorical photomontage was replaced in Soviet art during the latter half of the 1930s by monumental, static concepts whose objective

# Alexander Rodchenko

/1891—1956/

illustrations. This was only a short step from the beginning of his own photographic work. By 1924 Rodchenko was using almost exclusively his own pictures. His friendship with avant-garde artists whose work reflected the best in the experimental trends in European art of the period, and especially his close friendship with El Lisitzki his fellow teacher at the VKHUTEMAS, Moscow's School of Applied Arts, enabled him to keep abreast with contemporary experiments in photography made by Moholy-Nagy, Renger-Patzsch, Man Ray and others.
The new Soviet life brimmed with activity, promise and inspiration and Rodchenko showed things from a new point of view to which he also ascribed an ideological significance. He wanted to give expression to all that was new and young around him, he wanted to capture the spectator's interest and enrich his inner life. However, he was

'Genuine poetry must antecede life by at least an hour,' wrote the poet Vladimir Mayakovski in reply to critics who were either unable or unwilling to comprehend what it was his writings were about. The work of his friend Alexander Rodchenko can be said to have met this condition. The two artists shared similar fates. Both rejected the traditional means of expression and searched feverishly for new ones which would be capable of conveying the frenzied atmosphere of the times. Both were copied and rejected, celebrated and persecuted, honoured and ostracized. Both, however, commanded respect because they were ideological driving forces behind the creative endeavours in art and society of their time, and both always firmly believed in the artist's mission to be a catalyst for change.
Alexander Rodchenko was born in St. Petersburg, his father being a theatrical property man, his mother a laundrywoman. His love for the arts originated among the stage sets, in actors' dressing rooms, in the orchestra pit and in the circus ring where he grew up. Strangely, though, when old enough, he did not study theatre but painting, first at

an academy in Kazan, then at Moscow's Stroganov School of Applied Arts. By 1916 his paintings were appearing regularly at Moscow exhibitions side-by-side with those by other avant-garde artists like Malevich, Tatlin, Udaltsova and Popova. When the Revolution broke out, Rodchenko endorsed it passionately with all the impatience of his young soul. He sympathized with the new concepts of art which placed its fundamental values in utility, and soon surprised the public with his pioneering work in typography, book illustration, stage design, advertising and applied arts. His feverish artistic activity was matched by his deep involvement in public life, for in 1923 Rodchenko became one of the six founding members of the progressive grouping known as the Left Art Front. His opinions and works were published in the tribunes of Russian Constructivism, the magazines *Lef* and *Novyi Lef* for which Rodchenko did graphic design.
Rodchenko started his career in photography relatively early, employing the medium in his experimental typographical designs and photomontages for his posters and book

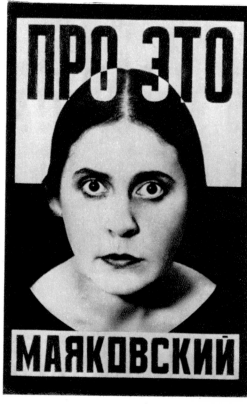

probably far too advanced to be understood. The ordinary man, accustomed only to descriptive representation, was naturally shocked by Rodchenko's work and rejected it as incomprehensible. Rodchenko was thus subject to great criticism, slandered and in 1931 even expelled from the photography section of the *Oktyabr (October)* art group. It was unfortunate: Rodchenko was an artist who had placed all his talent in the service of the ideals of the Revolution and now he was expelled for lacking ideology, for fostering formalism and aestheticism and for promoting taste alien to the proletariat. The injustice was quite painful to Rodchenko and he left Moscow to cure himself of 'aesthetic snobism' and formalism, and sought refuge in reportage work from the first grand projects of the early five year plans. Even here he remained an innovator, searching for a new photoreportage language which was ultimately copied even by his ideological opponents.

'Our duty is to experiment,' he wrote. 'There is nothing revolutionary in our photographing workers' leaders the same way as generals used to be photographed under the old regime ... Photography is a matter of common knowledge in any photographic club but how to do it is known only by few ... In brief, we must seek and find new aesthetics, enthusiasm and pathos with which to express our new socialist reality ...' Although criticized in his time, Alexander Rodchenko has not been forgotten.

120   A New Power Station in Moscow, 1930
121   Dust jacket for V. Mayakovski's poem *About This.*
        Photomontage, 1923
122   Illustration for V. Mayakovski's poem *About This.*
        Photomontage, 1925

# Jaromír Funke

out from the second university in a row, he founded with his friends a group called *Fotoklub Praha* and immediately found himself among the vanguard of the struggle for new photographic thought. He found a capable fellow campaigner in the person of

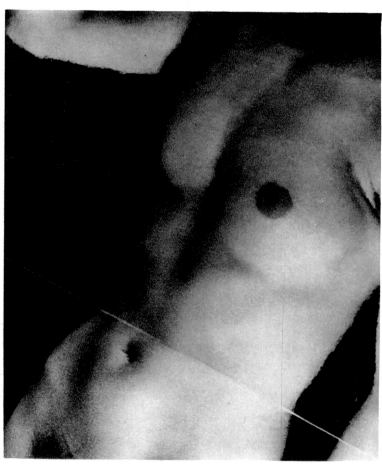

'He gave Czech photography exactly what it needed at the moment: a courage to experiment,' Karel Teige, an eminent Czech art theorist, wrote of Jaromír Funke. Funke, however, was not only a major impulse for Czechoslovak photography between the two World Wars, but also a major figure in the history of modern Czechoslovak photography, an ardent organizer of photographic life, a creative artist and

accomplished theorist. He seemed to attract controversy which was perhaps quite natural for a young man from a well-to-do intellectual family — the sons traditionally turned against the fathers. He kept switching schools as if he were not sure whether he wanted to be a physician, a lawyer or a philosopher. He had taken up photography as a hobby during his boyhood years spent in his native Kolín nad Labem, Bohemia. In 1922, when he dropped

Josef Sudek who, following the example of D. J. Růžička, had already started promoting straight photography. Soon, however, they were expelled from all amateur photographic clubs in Bohemia for their revolutionary principles and in 1924 established an independent Bohemian Photographic Society as a platform of modern photographic art. The foundations that Funke provided for modern Czechoslovak photography were built on his wise, sophisticated application of the principles of New Objectivity. Guided by his desire to satisfy the public interest as well as the needs of professional photographic education, Funke, who himself taught at art schools in Bratislava and Prague in 1931—44, published his theoretical speculation on the processes which lead from a mere photographic reproduction of the external

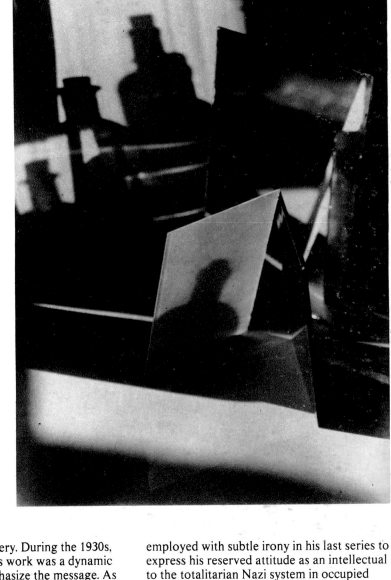

appearance of reality to an expression of the author's own feelings. Fundamentally a realist, Funke soon appreciated the valuable contribution of period experiments in photography, realizing that the emotional impact of photography lay primarily in its cognitive aspects. This always remained the basis of his photographic creed and it is in this light that his original rejection of Man Ray's photograms must be seen. Yet despite his rejection of the photogram, he found inspiration in it. In a similar manner he also assimilated and transformed other photographic experiments of the period. Funke, a man of versatile artistic interests and an intellectual background, became a catalytic mediator in the typically Bohemian melting pot of the time which amalgamated various avant-garde trends of European art. He was more than a mere intermediary or torchbearer, for he succeeded in making use of all these creative stimuli to develop the art of photography further. In this, his importance surpasses the limits of his national culture because his work amalgamated all major trends — Functionalism, Surrealism and social criticism — in European photography between the two World Wars into a unique ideological conglomerate. Despite its international roots and orientation, this bore the unmistakable features of a purely national culture. Funke succeeded in creating a rational, communicative, artistically imaginative and emotionally effective model for photography. His approach was that of

a constructor of imagery. During the 1930s, a typical feature of his work was a dynamic diagonal used to emphasize the message. As a rule, Funke arranged his photographs into series, often quite extensive ones, because he believed that the subject could be handled fully and communicated only when shown within the whole context.

Alas, many things he intended to try out in practice remained only theory. His death at the very end of World War II was one of those absurd banalities which he had

employed with subtle irony in his last series to express his reserved attitude as an intellectual to the totalitarian Nazi system in occupied Czechoslovakia. Such ironies had marked the last months of his life when he was forced to leave his teaching position and work as an unskilled labourer. Less than two months before the liberation of Prague, Jaromír Funke died because urgent surgery on his ulcerated duodenum had to be postponed because of an air raid.

# Jaroslav Rössler

/1902/

strove to combine photography with other forms of art, venturing in fact in the same direction as Man Ray and László Moholy-Nagy.

In 1925 he visited Paris for the first time and worked in the studio of G. L. Manuel frères on

At the age of fifteen Jaroslav Rössler started working as a laboratory boy in Prague's fashionable Drtikol's Photographic Studio. He soon mastered his teacher's technique and composition, grasping perfectly the specifics of Drtikol's concept of photographic portraiture but he remained unconcerned with his master's greatest problem in trying to make his photography an art. He was of a generation which remained uninterested in matters concerning the technique and motifs, concentrating rather on ideas and their interpretation. Rössler also understood very well that these things concerned not only photography but the whole modern concept of the meaning and function of all art.

In 1923 he met Karel Teige who urged him to join a new avant-garde art group *Devětsil* and he soon became an outspoken member of this modernist movement which encompassed not only photography but also typography, architecture, theatre, film, and so on. His photographs, drawings, typographical compositions, collages, montages and photograms appeared regularly in various avant-garde magazines of the period. Rössler's interpretation of the medium was never purist and unlike most Czech photographers of the period of both the traditionalist and modernist persuasions he

the bromoil transfer processes. The same year he returned to Prague to take photographs for the avant-garde theatre called the Liberated Theatre (Osvobozené divadlo) and commercial photography for a popular weekly magazine. In 1927 he returned to Paris, convinced that this was the place where he wanted to settle and work. He started collaborating with the experimental photography studio of Lucien Lorelle, producing advertising photography for major industrial companies like Gibbs, Michelin and Shell. His promising career in Paris was terminated by un unfortunate occurrence, however. When photographing a political

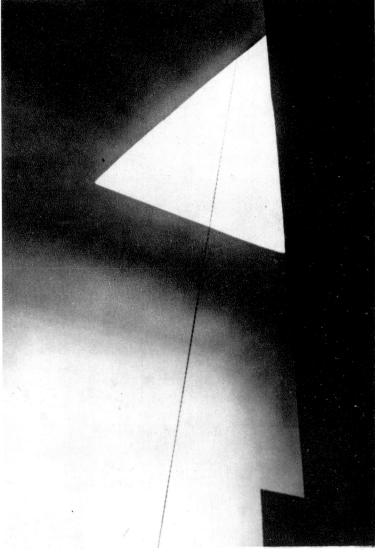

rally, Rössler was arrested and after six months' imprisonment deported back to Czechoslovakia in 1935.

The first great creative period in his life was over. Together with his wife he opened a modest studio in one of Prague's industrial quarters and, trying hard to make a meagre living, he remained artistically inactive for two decades. Whereas his work of the inter-war period had been under the sign of new functionalism and modern objective poetics, his work of the 1950s was totally different. The most striking examples of Rössler's postwar work are the so-called 'prisms', photographs made with the aid of a double-refracting prism. Although they were inspired by the breaking down of objective reality into linear and aereal elements, their overall character and concept is reminiscent of Surrealism.

Despite his advanced age, Jaroslav Rössler kept experimenting, using prisms to produce double images of fantastic, dream-like landscapes. He used solarization and the Sabatier effect and pigment processes to create work notable for its novel colour and image. Employing old means, Rössler thus discovered new poetics for photography as if he was trying to prove that nothing in art could be forgotten but must be constantly re-evaluated, utilized and given a new meaning.

Like Man Ray, László Moholy-Nagy and Alexander Rodchenko, Jaroslav Rössler was not merely a photographer. His approach was inter-disciplinary and his talent found its expression in various media even though Rössler was mostly a photographer. His work is a sensitive reverberation of artistic endeavours between the two World Wars, a period whose atmosphere marked even his post-war work. Within the Czechoslovak context, Rössler has remained probably the only photographer whose work in various media fully reflects the synthetic concepts of modern art. He provides a fitting end to the development of modern Czechoslovak photography started by Drtikol, Funke and Sudek.

# Karel
# Teige

/1900—1951/

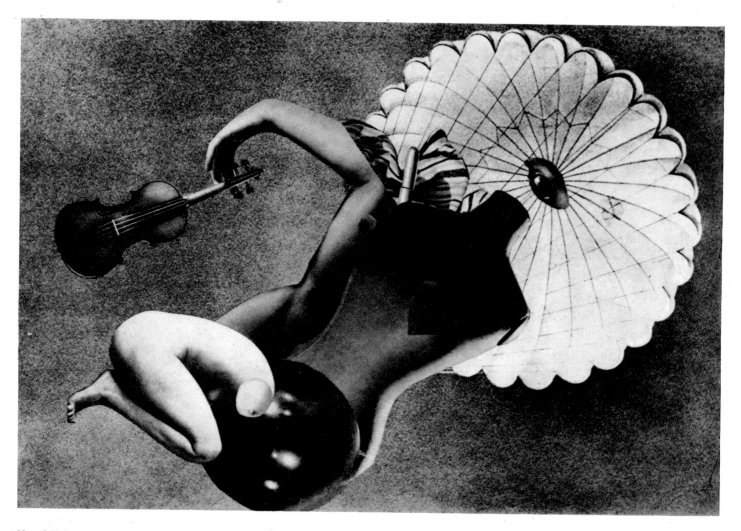

Karel Teige was not really a photographer, since photographs were for him just material for his phototypographical montages — which greatly influenced Czechoslovak magazine and book layout during the inter-war period — and for poetic collages, his semi-private Surrealist activity. These poetic collages, or picture poems as they were called then, constituted a sort of intimate diary by this theorist of modern culture; he used them in private to try out his theoretical concepts. Karel Teige's work for the development of photography and photographic thought was fundamental and his importance has surpassed the time-span of Czechoslovak avant-garde art to influence world photography.

Teige was a man of diverse talents: architect, graphic artist, publicist, art critic and theorist, a tireless spokesman for avant-garde art, a passionate promoter of modern trends in poetry. Born in Prague, he attended a Gymnasium with many later leaders of Czechoslovak avant-garde art of the 1920s and 1930s. The school spawned practically the entire *Devětsil,* an association of leftist and anti-bourgeois-oriented artists. It was with *Devětsil* that Karel Teige first appeared in public, becoming, together with the poet Vítězslav Nezval, the chief advocate of a new style called Poetism, conceived not only as an ideological basis for Czech avant-garde art but also a life style for future society.

In 1923 Teige started editing the magazine *Stavba* (*Construction*), transforming it into a major focus of European architectural avant-garde which adopted the principles of Functionalism to overcome the problems of residential architecture and interior design thrown up by the needs of modern life. Later, Teige also edited other magazines such as *Disk* and *ReD,* in which he voiced his thoughts on the new social functions of culture and on the fundamentals of creative art. In spite of Teige's leaning towards Marxism and his sympathetic views concerning the young Soviet state, his staunchest critics at the time were hard-line advocates of a Communist reconstruction of culture who called him an idealist and utopian.

In 1932 Teige was appointed associate professor at the Bauhaus School of Design.

The experiments of the Czech Poetists were aimed at the establishment of a universal poetics and attempted to fuse individual art disciplines and media together, but at the same time they took a lively interest in science and technology including photography and film. They were admirers of the new beauty produced by the age of technology and published photographs of ocean liners, automobiles and advanced architectural structures as typical examples of this new beauty. It was the designer and architect who were now praised as the greatest of poets and creators of a new utilitarian beauty. In addition to using photography for illustration and typographical design in magazines edited by Teige, the Poetists produced picture poems — unique collages composed of photographic fragments — and emotive film montages. Apart from the vast poetic work of Vítězslav Nezval and his peers, the centre of activity of Poetism — a trend akin in spirit to Dadaism and Futurism — lay in large graphical and theatrical productions. The theatrical production was mainly staged in Prague's Liberated Theatre, famous during the 1930s for the political satire and biting topical commentary of its founders and leading actors

and playwrights Jiří Voskovec and Jan Werich.

The book production of the Poetists was likewise impressive, again mainly thanks to Karel Teige who during the 1930s elaborated his original Poetist concepts into Surrealist ones. His and Nezval's Surrealist Group paralleled in importance the Poetist Devĕtsil of the 1920s. The Surrealist Group disintegrated only in the late 1930s when the internal differences of the Czech left were heavily influenced by the international political situation and the rift in fact threatened the unity of the cultural front against Fascism. Yet this was the time when Teige produced his most interesting 'private' collages revealing not only a dazzling humour and irony in a Dadaist vein but reflecting also the growing anxiety and scepticism so characteristic of the eve of World War II.

# Jindřich Štyrský

/1899–1942/

'My eyes constantly require food. They gobble it up, insatiable and brutal. And during the night they digest it,' wrote Jindřich Štyrský in his prose *Emily Coming To Me In My Dream* in 1933. For Štyrský, dreaming was a very important aspect of life which was enriching and facilitated an understanding of the essentials of the human soul. When, shortly before his death, he collected his literary and graphical accounts of his dreams into a volume (which he was never to see published), he included at the end of the book the jacket of an old French dream book, probably intended as the opening page of the prologue which he never lived to write. Nevertheless, the old picture, dominated by the French words *Clef des songes*, symbolizes aptly the source of Štyrský's imagination, fusing fiction and dream with reality.

Like so many of his contemporaries, the painter, poet and stage designer Štyrský put away his pencils and brushes at a decisive time in his life and for some time relied exclusively on photography to express his vision. Within an extremely short period, 1934–5, Štyrský succeeded in producing a remarkable self-contained photographic portfolio which represented a significant advancement for photography as an art. Although Štyrský always remained an amateur and for years used the camera only occasionally to record things, he became a photographer of international renown. Photography suited his creativity, for he was attuned to the specifics of the new medium, especially that indefinable inner tension and ambiguity in its translation of reality.

Štyrský's terse documentary style 'froze'

reality and made it speak for itself. His objects, isolated photographically from their real context, live their own surreal life and the pictures underline the absurdity of such a divorced existence, adding a flavour of mystery to random relations and context, sensed as a logic which defies definition. Extremely significant in this respect is not only the selection of objects but also the subject context which allows the dream to take its course. Štyrský's dreamland is an eerie carnival with sideshows full of mysterious symbols. There are shop windows cluttered with the strangest wares: a pharmacy with its vials and flacons; a hairdresser's with its promise of beauty; a shop selling prosthetic limbs. It is as if these strange objects revealed the romance of reality, that reality which for Štyrský was a 'tortuous, cruel phantom' and

96

which the critic Karel Teige characterized as a product of a 'tragic conflict of the inner and the outer reality causing so much anguish to modern humanity'.

His first two photographic cycles, *Frogman* and *Man With Blinkers,* were in fact Štyrský's response to the establishment of the Surrealist Group in 1934. The sixty-four pictures with a unifying theme were exhibited in Prague's Mánes Gallery in 1935. Another cycle entitled *An Afternoon in Paris* was exhibited only as late as 1938 and was Štyrský's last public exhibition. In 1941 an underground edition of a volume featuring Štyrský's photography and poetic prose by Jindřich Heisler appeared but the pictures were merely dramatically arranged selections from older works. Only retrospective shows held in Brno, Czechoslovakia, in 1966, and in Centre Pompidu, Paris, in 1982, put together from material collected by Štyrský's lifetime companion and co-author of Czech pre-war Surrealist concepts, Madame Toyen, gave full credit to Štyrský's exceptional photographic talent.

A graduate of Prague's Academy of Fine Arts; a leading member of *Devětsil,* an association for modern culture; director of design for the nonconventional Liberated Theatre in 1928—9; a versatile avant-garde artist living alternately in Prague and Paris, Jindřich Štyrský took up photography because he searched untiringly for new possibilities for artistic expression. In retrospect, his death during the tragic years of World War II seems to symbolize the painful conflict of dream and reality characteristic of his art.

# VI PHOTOGRAPHY CAPTURING THE MOMENT

Like film, radio or television, photography is a technical invention and its development has always been directly related to the technical advancement of the equipment. To capture an image of the world frozen in a moment was therefore only possible with the advent of light, easy-to-handle cameras, high speed lenses and films and, last but not least, a new generation of photographers capable of using the new techniques.

The first camera which permitted work under poor light conditions was the German Ermanox. This camera, which appeared on the market in 1923, was soon followed by Barnack's Leica. Cameras of the new generation could capture what had hitherto defied photographic reproduction and permitted the photographer to react spontaneously to whatever he saw in his viewfinder; pictures could also be taken in available light. Objects and people captured by photography were now as if frozen in time. A new form of visual communication, modern photojournalism, was ready to win the world. Naturally, neither the technological advancement, including the rotary print machine, nor the emerging new generation of photojournalists would alone have been sufficient for photojournalism to be born. Of equal importance was a new type of editor known as the picture editor who handled the selection of photographs, arranging and juxtaposing individual pictures to give the whole a new meaning. Thus, the 1920s saw the emergence of a new kind of journalism in which pictures played as important a role as the written word. The new genre of pictorial story, the photo-essay, appeared almost simultaneously in Germany and Russia, the two countries in Europe which were experiencing the greatest social upheavals of the time. 'Crush traditions! Photograph things and people as they are! This was the slogan of the new movement, a meeting ground of ideas from East and West, ideas that were decisive for the emergence of photojournalism,' wrote Tim Gidal in his book *Deutschland—Beginn des modernen Photojournalismus*. The traditional spiritual and social values of the bourgeois 19th century had died in the trenches of World War I and a new world was emerging from the social upheavals. The 1920s were therefore the right time for

photography to join the printed word as a herald of new mass movements and new ideologies. A mechanically operated piece of equipment, the camera, produced pictures whose credibility was something that the word could rarely hope to achieve, a property which made photojournalism a powerful communication medium capable of heavily influencing public opinion.

In Germany, the bastions of modern photojournalism were the *Berliner Illustrierte Zeitung, Münchner Illustrierte Presse* and the *Dephot* service which were the first to print the natural, candid photographs of Erich Salomon who specialized in pictures which for the first time in history showed the powerful and elite people of the period in unofficial, human situations. Other pioneers of the new style, Felix H. Man, Wolfgang Weber, Martin Munkácsi, Alfred Eisenstaedt and the emerging Hungarian-born photographer Endre Friedmann, who later became famous as Robert Capa, also appeared in these magazines as time went by. Their pictures had one thing in common: all captured unique, unrepeatable moments reflecting the joys, sorrows, passions, tragedies and hopes of human life as well as major historical events, characterized by a new, objective vision of life's reality.

The characteristic feature of this new style was that the pictures strove not only to capture an instant in time but also the invisible quintessential character of that moment. The photographer did not want to be a mere uninvolved observer. Unobserved, he would enter the situations to express his judgement. In these pictures the notions 'to see', 'to experience' and 'to report' become one. The basic documentary character of such photographs is tinged by the photographer's intellectual judgement and emotional involvement. Photographers tried to experience what they photographed, becoming involved eyewitnesses of the times. The new approach was most marked wherever illustrated magazines employed photography to tell a story. These photographic reportages, photo-essays or photo-sketches, as they were called in various countries, required that photographs on a given subject be arranged in a sequence which would offer a deeper and more

effective presentation of the theme than a single picture. These skilfully composed series using long, medium and close shots constituted a coherent message; the individual pictures partly lost their original meaning only to contribute to the new meaning of the whole. Photography could then tell a story in a manner similar to a film.

The photo-essay ultimately became the basis of modern photojournalism, an equal partner to the traditional written account, a joint product of the work of the photographer, the picture editor and the layout man. In a sense, however, it was the picture editor who became the most important element because it was he who gave the photographer the assignment, worked out the concept of the essay, selected the pictures and arranged them to give the story rhythm and drama. The picture editor became the director of photojournalism in which the selection and composition of pictures was as important as the pictorial material itself. The layout man gave the essay its final graphic shape, accentuating the aesthetic and intellectual message. In the 1920s illustrated magazines started to appear all over the world. The extent of pictorial supplements of magazines was no longer governed by the length of the text—it was now the dynamic pictorial story that determined the write-up.

The situation in Soviet Russia, the other cradle of photojournalism, was in many respects similar to that in Germany. Russian photojournalism was similarly emotional, marked by an effort to offer a piece of involved reporting. The photo-essay was known here as 'fotoocherk' (photographic sketch). However, unlike in Germany in the 1920s, Soviet photojournalism was from its very beginning utilized systematically as a state-controlled tool of propaganda and 'public education'.

It was in Germany — rather than America as was erroneously held for a long time — that the essentials of modern photojournalism were devised and developed, while Soviet Russia discovered it as a mass medium perfectly suited for the purposes of propaganda.

The further development of photojournalism was as dramatic as the times themselves. When the Nazis rose to power in Germany it looked as if photojournalism as a progressive, humanistic medium had lost its fertile soil for further development, but in the hands of Nazi ideologists it was expertly used and developed as the mouthpiece for promotion of totalitarian ideology. Many of those who had helped photojournalism to develop in Germany were forced to emigrate. Salomon settled in Holand, Munkácsi in Paris, Felix H. Man in London, Eisenstaedt in the United States, and Stefan Lorant, the first of the great picture editors, sought assylum in England. Thanks to these men, photojournalism took root in Great Britain and the United States, where it blossomed so abundantly that for years it seemed only natural that the style had been born there.

In 1936 the first issue of a new brand of picture magazine appeared on newspaper stands in the US. The name of the magazine was *Life* and its programme was: 'To see life; to see the poor and the gestures of the proud; to see strange things — machines, armies, multitudes, shadows in the jungle and on the moon; to see man's work — his paintings, towers and discoveries; to see things thousands of miles away, things hidden behind walls and within rooms, things dangerous to come to; the women that men love and many children; to see and take pleasure in seeing; to see and be amazed, to see and be instructed.' *Life* met with acclaim that surpassed even the wildest expectations of the editorial board; its format was a significant departure from its German and Soviet predecessors: the photo-essays were not composed of a number of small size pictures carried on a single page or a centrefold but consisted of large format pictures run on several pages. The compositon rhythm even took into consideration the fact that the reader had to turn the pages. Early US photojournalism differed from its European cousins in more than this one aspect. It preferred attractive, technically perfect large format photography, condoned flash and depended solely on stand cameras. American taste at the time also required that a good picture be razor-sharp. The new aesthetics of European small format photography — capturing the atmosphere of the scene — started gaining ground in the United States only after 1938 when the first issue of London *Picture Post* appeared. The picture editor of this magazine was Stefan Lorant who gave it a character and identity just as another German exile, Alfred Eisenstaedt, did with American photojournalism. It had been Lorant who had been instrumental in sending Robert Capa to cover the Spanish Civil War and it had been the *Picture Post* which was the first periodical to show war as it was — brutal, vicious and indiscriminate. Still, even during the World War that soon followed, American picture magazines sometimes carried cue-and-flash photography produced by stand cameras because American taste preferred spectacular views to raw reality expressed by earthy means.

With World War II, modern photojournalism reached maturity. It gave birth to great war photography in the West as well as in the East and ultimately also to one of the greatest eras in the entire history of the medium; this was humanist photography.

The subject of photojournalism is humanity; its main attribute a passionate defence of human dignity; its aim to be an appeal to human reason and heart, less interested in events in actual places and actual time, more in conveying a universal message concerning life. It is a kind of photography anticipated by André Kertész's pictures from World War I and the two post-war decades, by Brassaï's glimpses of Paris life or Bill Brandt's *The English at Home*. It was people like Kertész, Brassaï and Brandt who showed that the main objective of photojournalism was not to present beautiful pictures but rather to facilitate human communication, to make man an eyewitness of his time, to make him aware that, whether he wants it or not, he shares the responsibility for this world.

# Erich Salomon

/1886–1944/

photographers to click their shutters. Then, in 1928, pictures were published which toppled this tradition. For the first time the powerful were not presented as prim public figures but as living persons, captured in animated conversation or with faces drawn by fatigue. The author of these pictures was Erich Salomon, a photographer always impeccably dressed for the occasion, chatting amiably with ministers and diplomats about the problems at hand in fluent French, German or English, connected by five or six metres of cable to the release of his Ermanox stand camera placed inconspicuously somewhere in the corner. Holding the release button nonchalantly in his hand, Salomon remained fully concentrated, closely observing the situation, the motions and gestures of the negotiators, and when the tension reached its peak, he pressed the release. In order to disturb the scene as little as possible, he always relied on available light and had the release mechanism of his camera adapted to operate noiselessly. His subjects were always aware they were going to be photographed but could never be sure when. They soon realized that Salomon's unpretentious,

At a peace conference in 1930 the French Foreign Minister Aristide Briand asked the delegates to hold up the opening ceremony until Erich Salomon arrived. 'What's a meeting that isn't photographed by Salomon? People won't believe it's important at all.' Although the minister was only joking, he was right in a sense because by this time Erich Salomon had covered all major political and diplomatic negotiations in Berlin, Geneva, Paris, London and Washington. He had become famous for the cunning with which he penetrated even the most closely guarded meetings. If barred entrance, he would at the least try to take pictures through the window. This persistence had earned him the 'tribute' *le roi des indiscrets*. Before Salomon appeared on the scene of photographic news coverage, negotiations as a rule took place behind closed doors and photographers were at best permitted to take their pictures at special press conferences where the negotiators assumed dignified poses, stared benevolently at the cameras and waited for the

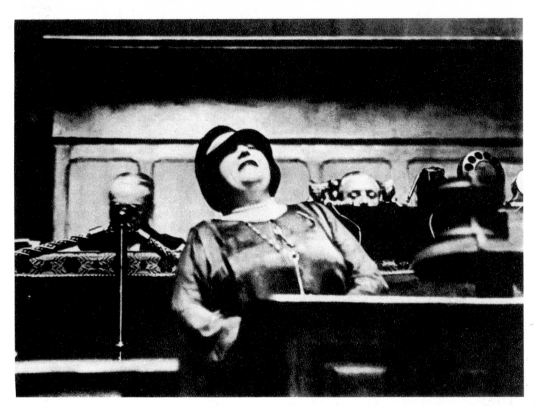

the courtroom with a camera hidden in a briefcase and they made him a photographic star overnight. At the age of forty-two Salomon realized that he had found his true calling.

His most famous photographs were taken between 1928 and 1932. In 1929 he was invited by the US press magnate William Randolph Hearst to come to America. Hearst was so impressed by Salomon's photography that he even ordered an Ermanox for each of his reporters. The results were disappointing, for Hearst did not realize that the camera alone did not make a star photographer.

When the Nazis came to power in Germany, Salomon moved to the Netherlands. An old diplomatic hand, he firmly believed that the Nazis would respect Dutch neutrality but he stayed until it was too late. In 1943 he was arrested in the Hague and deported with his family, first to Theresienstadt in occupied Bohemia and ultimately to Auschwitz, where he died.

spontaneous pictures were in fact valuable historical documents not only winning popularity for the negotiators but also gaining publicity for the event in question. Thanks to Salomon even the most private political talks became a matter of public interest and his pictures of politicians captured during a fiery oration or quietly enjoying their coffee often revealed more than official press releases. Salomon's work was widely acclaimed, earning his style the title of 'candid camera', which ultimately came to signify a whole new trend in informal photographic reporting. Erich Salomon was born in Berlin into the family of an important member of the commercial community. He studied law and at the age of 26 married his Dutch-born wife. When World War I broke out, Salomon went to fight for Germany and was taken prisoner in the First Battle of Marne in September, 1914. He returned home after having spent four years in various POW camps in France. His father was dead, the family money gone and Salomon had to look for a job, and ran this ad in the paper *Vossische Zeitung:* 'Lawyer Provides Tax Information in the Sidecar of his Motorcycle. Why not enjoy a ride in beautiful countryside while listening how to save money?' The advertisement turned out to be the turning point in Salomon's career for it attracted the attention of the promotion department of *Ullstein Verlag* and Salomon found himself with a new job. In 1927 he first encountered photography and was immediately captivated by it. His first assignment was to cover the famous 1928 Kranz murder case. Salomon took pictures in

# Martin Munkácsi

/1896—1963/

argument between an old man and an officer attracted his attention. He snapped the scene with the last unexposed picture left in his camera. A few days later when he returned from an out-of-town assignment, he happened to read in the papers that the old man had

Martin Munkácsi was born in Hungary in a working class family and died sixty-eight years later almost penniless in New York. Yet in his time he was one of the best paid photographers in the world with an annual income of over $ 100,000. He owned a fabulous Triplex studio in Manhattan and a dream residence in Long Island. Munkácsi's background is extremely difficult to trace because he did a great deal to make it obscure, most probably in order to receive more publicity. He held, for example, that he had been born in Discöszentmárton (Glorious St. Martin) although his real birthplace was Koloszvár. Another favourite story of his was that children at school had ridiculed him for

his dress because he wore subdeacon's clothes and his mother's high-heeled shoes. The fact remains, however, that Munkácsi's father was a housepainter whose original name was Mermelstein.

Munkácsi passionately longed for an education and kept running away from home, leaving his family forever at sixteen. He wrote poetry and by the time he was eighteen he was already working as editor of a Budapest daily, writing articles, pursuing interviews, commentating on football and also photographing. This might have remained his lifetime career had not chance changed his fate. In 1923 Munkácsi was on his way home from a soccer match. In the streetcar a heated

been accused of murdering the officer. Munkácsi's snapshot helped the defence prove involuntary manslaughter in selfdefence and the author became the most popular photographer in Budapest.

Munkácsi was a hard-headed man and one day after an argument with his editor-in-chief he left the office never to return. In 1927 he arrived in Berlin and, without any appointment or recommendation, went from the station straight to *Ullstein Verlag.* When he came out, he had a three-year contract in his pocket. In Germany a new kind of journalism was just emerging in which photographs were not merely entertaining illustration — they replaced text as the

message-bearing medium. This precisely suited Munkácsi's style because he had a natural talent for recognizing subjects which were interesting. His work appeared in many Ullstein publications, such as *Koralle, Die Woche* and *Die Dame,* but mostly in *Berliner Illustrierte Zeitung* which sent Munkácsi on assignments all over the world.

When Hitler rose to power in Germany, Munkácsi emigrated to the United States. He had been there before and his pictures were very much admired by Carmel Snow who edited *Harper's Bazaar.* It was she who commissioned Munkácsi to photograph his first fashion collection. Munkácsi took the models in their evening dresses out of the studio to Long Island beach. It was December and the unusual setting proved to be very effective. Miss Snow offered Munkácsi a permanent contract and in 1934 he found himself established as a fashion photographer in New York.

Munkácsi did more than just photograph fashion outdoors. He rejected the perfectly groomed and polished models, preferring to work with the healthy-looking, sweet girl-next-door types. In spite of his great success, he did not remain just a fashion photographer. A journalist at heart, he made his mark with his extremely popular series *How America Lives.* The feature ran for six years in *Ladies' Home Journal,* bringing a photo-essay on the life of a different American family each month. As a whole, the series was an acute social study of American life, presenting families from different places and of different status ranging from a black household to the President's family. The work proved to be exhausting and after suffering

a heart attack Munkácsi left photography, returned to poetry and started writing a semi-autobiographical novel. In fact, he retired just in time because the new post-war generation of picture editors, preferring younger photographers, did not appreciate his unusual ability to capture the right moment to best convey the message and render the subject in a formally perfect image.

Munkácsi died unexpectedly and tragically of a heart attack after a football game. The policeman who found him collapsed thought he was only drunk and did not hurry to call an ambulance. When it finally arrived, the once great photographer was dead. He was buried without ceremony in New Jersey.

# Felix H. Man

/1893—1985/

When Felix H. Man was hired as reporter in 1928, the picture editor of the then emerging *Dephot* service, Stefan Lorant, asked him to do entire photographic stories on given subjects. This was an entirely new concept because until then editors had been composing reportages of individual, unrelated pictures. Born as Hans Baumann, he needed a *nom de guerre* because his photo-essays were carried not only by *Dephot* but appeared also in the weekly *Münchner Illustrierte Presse* for which Lorant also worked. His new name Felix H. Man became the symbol of pioneer work in photojournalism dealing with the inner meaning of the photographed phenomena so typical for modern photojournalism.

Unlike Martin Munkácsi whose message was concentrated in a single, perfectly composed picture, Felix H. Man was one of those who supplied entire photo-essays to illustrated magazines. Man's essay on Berlin life between midnight and dawn, from 1929, in fact constituted the first night reportage, while his 1929 essay on Igor Stravinski in concert was the first dynamic series produced under natural light in which lack of sharpness was used as an important means of expression. Man's essays on major public figures photographed in intimate moments are also memorable: Mussolini at home, Charlie Chaplin in the street or George Bernard Shaw among his friends.

Felix H. Man was born in Freiburg and before World War I, in 1912—14, studied painting and art history in Berlin and Munich. He took his first pictures during the war, using a small pocket-sized camera. After the war he continued studying the applied arts, working simultaneously as a draughtsman for the

especially after World War II, provided ample space and support for the ideas of European photojournalists, proved that Felix H. Man, a pioneer of the photo-essay, was probably the most important representative of classical photojournalism. Yet Man had to wait until 1978, the year of his sixtieth anniversary of becoming a professional photographer, to have a representative selection of his lifetime work exhibited. In the catalogue, Man calls himself a pioneer of photojournalism, somewhat embittered that it had taken the world so long to realize that modern photojournalism had not been born in the United States and that it had been he, Felix H. Man, who created the first photo-essay.

Berlin noon daily *B. Z. am Mittag*. Contributing mainly to the sports section, he often used a camera to make sketches for his drawings. It was only in the late 1920s that he received a reportage Ermanox. Together with the leading photojournalists of the period, Munkácsi, Umbo, Weber, Eisenstaedt, Lorant and others, he helped change profoundly the existing practices in magazine and newspaper illustration. Like most of his friends he left Germany when he realized that politically *engagé* reporting, to which photojournalism naturally tended, was doomed in a totalitarian state where the authorities usurped the right to tell the truth. Thus, in 1934, he emigrated to England, where he helped Stefan Lorant transplant the ideals of German pre-Nazi photojournalism. At first he worked for *Weekly Illustrated* founded by Lorant, then he became chief reporter of the famous *Picture Post*. Still later he joined Lorant to shape the character and image of the US *Life* magazine. His cooperation with the British *Sunday Times* and the US *Life* magazine, which,

# Wolfgang Weber

/1902/

Wolfgang Weber always wanted to travel and early in his life he decided to become a musician because he thought this was the only way to make his dream come true. Later he realized that compared to the long hours spent practising, the rewards in terms of travel would be minimal and he switched to studying ethnology—to the great sorrow of his mother, a painter and ardent musician. In the end he disappointed even his father, an eminent ethnologist, professor at the University of Leipzig and director of the Ethnographic Museum in Munich, for he deserted ethnology as well. Yet it was thanks to his musical,

ethnological and philosophical studies in Munich that Wolfgang Weber became a photographer.

In 1925 he was sent by his professor to Africa to record for the musicological institute songs of the Wadchagga, a tribe living in the foothills of Kilimanjaro. Weber went to East Africa with five large suitcases containing a recorder and a large number of wax cylinders plus a 9 × 12 cm stereoscopic camera and 400 plates which he was commissioned to take for a panoramic theatre in Berlin. Once in Africa, however, Weber found himself more fascinated by the natives' way of life and the

general situation in the country than by bushmen's songs and on his return to Berlin he offered his unique photographic diary to *Berliner Illustrierte Zeitung*. The paper immediately published both his pictures and the accompanying text and since the five hundred marks that Weber received was a decent sum at the time, he started speculating whether he could make his old dream of travelling come true by becoming a journalist. Soon afterwards he was offered an advance of two thousands marks to produce a photo-essay on the battlefields of the Great War and he was hooked on

photography for life.

He travelled all over the world, never worrying much about the composition of his work; he did not even consider himself a photographer in the traditional sense of the word but rather a journalist using a camera instead of a typewriter, although whenever it was necessary he could turn out brilliant commentary and captions for his pictures. On assignments he was never accompanied by a write-up man as was customary later. His reporting always had two fundamental requirements for a good journalist in the field — perfect presentation of the subject or theme and accompanying background information. In his time, Weber ranked among the best paid photographers in Germany, receiving 350—400 marks per printed page. And yet the pictures he brought from all corners of the globe to the editorial offices on the second floor of the famous *Ullstein Verlag* were not sensational but records of ordinary life. While his colleague Felix H. Man sought subjects at home in Germany, Weber hunted for his exotic places. His famous series

included the coverage of a diamond rush in Africa; the wild animals of the savanna; the life of ordinary people in India, Madagascar, Java and Sumatra.

His activity was much curbed by World War II, since he remained in Germany trying hard to produce politically unbiased reportages. A typical example of his wartime work is his coverage of the transatlantic formation flight of Italo Balbo's squadron. Immediately after the war Weber took to the road again, although he did not now report on ordinary life. In 1945 he was appointed chief reporter of *Neue Illustrierte,* photographing

subsequently in Congo, Suez, Cuba, South Africa, Latin America and India as well as a number of other trouble spots. When the big illustrated magazine circulation started slipping in the 1960s, Weber switched to television.

Weber has been called a 'portraitist of the world' and the title is a well-earned one. Having started to make a portrait of our planet in the early days of photojournalism, Wolfgang Weber has been systematically adding to it for fifty years — a pioneer in new trends in journalism and an ideal photojournalist writer.

107

# Umbo

/1902—1980/

His real name was Otto Umbehr but everybody called this small, lively, rotund man Umbo. A good humoured practical joker, he was a great ladies' man and respected by men. His signature Umbo-Dephot appeared under countless pictures and series carried by the German and international press after 1927. The word 'Dephot' was an abbreviation for *Deutsche Photodienst,* a picture service founded by Simon Guttmann whom Otto Umbehr met one day in the Café Vienna, Berlin. The meeting proved decisive both for Umbehr and the emerging art of photojournalism.

Umbehr finished his secondary education right after World War I. The economic situation in Germany was uncertain and Umbehr decided to become a miner. However, he was restless and soon exchanged the miner's pick for the woodcarver's chisel, then for the potter's wheel and later even went on the stage. After this period of aimless

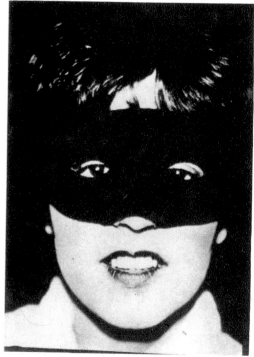

wandering he appeared in Weimar and enrolled as a regular student at the Bauhaus where he spent two years. Afterwards he worked as interior decorator, stage designer, circus clown and assistant director with a film company and perhaps would have spent his life drifting from job to job had he not asked his father to send him a camera. He started taking pictures and developing them himself in a darkroom which his Bauhaus friend Paul Citroën helped him to equip. Citroën at that time was experimenting with photomontage and his ideas inspired Umbo when he was working with Walter Ruttmann on his poetic documentary film *Symphonie einer Grossstadt (Symphony of a City)* which in its turn influenced Umbo's own photographic work. It was Ruttmann who arranged the meeting with Simon Guttmann which was the start of Umbo's years of work for the *Dephot* service, a new type of picture service which produced photographic reportage and photo-essay features for the German and international press.

Umbo's talent was universal for he was just as at home in photojournalism and documentary photography as when producing experimental photography, ironic collages of Symbolist and New Objectivity still lifes. His artistic inclinations led to his experimenting with new vehicles of expression: unusual perspectives, masks, close-ups, montage, etc., which introduced new features in photojournalism. The demand for personal viewpoint photography was growing and Umbo produced one series after another. Then the war broke out but Umbo remained working as a free-lance photographer until 1943 when he was drafted, spending the rest of the war as a lorry driver for the German army. The end of the war found him in Hanover 'naked as the day I was born' as he tersely used to comment on the inglorious end of his military career. His photographic equipment and files had been destroyed but a friend loaned him a Leica and the once famous experimentalist photographer had to make a living from photographing local news, advertisement work and an occasional commission from his old friend Guttman in London.

Later he taught photography in Bad Pyrmont, Hildesheim and Hanover. However, his restless nature prevented him from settling permanently in any one place and during the last decade of his life Umbo once again drifted from job to job, the last being that of a warehouse packer.

Even after he retired he used to spend his weekends selling admission tickets to exhibitions held by the Kästner Society for whom he once worked. Most probably he would have remained completely forgotten had it not been for the book by his onetime colleague Tim Gidal, who in 1972 placed the beginnings of modern photojournalism definitely in Germany during late 1920s and early 30s, giving due credit to Umbo's pioneering work.

# Alfred Eisenstaedt

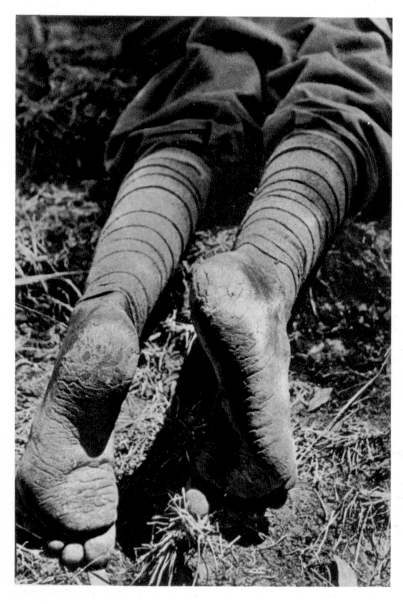

When Alfred Eisenstaedt came to the United States in the fall of 1935, he became a member of the team preparing the publication of a new magazine called *Life*. 'When he showed me the results of his first assignment . . . I was convinced that our ideas for the picture magazine would work.' The founder of the magazine Henry R. Luce later reminisced: 'Eisie showed me that the camera could do more than take a striking picture here and there. It could do more than record "the instant moment". Eisie showed that the camera could deal with an entire subject — whether the subject was a man, a maker of history, or whether it was a social phenomenon. That is what is meant by photojournalism.' Yet another of the pioneers of modern photojournalism in Germany had started sowing the seeds of the new style overseas.

Alfred Eisenstaedt was born in western Prussia, in the family of a businessman. He was educated in the harshly disciplinarian atmosphere of a Berlin Gymnasium of the Hohenzollern era and knew the mindless drill of the Imperial army. He survived the war with shrapnel fragments in both legs and since the post-war inflation turned the family money to so much worthless paper, he started selling buttons. In his spare time, he took up photography. He was a poor salesman; business did not attract him at all. Eisenstaedt was becoming more and more fascinated by

photography, devoting all his spare time to the hobby. He much admired Erich Salomon's candid photography made without using flash. He became fascinated by the ability of the medium to hold time still to relay a message. In 1929 he was hired by the Berlin bureau of Associated Press and became a professional photographer. His pictures started appearing in the press and were much admired for their frankness. The rise of the Third Reich represented for Eisenstaedt the end of a civilized Europe where he so enjoyed living and he emigrated to the United States and joined the staff of the then young *Life*, later one of the best known picture magazines in the world. Eisenstaedt brought to *Life* a style that had already become familiar in Europe but was at first misunderstood in the United States. For two years he was forced to use a stand camera and a flash to meet the requirements of the American notion of technically perfect, sharp focus photography. In fact what ultimately helped Eisenstaedt and

the other European photographers on the magazine to assert their own style was the rise of London *Picture Post* in September, 1938, a picture magazine in which Stefan Lorant and Felix H. Man continued the traditions of German photojournalism. Only then did *Life* reject the old aesthetics and venture in the direction paved by Eisenstaedt.

For *Life* Eisenstaedt made 1,800 reportages and eighty of his pictures found their way onto the cover. His photography brought the life of royalty, film stars, writers, scientists, musicians and other famous people into the homes of millions of readers.

His subjects were as wide as life itself, for Eisenstaedt photographed a waiter on skates twisting his way among the tables of a St. Moritz hotel; he waited patiently until four in the morning to snap Hitler and Mussolini shaking their hands at the conclusion of their first talks; captured the cold stare of Joseph Goebbels as well as the V-sign of Winston Churchill; he showed the world the cracked

feet of a totally exhausted Ethiopian soldier as well as the despair in the face of a Hiroshima mother. He loathed danger and yet did not hesitate to go to Kenya to photograph massacred Masai tribesmen, climb to the roof of a New York skyscraper or endure the giant mosquitoes in the jungles of Latin America. 'That was where the pictures were,' he once explained.

To look was the most important thing, but his look was always personal and committed. Life was all things for him but first was the reality that he was committed to observe and record. 'A photographer needs a short circuit between his brain and his fingertips. Things happen: sometimes expected, more often unexpected. You must be ready to catch the right split second, because if you miss, the picture may be gone forever ... It's really a matter of observing ... of being constantly alert to the sudden unexpectedness of life.'

# André Kertész

/1894 — 1985/

André Kertész was lucky to have been a self-taught amateur photographer, for when he started photographing ordinary life around him in 1912, this young Hungarian unknowingly rebelled against the beautiful soft focus photography that was the standard fare of the major photographic salons of the period. His photographs from World War I were made in the same unpretentious manner: no celebrations of victorious campaigns, no superhuman heroes, no shining brass, for André Kertész knew what it was to be a frontline infantryman, he was familiar with the muddy, raindrenched and vermin-infested trenches, with men exchanging cruel and bitter jokes while waiting to go over the top.

His photographs captured only ordinary people: a soldier enjoying his pipe between bombardments, a countryboy in uniform running across a meadow to pat a cow — a reminder of home. His pictures show trivial scenes that seem incongruously out of context in a war.

If the birth of photojournalism can be said to have been directly associated with the advent of small, easy-to-handle cameras, then a sense for unexpected detail, for the fleeting yet characteristic moment, must also be a partner of that birth, for this 'candid camera' approach had appeared in Kertész's photography long before the invention of the compact camera. 'I had played at being a photographer long before I had my first camera, telling myself if I had a camera I would take this or that so and so . . .' he once said to an interviewer. His lifetime work is in fact a pictorial diary of his life, a record of his fascination with the human condition, the significance of a moment, the beauty of the world.

In 1925 Kertész moved to Paris, becoming a member of the international bohemian community. Strolling through the streets of this centre of the arts, fashion and entertainment of the 1920s and 30s, he absorbed new ideas, trends and opinions yet remained true to his own creed that the beauty of photography was in its truth, taking pictures of vagrants sleeping under the bridges spanning the Seine; labourers in their bistros near the famous Les Halles; prostitutes on streetcorners; lovers whispering sweet nothings over marbletopped tables in

photojournalists considered one of the greatest pioneers of modern photography, an artist humbly observing and recording ordinary life.

His exceptional sense for form and composition always resulted in pictorial perfection which culminated in the outstanding pictures he made as an old man from the windows of his New York apartment. His compassion and respect for human dignity which influenced Brassaï, Cartier-Bresson and in fact an entire generation of great humanist photographers, have lent his visually perfect lyrical imagery a permanent value.

sidewalk cafés; vendors, street entertainers, jugglers, determined Popular Front rallies on the eve of the war—always expressing his personal impressions of various human situations, his feeling for universal human problems, developing what was later termed 'candid photography'.

In 1936 Kertész went to the United States on what had been intended as a one-year assignment. The war and his success in America made him stay overseas for almost three decades. For twenty-seven years Kertész thought his Paris files lost but a friend returned him the old box with his negatives which she had saved from the Germans and kept hidden in the cellar of a château in southern France. By then Kertész had become famous in the United States for his fashion, interior design and architectural photography while his reportage work had remained virtually unknown because American magazines had thought it to be too 'Central European in character, too lyrical and subjective'. He was vindicated only as late as 1964 when he had an exhibition in the Museum of Modern Art in New York. Kertész who felt remorse for the type of work which he had been doing to make a living in America was now hailed as a man whom

# Brassaï

/1899—1985/

Brassaï's photographic career started because he was a night owl, going to sleep with the dawn and getting up when the dusk started falling in the streets. He was captivated by Paris at night and so he wandered in its streets, alone or with a friend. Henry Miller took him to bistros and bars while Jacques Prévert showed him the picturesque world of street acrobats, clochards, vagrants, con artists, sanitary workers and labourers from the markethall. It was a world of laughter and sadness, bizarre festivals and human tragedy. For years he was haunted by these spectres of the night disappearing with the dawn, until André Kertész loaned him a camera.

He was almost thirty and until then had never been interested in photography. In fact, he had even despised it. Now he came to realize that the 'mindless mechanism' as he irreverently called the camera was able to capture the atmosphere of a moment and he immediately forgot his previous prejudice. He bought an expensive camera on credit — it was a 6.5 × 9 cm Bergheil with a Heliar 4.5 lens — and turned his apartment into a darkroom. As a rule he photographed at night, in smokefilled bars and under the eerie light of gas lamps. He was arrested several times during police raids because they refused to believe that it was possible to take pictures at

three in the morning. He in fact became a master at taking pictures under poor light conditions, a wizard with a camera who could make use of any light available. Thus he put together his first book, published in 1933 under the title *Paris de Nuit* (English edition entitled *The Secret Paris of the 30s*).
Henry Miller called him the 'eye of Paris' although he was not born in the city he so loved to photograph and was not even French by birth. Born as Gyula Halász in Transylvania, he studied painting in Budapest and Berlin. A talented but poor painter, he moved to Paris in 1923 and settled among the international artistic and bohemian

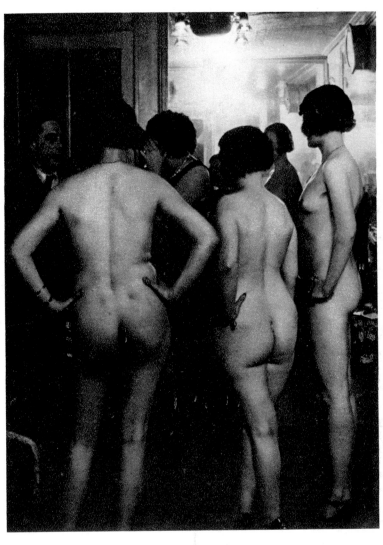

community of the Montmartre and Montparnasse district, associating with such people as Pablo Picasso, Paul Eluard, André Breton, Salvador Dali, Aristide Maillol, Georges Braque and Henri Matisse. He painted and wrote essays and since his name was too difficult for his French-speaking friends to pronounce, he adopted a pseudonym Brassaï based on his birthplace, Brasov, Romania. A painter, writer, sculptor and film-maker, Brassaï is remembered mainly for his photography of night scenes from Paris in the early 1930s.

'I'm no reporter because I do not photograph things that convey a message,' he once told an interviewer. 'I'm interested in what is universally human, what relates something about the human condition.' This simple statement aptly characterized what was later called candid photography and still later termed life-photography. Brassaï has never been interested in particularities but in generalizations, in actual phenomena typical of the atmosphere of the place and time. He said once that he did not care about psychology but his journeys into the Paris night probe deeply under the surface of reality, penetrating the souls of people, things, places and times.

The inner worlds, the stories hidden within — these were the mysteries that Brassaï the photographer was searching for during his sleepless nights.

Brassaï was always extremely considerate to his subjects because he knew only too well that laughter and sorrow, a costume and rags are but two sides of the same coin. Take for instance La Môme Bijou, Miss Diamonds, from the famous picture taken on a winter night in 1932. Once famous and rich, she was reduced to living from gifts and palm reading.

# Bill Brandt

/1904 — 1983/

The fate of this Englishman of Russian blood would probably have been quite different had he not chanced to meet Man Ray and leave with him for Paris when he was just twenty-four. The Roaring Twenties were almost over and photography in Paris was as international and experimental in character as was literature and painting. Paris was the place where the Hungarian-born André Kertész was searching for confirmation of his belief that the beauty of photography was in its truth; where another Hungarian, Brassaï, had just started his quest for the mysteries of the city's night life; and Man Ray, an American expatriate, was producing work which was to influence a whole generation. Primarily it was the ordinary look of Eugène Atget's pictures in Man Ray's studio that

compelled the young Bill Brandt to remain in Paris as Man Ray's assistant. And it was the inner warmth and poetic atmosphere, the magical mystery of Atget's dawns, that Bill Brandt took back home to England in 1931 as his new vision. 'The photographer must discover what really interests him; his instinct should be strong enough to carve its own channel,' Brandt said later.

Whether it was instinct or just need which made him work for the press after his return home remains unclear but the fact remains that he started as a freelance photographer. He considered everything around him worthy of his interest and soon produced a powerful photo-essay titled *The English at Home*, which was serialized by various magazines for which he worked at the time. With the erudition of

a professional storyteller and with the formal bravado of an accomplished graphic artist Brandt in this essay managed to illustrate the way the life of the rich differed from that of the poor in standards of living, education, work, leisure. His pictures are a report from a sensitive observer, as much at ease at Royal Ascot as in the dockyards, in the drawing room as the kitchen. His pictures do not criticize or press an opinion, they merely present the scene he perceived it. It was this personal interpretation of observed phenomena that was needed in the British photojournalism then emerging. In 1937 Brandt made a tour of the traditionally poor mining and industrial areas in north-eastern England. In Newcastle, Jarrow, Halifax and other places, his camera captured the grim

116

atmosphere of factory towns, the hard existence inscribed in people's faces, their despair on the verge of poverty and starvation. What Brandt produced was not a document as were the projects of the US Farm Security Administration. His images are seen through the prism of personal mood and experience. They are characterized by an almost Atgetian wizardry with light and a tone scale ranging from ultralight greys to ebony blacks. This was Brandt's own poetry, a personal vision of human happiness, joy and sorrow.

It was probably the two strong influences from his early photographic career — Man Ray and Atget — that caused the two features which have always remained strong in Bill Brandt's work: truth and artistic creativity.

During the war Brandt was a reporter and what interested him most was not so much the heroics and horrors of war but the silence before the planes appeared and bombs started descending. Deserted London streets; hordes of people lying side-by-side on tube station platforms; an old lady who would not forget to take her umbrella even to an air-raid shelter; these photographs are first of all governed by the photographer's emotional experience from universally human situations. In the post-war years Brandt's interest shifted to portraiture, nudes, landscapes and natural objects. In his later efforts to express the purity of line and form he evoked Surrealist sculptures, using the distortion of the wide-angle lens. He escaped with his camera from overcrowded cities to the countryside.

# VII  PHOTOGRAPHY AS PROPAGANDA

The social uses of photography were — among other things — motivated by political concerns. As photography came to play an increasingly important role in the press, it asserted itself as a major tool of the ideological struggle, especially in countries shaken by revolutions that had resulted from World War I. Thus photography either helped reinforce the age-old existing social system or rallied any opposition forces determined to overthrow it; or, as in the case of the young Soviet state, it helped the establishment of the new order. In all cases, however, photography fulfilled the role of an agitator or propagandist trying to influence public opinion. 'We, worker photographers, are the armed troops of the class struggle,' stated a special issue of the magazine *Der Arbeiter-Fotograf (The Worker Photographer)* published in 1931 to commemorate the national German conference of worker photographers and an international exhibition in Berlin.

Worker photographers were not merely amateur photographers who happened to be workers by profession or class background — although these indeed constituted a majority — but people who placed their private hobby in the service of practical politics. Unlike a regular amateur photographer, a worker photographer did not take pictures for fun but because he was firmly convinced that photography was a powerful tool to be used by the working class in its political struggle. The worker photographers' movement became a mass phenomenon during the late 1920s and especially the early 30s, i.e. during the Great Depression. It emerged in various European countries including Germany, Hungary, France, Czechoslovakia, the Netherlands, Switzerland, Great Britain, the United States and Japan. For the first time in history the workers and their situation were photographed not by members of other social classes but by workers themselves. Using the camera, workers now started gathering evidence for a social critique.

The worker photographers had in fact been born during the dramatic developments of the Russian Revolution in 1917 when photography was given a precisely formulated assignment: to inform, educate and agitate the masses. The task stemmed from the pressing

needs of the moment because there was no other instructive, illustrative and educational medium that could inform the people in this vast country of the meaning of the recent developments, especially since the overwhelming majority of the people were illiterate. The Soviets decided this was the medium which could affect the consciousness, thought and sentiment of the masses; thus Soviet Russia was the first to use photography as a tool for carefully planned, centrally controlled and didactically oriented agitation and propaganda. However, the Soviets needed more photographers than they had at their disposal at that time. A huge campaign was therefore launched among workers and peasants to educate new photographers. As early as December 1917, immediately after the Soviets had taken over in Russia, a department of cinematography and photography was established under the auspices of the State Commission for Popular Enlightenment in St. Petersburg, where lectures on photography were provided. The following year the High Institute of Photography was opened in St. Petersburg, the first institution of higher learning in Europe to offer a full curriculum in photography. In the fall of the same year the Soviet government established special departments of photoreportage at the cinécommittees in St. Petersburg and Moscow; the departments were expected to cover current political events and to use the photographs taken for propaganda purposes. Within less than 3 years an archive of more than 15,000 exposed negatives was amassed. To materialize Lenin's idea of incorporating photography — and cinematography — into an integrated system of propaganda was not an easy task because war-wrecked Russia, plagued by extreme economic difficulties, even lacked newspapers at first. Eventually, with the development of posters and graphics, ROSTA (Russian Telegraph Agency) and its 'Satire Windows', photography took to the streets in the form of pictorial poster newspapers. These so-called 'agitdisplays' with pictures of recent newsworthy events were hung weekly on streetcorners in major Russian cities. In Moscow alone about sixty such displays were circulated simultaneously, with twenty or so in St. Petersburg. Yet this

was not enough. 'Agittrains' and 'agitsteamers' started criss-crossing the country, pictorial albums were issued, exhibitions were organized and collage and montage were discovered. This method of propaganda raised agitation to the level of an art, using not only photography but also literature, painting, film and graphics.

'No other photographic genre had a greater impact than pictorial news. Landscape and portrait photography practically died out,' wrote Sergei Morozov, a Soviet historian of photography. This socially oriented photography naturally left its imprint on the then emerging amateur photography movement which later became a model for the world-wide organization of worker photographers. In spite of its deliberate anonymity, the worker photographer movement produced indisputable talents in creative photography such as Walter Ballhause, Eugen Heilig and Ernst Thormann in Germany, Erich Rinke, the author of *Fotografie im Klassenkampf (Photography in the Class Struggle)*, and the Slovak organizer of the *Sociofoto* movement, Irene Blüh.

The mid-20s became a milestone because at that time Soviet photography began consciously to place the photographic image side-by-side with written reportage. In 1923 the picture weekly *Ogoněk (Small Fire)* was founded, followed by the *Sovetskoe Foto (Soviet Photography)* and *Fotograf* in 1926. The same year *Soyuzfoto,* Soviet picture service, started working. In 1930, on the direct initiative of the famous writer Maxim Gorki the magazine *SSSR na stroike (USSR in Construction)* appeared both in Russian and in foreign language editions. The magazine became a platform for photographers like A. Shaikhet, M. Alpert, G. Zelma, G. Petrusov, S. Fridlyand, B. Ignatovich and others who employed the so-called *fotoocherki* (photo-sketches or photo-essays) to relate complete stories about the new large projects of the first five year economic plans and the new life of the country. One of the first full-length essays of this type was the series *Twenty-four Hours in the Filippov Family,* relating the events of an ordinary day in the family of a Moscow worker. The piece of propaganda in the end served as a model for propaganda campaigns aimed at the outside world.

As early as 1921 the *Arbeiter Illustrierte Zeitung (Worker's Illustrated Newspaper)*, a workers' picture magazine, known popularly as *AIZ*, appeared in Germany. Following the example of Soviet worker photographers, *AIZ* soon started carrying reportage series produced by worker photographer groups which commented on the complicated and uneasy political developments in the Weimar Republic. In 1926, under the auspices of *AIZ*, the first issue of a new magazine, *Der Arbeiter-Fotograf (The Worker Photographer)*, appeared. The magazine in fact stemmed from the results of a photographic competition of proletarian and leftist intelligentsia amateur photographers. At the turn of 1928 and 1929 German workers' photographic clubs united, forming an impressive base for German proletarian photography; the Union of German Worker Photographers' was composed of 45 groups with a total membership of 1,480 people and some 5,000 potential members and willing collaborators. Through its foreign relations department and the magazine *Der Arbeiter-Fotograf*, the Union maintained close contacts with photographers and photographic magazines in the USSR and other countries, exchanging material and publications and providing exhibition space.

At about the same time a similarly oriented *Szociofotó* movement originated in Hungary under the guidance of the Slovak-born writer, poet and critic Lajos Kassák. The movement concentrated around the magazine *Munka (Labour)*. Likewise in Slovakia a movement with the same name — *Sociofoto* — was established by Communist pictorial propagandists led by Irene Blüh and by members of the photographic section of the Slovak German club known as *Naturfreunde (Friends of Nature)*.

Members of this widely based international photographic movement in fact performed sociological research into the conditions of life in urban and rural areas, publishing the results of their work in German, Hungarian, Czech and Slovak leftist press, and also in *AIZ* whose editorial offices had to be moved to Prague after Hitler's rise to power. Social critique photography was likewise utilized by leftist architects, members of the Left Front, who held large exhibitions in Czechoslovakia and, during the black years of depression and mass unemployment, confronted the reality of urban tenement housing with the bright possibilities of state-controlled housing programmes. These exhibitions were sometimes forcefully closed by the authorities who considered them too radical.

In Bohemia the activities of socially concerned photography took place within the film and photo section of the Left Front but proletarian photography never became a mass movement as it did in Slovakia, Hungary and Germany.

Yet it was Prague where, in April 1933, the International Exhibition of Social Photography was held. This clearly outlined the task for socially oriented photography: to become a social factor and a promoter of the new *Weltanschauung* (World Explained), dialectic materialism. In the preface to the exhibition catalogue, Lubomír Linhart, the driving force of the exhibition and spokesman for the Czech Film-Foto Group of the Left Front, wrote: 'We take photography for what it has truly become today, an important social force ... affecting profoundly socio-political and economic problems ... What we want is to give photography a new, healthy, socially positive content and a fighting spirit ...'

This idea had been influenced by both Soviet and German photography, and in fact by the entire international movement of socially concerned photography. The exhibition displayed not only Czech photographers but also works of the members of the Slovak *Sociofoto* movement, Soviet photojournalists, French proletarian photographers and many others. Only the collection of German worker photographers was missing because the presentation was prevented by the Nazis. Despite this, the exhibition turned out to be a manifestation of socially and politically minded photography which, during the years between the two World Wars, united the efforts of the European Left and influenced the emergence of similarly oriented movements in the United States (the Photo-League) and Japan.

This 'social', 'proletarian' or 'socialist' photography, as it was termed in various countries, was a mass international social and political movement. In some countries it was a tribune for the oppressed who called for social reform, in the USSR it became intoxicated with revolutionary fervour, reflecting the naiveté and romantic sentiment of the new era as well as the fatigue from too rapid a change, but most of all it viewed the future with confidence. This social photography was photography that informed, educated and agitated.

Before long, however, the clamour of arms of the coming World War II began to be heard all over the continent. Naturally, the war effort also relied heavily on the power of photography as an effective tool of agitation and propaganda. On one hand, Helmuth Herzfelde, forced by the political developments to leave his native Germany, used his pictures as John Heartfield to reveal the inhuman face of Nazism, on the other hand photographers of German *Propagandakompanien* (propaganda companies) did everything to enforce the false myths of the thousand years' Third Reich. These were but two aspects of the same thing: photography as propaganda.

# Irene Blüh

/1904/

as background material and evidence for his interpellation to parliament.

The work of the young lady photographer soon aroused the interest of the local gendarmerie. A banking clerk by profession, Miss Blüh was constantly transferred from place to place until 1931 when she decided to go to Germany, partly to avoid imprisonment for her activities as a photographer. She enrolled in the Bauhaus School of Design where she studied modern photographic and typographical forms of promotion. The two years spent at the Bauhaus left a lasting impression on her life. Her photography now changed. Gone were the simple frontal shots; in her photography she started to render reality with sophisticated vision, dynamic form with a very personal touch.

After her return to Czechoslovakia, she started a Communist bookstore in Bratislava which became a meeting place for radical students, writers, artists, poets and journalists. From here political posters, photomontages, pictorial documents and other forms of modern pictorial propaganda were disseminated not only throughout Czechoslovakia but also Austria, Poland,

When Irene Blüh took her first pictures of the life of Horná Mariková, a little Slovak village, in 1925, she could hardly know that she was earning a place in the annals of what is called today social or proletarian photography. She was only twenty-one and totally ignorant of the people who had employed this type of photography before in various parts of the world. What she did know about was the poverty of her native country, the cries of famished children, the back-breaking work in steep stony fields, the incessant struggle against the elements for a few sacks of potatoes, the staple food of Slovak villagers. Unlike her predecessors in this field of photography she did not use her primitive Goertz-Tenax plate camera to argue for social reform. The lithe but energetic girl wanted much more than just reform or compromise: a fervent Marxist, she attacked the very foundations of the system of social inequality, becoming a revolutionist. Her first photographs of the little village of Horná Mariková were used by a Communist deputy

120

Hungary and even Germany. Moreover, the bookstore became a home base of a group of photographers who decided to carry out long-term systematic sociological research of the most backward and undeveloped districts of Slovakia according to a plan devised and controlled by the Communist Party. In 1934 the group presented the results of the project at an independent exhibition called *Sociofoto* after a similar *Szociofotó* movement in neighbouring Hungary. As a result of the untiring efforts of Irene Blüh the movement grew rapidly, uniting various groups and individual sympathizers with the Leftist cause for which photography became an important tool of political work.

Irene Blüh's name did not appear at the time because, although she published her photographs in practically all the leftist magazines and newspapers of the period, including the Czech *Tvorba* and *Rudé právo,* the Party daily, the Slovak *Dav,* Hungarian *Az Út* or German *AIZ,* she, just as other members of the *Sociofoto* movement, published her work anonymously because the movement

wanted to advance a cause rather than individuals. Thus Irene Blüh, Barbara Zsigmondi, Rosi Ney, Friedrich Stroh, Karol Aufricht and others considered themselves just parts of a whole, contributors to the common cause, and it was as a group that they presented their work at two international exhibitions of social photography in Prague, in 1933 and 1934.

After World War II Irene Blüh reappeared on the Czechoslovak political scene. She was appointed director of the Party press in

Bratislava, was elected into the parliament and held other important public offices. Although she continued with photography, her real contribution to the art was in the 20s and 30s in the development of photography as a tool of modern propaganda in Czechoslovakia.

# Walter Ballhause

/1911/

The unemployed sitting in quiet desperation on the curb; a blind beggar on a streetcorner; a long queue of men and women waiting on their luck in the yard of a labour exchange; such were the photographs published by Walter Ballhause in the workers' press, especially the *Arbeiter Illustrierte Zeitung (Worker's Illustrated Newspaper)* and *Der Arbeiter-Fotograf (The Worker Photographer)*, during the 1920s and 30s. At eighteen he joined the Social Democratic Party and at nineteen he started taking photographs of things around him, using a borrowed Leica. Like other German worker photographers at the time, he did not take up photography merely as a hobby but because he considered the medium a powerful tool for political struggle.

He was born in Hamelin, Lower Saxony, and at fourteen he joined the Workers' Gymnastics and Sports League and enjoyed tremendously the atmosphere of a group of people bound by a common interest. Then he and his mother moved to Hanover and he had to contribute to the family budget.

Although he did not photograph for long — in fact, only for three or four years before the Nazis came to power — his pictures represent a deeply involved testimony of the times, revealing much about the author himself since,

after moving to Hanover, he was one of the countless army of unemployed during the depression.

As a self-taught photographer, Ballhause was chiefly interested in the pictorial content of the photographs rather than aesthetic effects. His short career as a photographer was remarkably successful. The Social Democratic paper *Volkswille* printed most of his pictures and some were also carried by the Austrian workers' press in 1932. Some of his pictures were exhibited at the *Kunsthaus* in Hanover along with works of amateur salon photographers.

The advent of Nazism as the state ideology in Germany brought Ballhause's photographic activities to an end. Several prominent Nazis who were familiar with the impact of Ballhause's vision tried hard to win the author over to the cause of the new regime since they needed propaganda photography and people able to produce it. Ballhause refused all offers on the grounds that he was too busy studying chemistry and in the end he dropped photography altogether, but unfortunately it was too late. He was denounced as an anti-Fascist and although he tried to keep a low profile and even moved to Plauen, he was arrested in 1944 for alleged underground activity and 'undermining the military morale'.

Ironically, it was the huge Allied bomb raid on Dresden during which scores of thousands of people were killed that saved him from execution.

After the war Walter Ballhause worked as an industrial chemist and remained practically forgotten until 1971 when his work was rediscovered, making him practically overnight one of the most celebrated figures of pre-war German worker photography.

# Arkadi Shaikhet

/1898 — 1959/

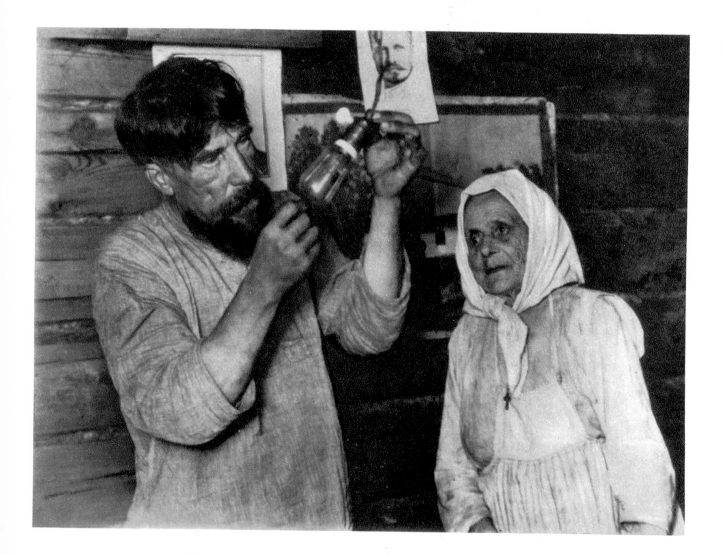

Arkadi Shaikhet was a shipyard mechanic before he started his photographic career with retouching jobs in the darkroom of a Moscow studio photographer. Five years later he won prizes at the Moscow Jubilee Exhibition and in London, at a time when opportunities were such that life could completely change overnight.

It was in 1924 that the first Soviet illustrated magazine *Ogonëk* carried pictures by this hitherto unknown photographer. Since then his name has always been associated with early Soviet photojournalism. He was one of those who were given the chance of a lifetime by the new system. As hydroelectric schemes cropped up on rivers with exotic names, industrial complexes were built in Siberian wastes and irrigation canals dissected arid Central Asian steppes, Arkadi Shaikhet was on the spot to witness the illiterate Russian *muzhiks* entering the 20th century. Essentially a story-teller, given to the traditional Russian preference of broad epics, day after day, month after month he kept filing his record of the times.

He photographed gangs of wild, dirty, hungry orphans who roamed the streets of Russian towns in the years following the Revolution; *muzhiks* in traditional dress, with burlap bags over their shoulders and their feet tied in rags as they walked long distances from all corners of Mother Russia to Moscow to help reconstruct the economy destroyed by war; the column of the first Soviet-made automobiles en route from Nizhni Novgorod (Gorki) to Moscow; peasants waiting patiently for Premier Kalinin to discuss their problems; old peasants staring at an 'Ilyich's lamp' as the electric lightbulb hitherto unknown in rural areas was nicknamed. Shaikhet was not so much impressed by the large and fast-growing industrial projects as he was deeply attracted by the emotions and experience of ordinary people. He never embellished his pictures because what Shaikhet was most anxiously

Oder; German POW's plodding through snowdrifts in fog; the bulk of a tank, its gun pointing silently to the Kursk skies.
The work of Arkadi Shaikhet, represented by thousands of photographs disseminated through a variety of magazines and newspapers and covering a period from the early 1920s until the late 1950s when he died while still working, is a testimony to a man who witnessed great historic changes and upheavals yet managed to produce photographic work that remains deeply human.

trying for was credibility. Starting in the 1920s his work is a unique testimony of a life style, a testimony marked by revolutionary romanticism but not overburdened with later schematic stylization.
*Ogonëk, Proletarskoe foto (Proletarian Photography), SSSR na stroike (USSR in Construction), Nashi dostizheniya (Our Achievements)* were the magazines in the vanguard of a great era of Soviet photojournalism and now constitute a vast, albeit dispersed, catalogue of Shaikhet's work. This list of magazines would be incomplete without the German *Arbeiter Illustrierte Zeitung* which was the first to print one of the first Soviet photo-essays, the famous *Twenty-Four Hours in the Filippov Family*, of which Arkadi Shaikhet was one of the co-authors. Even during the 1930s when the initial simplicity and authenticity of photography used by Soviet picture magazines was replaced by calculated, bombastic monumentality, Shaikhet's style changed little.
When World War II broke out, Arkadi Shaikhet was forty-three and it seemed his work no longer shocked or surprised. Yet the war years represent the culmination of his career as a photographer. Once again, he remained unimpressed by pomp and heroics but entered the annals of combat photography by his uncomplicated presentation of ordinary wartime days and anonymous human beings: an infantryman hugging his wife and mother; men building a pontoon bridge, and up to their waists shivering in the ice-cold water of the

# Max Alpert

/1899 — 1980/

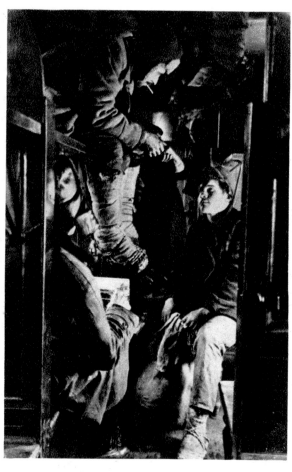

Max Alpert was sometimes called the chronicler of Russia. It was a hard-earned tribute because his camera was always where the action was, sometimes in the most remote places. It was his camera that immortalized the pick-axes that broke the dry soil of Central Asia to build the Fergana Irrigation Canal; took pictures of the first pioneers who arrived in the inhospitable wastes of the Urals to build the huge steeltown of Magnitogorsk; the laying of the 1,500 km long Turksib railway linking Turkmenia with Siberia; the construction of the Dneprogress hydroelectric scheme. He captured the return of Maxim Gorki from Italy; the crowds cheering the flier Valeri Chkalov, the first aviator to fly over the North Pole; and many more heroic achievements.

Throughout his long life, Max Alpert was a photojournalist. In 1924, with the Revolution barely over, his pictures first appeared in the Soviet press. It was a time when everything was changing, when people were building a new life in the ruins with their bare hands. Perhaps because it was an era of strong emotions, dramatic changes and daring ideas, photographers had no time for speculation and, totally unprepared, had to start recording everything around them. It is only today that their work is viewed as the earliest form of life-photography which became strongly involved in the fascinating depiction of life in Soviet Russia, a depiction which attracted wellwishers and enemies alike. Together with other photographers of his generation, A. Shaikhet, G. Petrusov, S. Fridlyand, G. Zelma and others, Max Alpert was one of the fathers of Soviet photojournalism. He co-authored the famous *Twenty-Four Hours in the Filippov Family,* one of the first large photo-essays in Soviet photography. At that time he worked as photoreporter for the Party daily *Pravda,* the *Soyuzfoto* service and the picture magazine *SSSR na stroike (USSR in Construction)* and he was an obvious choice when it was decided that a photographic essay should be taken of the life of an ordinary Moscow worker's family. The photographers selected for the project, Alpert, Shaikhet and Tules, moved in with the family of a metalworker named Filippov and spent long days there recording the events and comings and goings of the family. The essay, comprising almost eighty pictures, was exhibited in Vienna in 1931, then in Prague and Berlin and ultimately brought to an untold number of homes by the *AIZ* magazine. Alpert often used the format of an essay for his work. Remarkable, for example, is his pictorial sketch of Victor Kalmykov, one of the

126

thousands of young illiterates who came to the Urals to look for work in the Magnitogorsk steelworks project, finding not only a job but also an education and professional qualification. Of course, these essays had to be arranged beforehand to a large extent to have the desired propagandistic impact in the press, but they also constitute a period testimony, a pictorial chronicle of the times.

World War II started a separate chapter in Alpert's work, producing his best-known picture titled *Combat*. Even here Alpert was more of a newspaperman with a precise idea of the intended impact than a sensitive social seismograph like Shaikhet, as if this picture of a company commander, his arms open wide as though ready to dance the wild *kazachok* dance of the Cossacks, yet clutching his pistol firmly in his fingers, was calculated to appeal to the spectator to come, stand up and fight for his country.

# Boris Ignatovich

/1899—1976/

'Everybody has a wild imagination when he is young and I would have believed anything but that I would be a professional photographer,' Boris Ignatovich once admitted.
He confided how he started photographing: 'A friend gave me a pocket Kodak. I took it to the editorial office and Mikhail [Zoshchenko] came and I asked him to pose for me. When we went home Mikhail stopped by a kiosk because he wanted to buy some apples and I pointed the camera at him. This was my first reportage snapshot. It was in the spring of 1923 . . .'

By this time Boris Ignatovich already had behind him a career as a writer and editor of three Leningrad satirical magazines around which he had rallied authors like Vladimir Mayakovski, Mikhail Zoshchenko, Andrei Bezymenski and Mikhail Bulgakov whose acute sense of humour provided a biting commentary on the life in Soviet Russia in the post-Revolution period of great social changes. Ignatovich had already become renowned as a journalist when photography attracted him with the possibility to report visually the dramatic atmosphere of the

historic epoch and its heroes. He knew he would have to start his career again from scratch but did not hesitate to swap the pen for the camera.
His close friendship with leading writers, poets, artists and film-makers as well as his deep understanding of the problems of the moment soon made him seek those who strove for a new vision in photography, searching for novel means to express the unprecedented things taking place in Russia. Ignatovich started collaborating with Alexander Rodchenko, Eleazar Langman,

128

subject, unusual camera angles and close-ups. Together with his wife, his sister and other photographers he founded a photographic 'brigade', a team which worked for the *Soyuzfoto* service. As befitted the period tendency to subdue all individuality, the members of the team signed their work collectively 'Brigade of Boris Ignatovich'; in fact, their work is so similar in style that even today it is sometimes difficult to tell the authors apart.

At the beginning of the war, Ignatovich — like all Soviet reporters — began working for the army. He was assigned as frontline reporter to

Abram Shterenberg, joined the photographic section of the *Oktyabr (October)* group and after Rodchenko's dismissal from the latter for alleged formalism, he became the group's leader although he too did not escape criticism from the guardians of Soviet culture. In fact, he had much in common with Rodchenko. Both were fond of detail, close-up and steep picture angles — the close-up probably being the influence of Soviet cinematography for which Ignatovich also worked as cameraman and director of photography — but whereas Rodchenko was a visual designer-constructor of the image, Ignatovich's work retained the immediacy of the reporter's approach.

A native of Ukraine, he was always strongly attracted by the subject of rural parts of this area: *muzhiks* in a tearoom; a mother with a child on a riverbank; a colt seeking shelter with the mare; village children perched on an oven; a rack-waggon dragging in the mud of a rutted track. All these are vignettes of traditional village life but Ignatovich also paid attention to the new aspects of rural Russia: a rural commune lunching together; a relaxed evening with accordion music in the 'Red Corner' of a rural cultural club; and commune leadership in session lit by a kerosene lamp. The transition of the Russian village, the conflict of the old and the new, mistrust and enmity contrasting with faith and enthusiasm, all these things fascinated Ignatovich because he saw them as contradictions within the historic upheaval. With a similar emotional involvement, guided by his desire to capture the atmosphere of the period, he also paid

homage to the beauty of things made by human hands. His photographs of Leningrad's architecture are an ode to labour, his records of large industrial projects a celebration of man. He created the pictorial ideal of the 1930s: his photography from this period is packed with motion, the dynamism of the

the paper of the 30th Army Corps. His photograph *Horse-driver* will always remain a pathetic symbol of man forced to leave his native village to fight in a war, a man whose role of warrior is so incongruous with his true nature revealed by his wide, good-humoured Slavic grin.

# Georgi Zelma

/1906 — 1984/

A native of Tashkent, Uzbekistan, it was here that Georgi Zelma spent his childhood and here that he kept returning with his camera. At fifteen in 1921 he had moved with his mother, brothers and sisters to Moscow, where he received his first camera in the photographic club at his school. It was a 9 × 12 Kodak which opened new world for him. His interest in photography led him first to the *Proletkino* film studios, then to the *Russfoto* service where he learned the trade thoroughly. Unfortunately, his family did not fare well in Moscow and in 1924 the Zelmas returned to

Tashkent where Georgi became the Central Asian correspondent of the *Russfoto* service. It was probably this job that had the greatest influence on his emergence as a new photo-journalist because Central Asia was a place where things began to happen and a place with which Zelma was familiar.

As the Central Asian woman removed the traditional *parandji,* the horse hair veil, entire Central Asian nations started breaking the age-old yoke of superstition, illiteracy and disease and it was Zelma's photographs which showed the woman emerging from the

seclusion of the household. We see an old man pressing his ear unbelievingly to the earphone of a primitive crystal receiver; a farmer who has just read a governmental decree syllable by syllable to make sure that the new government is really going to give him land; a boy training on a makeshift horizontal bar. It was an era of new things, full of change and surprise, and Zelma's photography sounded with an echo of the *muezzin's* call summoning the people to the daily prayers. One of the reasons why Zelma was able to produce these photographs of Asian life was that he spoke the language and dressed in the traditional dress. 'People didn't even realize what I was doing, they thought I was a surveyor because of the tripod, and the camera looked more like an accordion,' he once reminisced.

His greatest fame dates from World War II, when he became widely known as the man who took photographs at Stalingrad. When

the war broke out, Zelma first photographed in Odessa, then his newspaper sent him on an assignment to the north where he photographed combat action on the Rybachi and Sredni peninsulas. This is where he met and collaborated closely with the famous war correspondent and writer Konstantin Simonov. Then he was transferred to Leningrad and photographed at Tikhvin and Voronezh. His next assignment was Stalingrad. He arrived there shortly before the city became engulfed in heavy fighting, staying until the end of the battle. His emotion-packed reports from 'hell' concentrated on a few square kilometres of ground constantly won, lost and retaken, revealed Zelma as an agile reporter willing to risk his life in direct fire to capture the historic moments of the battle waged for 'every single house, every single floor, every single room'. Of all war photography it is perhaps Zelma's Stalingrad cycle that reveals most about the people who had to live through the hell of war whichever side they were on, for at Stalingrad even the hard-core Nazis became human. The tragedy of the heroic defence of a perimeter from which there was no retreat, the relief of deliverance, the taste of defeat, the last piece of bread broken in two on the day of victory to share with the enemy who was as exhausted and hungry as the victor — such pictures constitute Zelma's Stalingrad epic and together with his social documentaries of the 1920s and 30s won him a permanent place in photography's hall of fame.

# Moisei Nappelbaum

/1869—1958/

and Eupatoria. Afterwards he went to the United States, holding jobs in New York, Philadelphia and Pittsburgh. In 1895 he decided to return to his native Minsk and

Moisei Nappelbaum was known as an ascetic of photography for although he was thoroughly familiar with all technical means of photography and could use them to brilliant effect, he relied on them only very rarely. As a rule he used only a single lamp and it was this obstinate custom which gave his portraiture a unique character. It was light that was the essential source of the individuality of each face, the unique rendition of the model's inner life, his spiritual and intellectual attributes. The most distinct feature of the physiognomy of his models is the face dominated by the eyes, for

Nappelbaum faded out the torso and the posture, suppressed the surroundings, and only rarely did he divert the spectator's concentration by also lighting the model's hands, as he did intentionally in his famous portrait of the painter Vladimir Tatlin. He was a thoroughly trained photographer. He had learned the trade in the Minsk studio of the Italian photographer Boretti whose apprentice he became in 1884. When his apprenticeship was over, he decided to see the world and gain professional experience, working in Smolensk and Moscow, then moving to Odessa, Warsaw, Vilnius (Wilno)

opened a portrait studio of his own there. Fifteen years later he started working for the press. By this time he had established himself in St. Petersburg and his portraits, printed by one of the best illustrated magazines of the period, *The Sun of Russia*, achieved great popularity. Nappelbaum's portraits from this period reveal his acute ability to recognize a strong personality and character. This feature of Nappelbaum's work, discernible even in his earlier portraiture, is characteristic especially of his best works — portraits of his friends and outstanding personalities of the period.

It was during the first weeks after the Revolution, in January 1918, that Nappelbaum took a portrait of Lenin. Although, according to the newspaper custom of the time, the oval of the face was supplemented with the drawn outline of the bust, the picture remains the first official portrait of the leader of the young Soviet state, a man whose name was spelled in newspapers all over the world but whose likeness was still largely unknown.

In the spring of the same year Nappelbaum had a large exhibition at the Anichkov Palace in St. Petersburg. His portrait of Lenin was displayed side-by-side with other works, and it was seen that in a world of shaken values, Nappelbaum's portraits were not only a reliable indicator of good photography but

also attracted public interest to a new medium given a new importance by the Revolution. Nappelbaum then gradually produced a series of portraits of the leaders of the Revolution — A. Lunacharski, V. Vorovski, F. Dzerzhinski. V. Kuibyshev — and major figures of Russian culture, art and science — A. Blok, A. Akhmatova, M. Gorki, S. Esenin, S. Eizenstein, V. Meierkhold, B. Pasternak and many others. These pictures constitute a gallery unparalleled in the history of Russian photography. The portraits were mostly produced in the first state photographic studio in Moscow, founded by Nappelbaum with the support of Y. M. Sverdlov, Chairman of the All-Russian Central Executive Committee, the titular head of state. Moscow was chosen

because in 1919 it again became the capital of the country.

In the early post-Revolution period Nappelbaum's portraiture work served the same function as reportage, for it documented, informed and promoted the new system by popularizing its leading representatives. True enough, Nappelbaum enjoyed a unique transitory position because the traditional classic of photography, portraiture, was soon rapidly suppressed by the new, emerging genres and in the end was even rejected for some time as a 'bourgeois relic'. Yet it was Nappelbaum who was to help the rehabilitation of portraiture in Soviet photography.

In 1958, the year of his death, Nappelbaum's book *From a Trade to an Art* was first published, a story of Nappelbaum's life with discussion on his opinion of portrait photography; both his photographs and opinion make it interesting reading even today.

# Abram Shterenberg

/1894—1978/

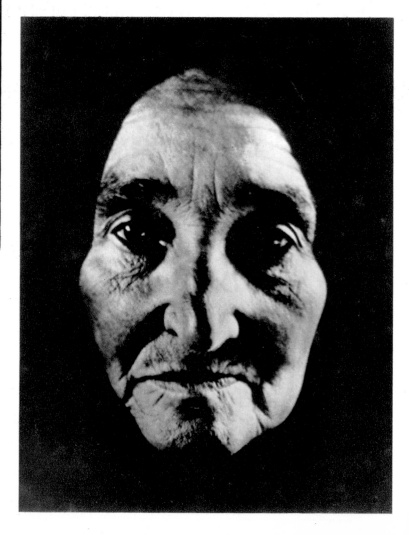

junk' did he for a short time leave his beloved genre. For a time he followed the example of his friends, members of the progressive *Oktyabr* group like A. Rodchenko, E. Langman, B. Ignatovich and others, and took up photojournalism which was officially deemed to be the only genre worthy of the 'great times', trying to record the social, political and economic events shaping the Soviet existence.

He made portraits of a number of famous as well as relatively unknown people. The typical feature of these masterpieces is a large detail of the head or the face which, supported by creative lighting and accentuation of the surface texture, produced an expressive

Unlike most leading Soviet photographers of the inter-war period who indulged either in documentary photography and photojournalism or in art experiment, Abram Shterenberg dedicated his life to portraiture, still life and landscape. It was portraiture which brought him most fame, for it had been with portraits that he had started his career as a professional commercial photographer and which he continued developing after the Revolution although working as a photographer for the Red Army. He remained faithful to it up to the 1970s when he died. Only during the period of the severest schematism of the latter half of the 1930s when portraiture — together with still life and landscape — was proclaimed to be 'worthless characterization. Especially strong in this respect was his sense for light. Shterenberg employed light to suppress the superfluous and disturb the motif, and to emphasize the essential. Although he relied mostly on lateral lighting, he sometimes resorted to back light. His portraits intentionally lack any lit background so that more often than not robustly modelled faces just emerge from the darkness. Whereas his 1919 portrait of the poet Vladimir Mayakovski features the head contoured by light and his 1925 *Violin Player* uses illumination to accentuate the lines and also the surface of the hand and the instrument, his 1935 portrait of the photographer and painter Yuri Erëmin concentrates exclusively on the dramatically lit demonic face. His photograph called *Mother* is merely an expressive oval of the wrinkled face floating like a mask on jet black background. A similar approach is used in his portraits of Henri Barbusse and Rabindranath Tagore in which the picture is entirely dominated by the highlights of the face which in the latter case seems as if lightly drawn by a brush. Shterenberg also used other means of characterization, such as head movement in the portrait of the Georgian primaballerina Maka Macharadze, or a slightly ironic accentuation of the traditional stiff collar in the portrait of the English actor, director and theatre critic Edward Gordon Craig, or an

intentionally straightforward look in the face of Sergei Eizenshtein, the famous film director.

Shterenberg's portraits are studies of human spirit rather than physiognomy. They seem to be from another world, reflecting the model's unique destiny in his portrait. Shterenberg's Maykovski is the personification of revolutionary fervour and dedication; his Erëmin is a symbol of a sensitive, day-dreaming and therefore vulnerable artist; his *Mother* is a paragon of goodness and sacrifice of humanity while his photograph *Worker* is an optimistic and confident, albeit fatigue-drawn look into the future.

Each of Shterenberg's photographs is a unique work of art, a meticulously prepared original to be exhibited rather than reproduced since Shterenberg valued only author's prints in which the selection of the paper and chemicals played an important role. The only manipulation that he condoned was the possible use of a mask. This made Shterenberg a unique phenomenon in Soviet photography which tended to favour ease of reproduction for mass dissemination in the press.

# John Heartfield

/1891—1968/

John Heartfield's real name was Helmuth Herzfelde; he was a German by birth who became a naturalized Englishman. Legend has it that the idea of photomontage was born in his mind by necessity. His letters from the front in World War I were assembled from newspaper photography cutouts to fool the censors. This made him realize the pamphleteering potential of a simple association of different photographs. On the other hand, Georg Grosz once said that Heartfield and he discovered the principle of photomontage at 5 o'clock on a May morning in 1916 in Grosz's studio; he insisted that it was then that they both realized the enormous possibilities of photomontage. Whichever version is more likely, one thing remains sure: Heartfield's photomontages are sharp, direct and stunning and he produced numerous posters, magazine covers (mostly for *Rote Fahne* and the *Arbeiter Illustrierte Zeitung*) and illustrations attacking inhumanity, violence, political trickery, lies and demagogy.

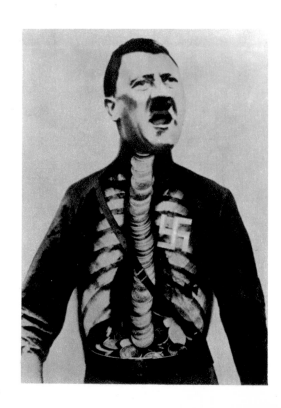

Gewidmet dem »Schwarzsender«, der Abend für Abend »trotz Gestapo« den Kampf für Frieden, Freiheit und Demokratie führt.

**Die Stimme der Freiheit in deutscher Nacht – auf Welle 29,8**

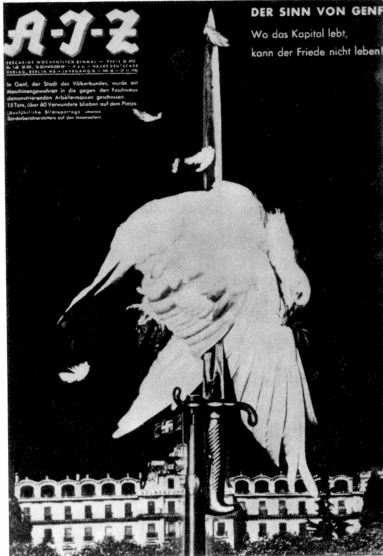

A-I-Z

ERSCHEINT WÖCHENTLICH EINMAL — PREIS 20 PFG.
Nr. 1.40, 30 GR., 70 SCHWEIZER RP. — V.b.b. — NEUER DEUTSCHER
VERLAG, BERLIN W8 — JAHRGANG XI — NR. 48 — 27. 11. 1932

In Genf, der Stadt des Völkerbundes, wurde mit
Maschinengewehren in die gegen den Faschismus
demonstrierenden Arbeitermassen geschossen.
15 Tote, über 60 Verwundete blieben auf dem Platze.
(Ausführliche Bildreportage unseres
Sonderberichterstatters auf den Innenseiten.)

**DER SINN VON GENF**

Wo das Kapital lebt,

kann der Friede nicht leben!

Heartfield was born into the family of a Socialist who wrote poetry, prose and plays under the name Franz Held. His mother was a textile worker and she had met Heartfield's father at a Berlin strike rally. The Herzfeldes lived in Switzerland and Austria and when his parents died Helmuth and his younger brother Wieland were taken into the care of friends and relatives of the family. Heartfield studied at art schools in Munich and Berlin and together with Georg Grosz started a new magazine called *Neue Junge (New Youth)*, at the same time taking up photography as a hobby. In 1917 he and his brother Wieland founded the later famous *Malik Verlag* which published works of Leftist writers and artists, which Heartfield illustrated. Together with Georg Grosz and Richard Huelsenbeck he became involved in 'trick' moving pictures and became an important figure in the European Dadaist movement. In 1918 he joined the German Communist Party which helped shape his understanding of photography as a weapon in politics.

During the 1920s he produced his first great photomontages, illustrations for *Malik Verlag* editions and designs for Max Reinhardt's and Erwin Piscator's theatrical productions in Berlin.

In 1935 Heartfield left Germany after a dramatic flight from the Nazi police, settling first in Prague and then in London. It was in exile that he produced his most effective anti-Fascist photomontages, mostly for the *Arbeiter Illustrierte Zeitung* whose editorial offices had moved to Czechoslovakia. In the spring of 1934, an exhibition of Heartfield's work was held in Prague. The exhibition infuriated the Nazis in Germany and they exerted so much pressure on Czechoslovak authorities that the most scathing lampoons of Hitler had to be removed from display. A similar exhibition opened in Moscow in 1936 and it was also here that the first monograph on Heartfield was published by Sergei Tretyakov.

In 1950 Heartfield returned from exile via Prague but as his brother Wieland later reminisced, his works were deemed too 'formalist' in post-war East Germany. Despite two coronaries, Heartfield resumed his work and in the end lived to be re-discovered and officially recognized, appointed member of the German Academy of Arts in Berlin and received a full professorship and two medals.

# HUMANIST PHOTOGRAPHY

'The first cry of a newborn baby in Chicago or Zamboanga, in Amsterdam or Rangoon, has the same pitch and key, each saying, "I am! I have come through! I belong! I am a member of the Family..." People flung wide and far, born into toil, struggle, blood and dreams, among lovers, eaters, drinkers, workers, loafers, fighters, players, gamblers, huts and skyscrapers, jungle hunters, landlords and landless, the loved and the unloved, the lonely and abandoned, the brutal and the compassionate — one big family hugging close to the ball of Earth for its life and being,' exclaimed the catalogue of perhaps the most famous exhibition in the entire history of photography, *The Family of Man.*

From the suffering and despair of World War II, from the disillusion and ruins of moral values, a desire was born to show that life was beautiful and good people lived everywhere. This was the gist of the speech with which the creator of the exhibition, Edward Steichen, opened the show in Moscow, 1959. 'I trust that this exhibition will be yet another argument for how much people need peace.'

The preparations for the exhibition started as early as 1952 when Edward Steichen visited Europe and searched archives and files of professional and amateur photographs alike for material that would reflect the message of the intended exhibition. Thousands upon thousands of pictures were sent to him by post. It was long and exhausting work before Steichen and his assistant Wayne Miller shaped these photographs into the legendary exhibition *The Family of Man.* In the final version, the exhibition included 503 pictures by authors from 68 different countries. *The Family of Man* opened in New York's Museum of Modern Art in January 1955, and after a long, triumphal tour of the United States it was shown in more than forty countries. The exhibition was seen by some ten million people. Its book edition was one of the bestsellers of the 1950s. The success was enormous but as Steichen explained it, 'The audiences not only understand the visual presentation, they also participate in it, and identify themselves with the images...'

In all respects it was a magnificent show. Works by famous authors hung there side-by-side with those of virtually unknown photographers, fame meaning little to the selectors. What was important was not so much the photographs themselves but the collective photographic message of mankind. For the first time in its history photography showed its humanist mission in a grand manner. It questioned the human condition, the moral responsibility of man for mankind. Humanist photography became a household word.

Since then, *The Family of Man* has been recognized as a milestone in the development of photography as an art. It represents the end of one period and the beginning of another. However, this milestone had been preceded by one of the darkest times for mankind: World War II had to take place first. This, the most tragic event of modern history, gave birth to great photography in the West and East alike. The visual report of the war filed by countless reporters on the spot will forever remind the world how cruel human beings can be to each other. Undoubtedly the most unforgettable pictures from the war are not those which document the actual bloodshed but those relating the horrors of war through grief in the face of a mother, terror in the eyes of a child, resolution in the gesture of the just, pictures documenting the impact of war on human fate with compassion and involvement. The greater the emotional experience of the photographer, the greater the emotional impact of his picture.

These war pictures are tragically sad. The photographers went to war because they loathed violence and many paid with their lives for their courage. They knew the essence of war could not be reflected in purely didactic photography, for war is emotion and thus they tried to capture this emotion. 'War is like an aging actress: more and more dangerous and less and less photogenic,' said Robert Capa in his typically terse manner. His Russian colleague Dmitri Baltermants said the same thing, albeit with the pathos so typical of the Russian nature: 'War is not to be photographed because it is but immense grief.' For a long time, the world was familiar only with the war and combat photography of Western authors like Robert Capa, David Seymour (Chim), Alfred Eisenstaedt, David Duncan, Eugene W. Smith and others. Then, almost thirty years after the war, the world stood speechless, stunned by the message

from the other side of the continent, discovering names like Dmitri Baltermants, Boris Kudoyarov, Mikhail Trakhman, Anatoli Garanin, Georgi Zelma, Max Alpert, Evgeni Khaldei and other Soviet photographers whose work embraced 'Soviet war photography'. In 1977, the British historian A. J. P. Taylor hailed the English edition of *The Russian War* in the words: 'I imagined that I had got beyond surprise and knew all the visual aspects of the Second World War. I was wrong. The collection of Soviet photographs has stunned and inspired me. It has no parallel. This is not a record of war from on high as seen by the commanders of the time and by historians later. It is the record of a people at war and of their experience... British and American cameramen were devoted reporters... But their purpose was to record what was happening for the benefit of people at home. For the Soviet cameramen the war was everywhere. Their purpose was not to serve a distant public, but to assert the deep involvement of the Soviet people in the war.' Soviet war photography is passionate because it reflects the individual's grief from the suffering and death among his fellow men. It is this deep emotional experience of the photographers that places Soviet war photography on an equal footing with famous Western war reporters in their common plea for humanity.

Since the end of World War II, however, the world has been anything but a peaceful place: Korea, Congo, the Middle East, Vietnam, Bangladesh, Biafra, Chile, Cyprus, Afghanistan. Moreover, human suffering is not born of war only. There are other plagues strangling mankind: hunger, poverty, racial intolerance, violence in all its forms. Thus in 1947 an international association of photographers was born under the name Magnum Photos as a platform for photographers who wanted to place their talent in the service of humanity without having to rely on the financial support of the utilitarian interests and political orientations of the press. These photographers were guided by their desire to assert their own concept of concerned photography, to offer a 'human view' of the events of our time, to appeal to morality. In its efforts to feel the pulse of the times Magnum Photos became a living legend.

Magnum was founded by three mighty figures of modern photography: the Hungarian-born Robert Capa, Polish-born David Seymour (Chim) and Henri Cartier-Bresson, a Frenchman. The result of their happy post-war reunion over a magnum of champagne — hence the name — was their decision to establish a picture service of a new type which would provide support for its associates yet give them a free hand as authors. The trio was soon joined by George Rodger, an Englishman. The Swiss-born Werner Bischof and Austrian-born Ernst Haas joined Magnum in 1949, followed by many other photographers of different nationalities. All of them, however, were united by their desire to present to the world a humanistic testimony of contemporary life on our planet. Magnum's first project was a large series entitled *People Live Everywhere* serialized in magazines in 1950—51. The success paved the way for other projects like *Youth of the World, Women of the World* and *The Child Generation*. Since then, Magnum members have published work in leading magazines, published books and held shows attended by millions of spectators. Werner Bischof produced his tragic report on famine-stricken Bihar; Eugene W. Smith produced his classic essays *The Spanish Village* and *Man of Mercy Albert Schweitzer*; George Rodger a large series on African life and Henri Cartier-Bresson his lyrical essays on Paris and the Seine.

It was especially Henri Cartier-Bresson's style which shaped a new type of photography called 'life photography'. As immediate and spontaneous as reportage, life photography observes without interfering but where reportage is, as a rule, concerned with actual events in actual places and time, life photography offers a concentrated view of the human situation in general. It is interested in recording the current problems of humanity and its aim is to communicate a universal humanist message, be it by a series or a single image.

To report on the human condition is very demanding on the photographer, for he must be involved, compassionate and humble. Even the method is demanding because the photographer cannot manipulate reality to suit his message but rather has to wait patiently for the right moment to reveal the essential character of the phenomenon or event. This is the proverbial Bressonian 'decisive moment', the right selection of a single instant from the countless possibilities of the event-in-the-making, the right selection of a single split second capable also of expressing the whole context, that which preceded the moment and that which will inevitably follow. The method which has become so typical of humanistic photography was in fact anticipated by Atget's Parisians or Kertész's early photography from his native Hungary. It became characteristic of the work of Elliott Erwitt, Marc Riboud, Werner Bischof and many other authors who were on the spot to capture — each in his own inimitable way — a visual message on the life on our planet. The grand era of humanistic photography which opened with Steichen's famous *Family of Man* has not ended but since the late 1960s its original proclamative humanism viewing the future of mankind essentially with optimism, has been subdued. This has been the effect of numerous wars and armed conflicts that have taken place since the end of World War II. The most protracted of these conflicts, the war in Vietnam, has more than any other modern wars shaken the optimism of not only the United States but the whole world. Photography has now become more matter-of-fact, more sober and more brutal. Don McCullin need not approach human agony and death with chaste modesty when brutally naturalistic television coverage daily floods our living rooms with eyewitness reports of annihilation, atrocity and attrition. Today, the photographer does not hesitate to take close-ups of torture, execution and murder. Don McCullin, Philip Jones Griffith, Kishor Parekh, Tim Page, Abbas, Magubane, Susan Meiselas and others have recorded, with brutal openness, the taste of fear, death and famine, be it in Biafra, Kampuchea, Congo, Bengal, India, South Africa, Iran, Lebanon, Nicaragua or El Salvador. Photography of this kind more often than not analyses the conditions of life in various social strata and under different political systems, noting social determinants and interpersonal relationships, identifying reasons why our planet lives the way it does. Often the photographer is less of an reporter and more of a scholar, a sociologist or political analyst. Bruce Davidson who photographs the blacks of New York's Harlem does not rely on the decisive moment to deliver his message; his work resembles a long-term research project mapping out the life style and mentality of the ghetto.

The humanist aspect in photography has had a long and noble tradition for it records the debasement of humanity and man's undying thirst for life. It is in the name of life and human happiness that this type of photography asserts the basic qualities of existence. In this lies perhaps the ultimate mission of the medium, as aptly formulated by Edward Steichen, the creator of *The Family of Man*: 'The mission of photography is to explain man to man and each man to himself.'

# Robert Capa

/1913—1954/

1931. He was fortunate because this was the time when what was later called photojournalism was being born in Berlin; young Friedmann gained his first experience as a reporter in the employ of *Ullstein Verlag*. When the Nazis came to power in Germany, he moved to Paris: here the legend of Robert Capa was born.

Friedmann knew that a young, unknown and poor emigré would face tough competition in France and thus styled himself Robert Capa, a rich, talented and famous American photographer who visited Paris from time to time, willing to sell his talent albeit at rates three times as high as the customary ones. Friedmann then successfully repeated the same hoax in the United States, posing as Robert Capa, a famous French photographer. Needless to say, Friedmann had exactly what his alias Capa was offering, talent, and thus the hoax soon became the truth.

When the Civil War broke out in Spain in 1936, it was here that Capa first witnessed the terrible impact of war on an innocent civilian population and it was here that his wife Gerda Tavo died under a tank. His experience in Spain made him decide to become a professional war photographer so that he could express his loathing for war. In Spain he met Ernest Hemingway and while Hemingway found there inspiration for his famous *For Whom The Bell Tolls*, Capa obtained material for his first book *Death in the Making*, which contained his best-known picture *Death of a Loyalist Soldier*. Legend

When Robert Capa, perhaps the greatest of war photographers, was killed at Thai Binh, Vietnam, John Steinbeck wrote in the obituary: 'Capa's pictures were made in his brain — the camera only completed them... Capa knew what to look for and what to do with it when he found it. He knew, for example, that you cannot photograph war because it is largely an emotion. But he did photograph that emotion by shooting beside it. He could show the horror of a whole people in the face of a child...'

Robert Capa was in fact his *nom de guerre*, for the great photographer was born as Endre Friedmann, the son of a Budapest tailor. As a youth he had advocated world revolution and since his sympathy for the Leftist cause made him a highly suspect person in the eyes of the Hungarian police, he went to Berlin in

this compassion that compelled Capa to join his friends in establishing Magnum Photos in 1947.

Robert Capa was never out of work, which was the way he wanted it, but in the end war caught up with him. When he finished his day's work on that fateful day at Thai Binh, Vietnam, he stepped out from his jeep and went for a walk. After a while a mine explosion roared in the rice paddy and the Vietnamese lieutenant assigned to the team told Capa's write-up man: *'Le photographe est mort.'*

has it that during this first battle Capa placed his camera on the breastwork of a trench and ducking from machine gun fire he released the shutter without looking. He sent the exposed film to Paris to be developed and this single picture made him the rich, talented and famous Capa of the alias he had invented. 'If your pictures aren't good enough, you aren't close enough,' was his famous dictum. What Capa meant was not only physical but also emotional closeness. His close-ups taken from the shortest distance possible have become classics.

During World War II Capa came to Europe, travelling from one operations centre to another, filing on-the-spot reports as he went. In Tunisia he applied for permission to be parachute-dropped with the first wave of assault troops invading Sicily. He had never parachuted before but he wanted to be the first to shoot American troops in action in Italy. He became an expert on war. His D-Day pictures also have a fascinating history: he photographed the Allied troops wading ashore with his back turned to enemy fire. The dramatic, slightly blurred pictures of the landing troops are characterized by the typical anti-technical approach of all Capa's greatest pictures. Out of one hundred exposed pictures made on D-Day, only eight survived because a nervous laboratory technician overdried them. One of those eight pictures has since become universally accepted as the symbol of D-Day.

Capa had many famous friends and people like Hemingway, Saroyan, Steinbeck, or Picasso were proud of his friendship. They admired Capa's greatest asset as a person, his compassion for human suffering. It was indeed

# Dmitri Baltermants

/1912/

to the last moment of truth. The tragedy of the moment is emphasized by the dramatic skies and another woman in the background who has fared similarly.

The series of photographs remained long hidden in Baltermants' files. Such emotional pictures were not needed during the war since the magazines and newspapers for which Baltermants was working wanted pictures recording the situation at the front, providing information on the advance of Soviet troops and showing exemplary heroic deeds. The events photographed at Kerch were only a single link in the long chain of experience of a war photographer. *Grief*, presenting war as the grossest of inhumanities, came to be appreciated only in peacetime.

'War is nothing but immense grief,' Baltermants summarized his feelings in a similar way to his colleague Robert Capa; he went on, 'I kept photographing war for several years but I know that during all this

'A Soviet Robert Capa!' exclaimed the Italian press in 1965. *Life, Stern, Paris Match*, all the big picture magazines were suddenly asking this little known Soviet reporter for permission to print his photograph *Grief*. Overnight, Dmitri Baltermants' name became famous, more than twenty years after he had taken the picture. *Grief* was in fact part of a large series which he had made in Kerch in 1942 immediately after the Germans retreated from the city. The picture shows women and children approaching an open mass grave to search for their fathers, husbands, brothers and sons among the dead. An instant of immense human grief, when last hope is lost, a moment of shattering truth: a lasting testimony to what war is. Baltermants handles the subject as if he were viewing the scene through the eyes of the searchers. A woman in a white kerchief, who has crossed the field full of corpses, still looking, knowing what she is going to see in the end, yet still hoping. The photographer follows her with his camera up

time I made only five or six real pictures. War is not to be photographed, you know.' Baltermants, whose nation suffered the biggest casualties during the war, hesitated for a long while before unveiling the suffering captured in his photographs. It was only years later that he took *Grief* out of his files and entered it in a world-wide photographic contest entitled *What Is Man?*. The spectators' prize which the picture won was the first indication of his new stardom as a war photographer, a stardom comparable perhaps only to that of Robert Capa.

It is perhaps ironic that the war years which produced his best photography were the beginning and at the same time the culmination of his career as a photographer. Prior to 1939, when Baltermants joined the army as a photographer, he had been professor of analytic geometry at a military academy, photography being merely a hobby and an occasional source of extra income. He spent the whole war at the front, first as combat reporter for *Izvestiya*, then for an army daily. He photographed the defence of Moscow and Sevastopol, he was at Stalingrad,

he recorded the liberation of the south of Russia and of Poland, ending his war odyssey in Berlin.

Like *Grief*, his other war photographs have become an appeal for peace. *The Trail of War, Attack, Tchaikovski, Crossing the Oder* — these pictures never leave the viewer dispassionate. The experience of taking these pictures helped him formulate the creed which he offered to his young colleagues from *Ogonëk* magazine: 'To be a photoreporter is not a profession but a way of life, behaviour and thinking.'

# Mikhail Trakhman

/1918—1976/

Had Mikhail Trakhman been able to remain a war photographer, he would probably have become a star. His pictures differ from those taken by his colleagues D. Baltermants, A. Shaikhet, G. Zelma, M. Alpert, A. Garanin and others with whom he helped create what is now termed Soviet war photography. He never photographed the 'theatre of war' and its leading characters, the soldiers, but remained hidden in the wings. Intentionally, he sought the essentials of war experience not in the combat fire but rather in more ordinary wartime events and his pictures are symbolic mementoes of the impact of war on ordinary life.

When World War II was over in Europe, Mikhail Trakhman was one of the few army photographers who were transferred to the Far East. However, he refused to go. He had had enough. He could not know that with this act of insubordination would end the most important chapter in his life as

144

autumn countryside, pulling hay carts loaded with all their earthly possessions, seeking refuge: how many times have they had to flee already? Belorussian partisans in an earth cellar with a kindling throwing meagre light in the face of a nurse keeping vigil at the bedside of her wounded charges. An old woman, her arms open wide with grief and desperation, asking wordlessly: why?

a photographer, for never again was he able to produce such strong work. A photographer in uniform is subject to military law and Trakhman's insubordination complicated not only his military life but also the start of his post-war existence as a civilian. Yet even without complications, he would probably have been at a loss to find a subject which could match his previous deeply involved, sensitive and thoughtful vision of humanity in wartime.

Before the war, Trakhman worked in documentary film. This specific approach to life and the spontaneous reaction of a documentary cameraman lent a special flavour to his war photographs which often resemble movie picture takes. Trakhman used close up, medium shot and long shot simultaneously, juxtaposing the action of the first plane with that of the second, often using several internally associated action determinants. Such rich action produces an image brimmimg with inner meaning. Trakhman's handling of a still resembles a continuous action shot and each of his pictures implies the context of the action, both the previous and subsequent developments of the event recorded.

During the war, Trakhman was dropped by parachute among the partisans of the Leningrad, Kalinin and Pskov regions. As the Germans were retreating, he advanced with the guerilla spearhead columns into Belorussia, Ukraine and Poland. He worked deep behind the enemy lines, often as far as 300 or 400 kilometres from the front. The territory was still held by the Germans but immediately around him were the Russian forest, fields and farms and people still trying

to cope with everyday problems. Prisoners taken by the partisans during their sorties from guerilla-controlled forest often could not understand what had hit them: the Russians were still thought to be several hundred kilometres away.

Trakhman's pictures constitute a chronicle of ordinary days behind the enemy line. A mother tenderly embracing her son who is leaving with his gun to join the guerilas in the forest, perhaps never to return. Ragged women and children stumbling through

Actually, Trakhman's pictures, brimming with human emotions, were not at first intended for publication. As a special reporter of the *Sovinformburo* (Soviet Information Bureau) he was to record the situation in enemy-held Soviet territory and all his films bore the code NDP (Not For Press) because they could contain classified information. Yet these for-official-eyes-only reports produced a moving testimony of the quiet drama of a people whose ordinary days were shaped by war.

# Boris Kudoyarov

/1903—1973/

simplest of things came to signify immense happiness.

In Leningrad, Kudoyarov exposed three thousand negatives which now constitute an unparalleled report on people who were half dead from cold and starvation but who still did what had to be done, be it with a gun or their bare hands. Kudoyarov's camera looked into the faces of mothers bending over the lifeless bodies of their children but still having enough strength to line up for hours on end to receive food and frozen water to bring to those at home who still survived. His pictures are witness to man's immense will to survive. His paper, the youth daily *Komsomolskaya pravda*, dispatched him to Lenigrad on the very first day of the war. Air routes to the city had already been severed and Kudoyarov had to travel by train via Vologda and make a detour around Lake Ladoga. When he

For nine hundred days Leningrad lay besieged, and for nine hundred days Boris Kudoyarov lived, worked and suffered with the inhabitants of the city, taking pictures in the freezing cold, under constant artillery fire, with an ever empty stomach, in situations where death was more common than a piece of bread and a sled laden with corpses a more familiar sight than a streetcar. It was a time when everything which had been commonplace before the war — a warm stove, a shining lightbulb or just food — acquired a totally new value, when the arrived, he saw a city preparing to defend itself as the enemy rapidly advanced. Soon the city was surrounded. The long siege reached its gravest point in 1941 when the daily bread rations had to be reduced to 100 grammes because emergency foodstores had been burned to the ground by enemy fire. The city practically had no ammunition left. The only supply route left open had to negotiate Lake Ladoga using boats and ships in summer but in winter truck convoys had to cross over the ice. The route was called the 'Road of Life'. It brought life into the besieged city but often took the lives of the fearless men who made the trip, especially during the thaw when the ice was too soft to support the heavy trucks pulling huge fully laden sleds.

As war photography, Kudoyarov's Leningrad epic is unique because what it lacks in dramatic combat action is made up for by the sheer multitude of those who died. Kudoyarov's approach is a documentary one, a report that is deeply human because the documentarist lives the life of his subjects. Kudoyarov started photographing long before the war. He had joined the Red Army at seventeen, fighting at the fronts of the Civil War which ravaged the country after the Revolution. What had been decisive for his future career was his return to his native Samarkand where he was appointed head of the local police. In Samarkand he had enough time to spend on his two favourite hobbies, soccer and photography. In time the two became one and Kudoyarov the police officer became a sports photographer for the *Russfoto* service. In the early 1930s he started photographing other subjects and, sharing the ideals of experimental Soviet photography, he joined the avant-garde *Oktyabr* association, trying to enliven the officially promoted construction propaganda with novel forms. When the war broke out he was an experienced professional. Yet it was only then that he reached the zenith of his career as a photographer. In an extraordinary situation his sense for drama nurtured for years by his love for sports, sudddenly soared to produce the best proof of his talent: an emotionally profound expression of the inner drama of human fate. His pictures are quite calm on the exterior but hide deep compassion, sensitivity and understanding. Kudoyarov's approach is simple and humble because the author of these pictures intuitively knew that this reality was stronger than any speculative manipulation of the image. He photographed man down on his knees, yet man undefeated. The post-war years were for Kudoyarov what they were for so many of his colleagues: never again did his work show such spontaneity and strength as his wartime photography. He died where he was born, in Central Asia, when he was travelling on an assignement — a fitting death for a reporter.

218   Nevski Boulevard, Leningrad, 1941
219   Fetching Water, Leningrad 1941
220   Volkovo Cemetery, 1942
221   After an Air Raid, Leningrad, 1942

147

# Werner Bischof

/1916—1954/

A boy wearing a hat and playing a pipe, walking through the countryside with a bag on his shoulder: a symbol of eternal youth going straight ahead regardless of obstacles. The picture was taken somewhere on the road between Cuzco and Pisac, Peru, in 1954. Soon afterwards, a car failed to negotiate the sharp bend in an Andean road and plunged deep into a ravine, bringing death to its three passengers: a native driver, a geologist and a thirty-eight-year old Swiss-born photographer named Werner Bischof. An aesthete by nature and painter by education, Bischof never sought events but

rather what was permanent, what constituted a universal message about man and his life. He travelled all over the world and always photographed his subjects in such a way as to make them universal: a begging Bihar woman with a child on her arm a symbol of all the starving in this world; the unnaturally serious, tearstreaked face of a little Hungarian girl a personification of all the suffering of innocent children; the huddled figures of prisoners the embodiment of all human despair and the ground littered with emaciated bodies a screaming accusation of human want. In these pictures the

photographer unambiguously sides with the meek and the oppressed. He does not question the reasons or analyze the causes but, compelled by compassion, he commemorates the human situation.

This was the way Werner Bischof photographed the eternal symbols of motherhood, hunger, childhood or poverty and it is quite unimportant whether the scene is India, Greece or Hong Kong. The people in these pictures always retain their dignity as human beings and it often seems as if the suffering gives them a moral status and beauty. Bischof's images are never dynamic;

their inner tension stems not from action but rather from an inner emotional charge. Werner Bischof took a long time preparing for the role he was to play in modern photography. Born in Zurich, he defied his father's wishes to take over the family business and enrolled in a school of applied arts. For a long time he experimented with light in photography, working out new aesthetics of natural form and structure. 'I first started photographing people in 1940. I had never thought I would photograph people. I did pictures of shells, sand, natural beauty ...' Everything he did before he was twenty-eight had been in search of a new means of photographic expression, an overture to the main act in which the leading character was to be man himself.

Bischof started photographing people on commission from the picture magazine *Du*. He approached his new subject timidly at first but with the thoroughness so characteristic of his nature he studied it in all its aspects, searching for his own approach. Already his first monothematic series on invalids and refugees reveal his future philosophical and aesthetic approach to photography. After the war

Bischof travelled for three years through areas devastated by war and his quest for understanding unknowingly brought him into the fold of life photography. His pictures were now printed not only by *Du* but also in *Life*. *Picture Post* and *The Observer*.

In 1949 Bischof joined Magnum Photos as its sixth associate. He began travelling incessantly all over the world, photographing in Italy, France, Korea, Iceland, Hong Kong and spending a whole year in Japan. In 1951 he visited northern and central India and collected material for the most famous of his essays, a report on famine-stricken Bihar. Afterwards, he planned a long trip through Central and South America. The trip took place in early 1954. His last subject was Machu Picchu, the sacred city of the Incas; the sombre character of the pictures seems to anticipate the photographer's death.

# David Seymour (Chim)

/1911—1956/

He was born in Warsaw, Poland, as David Szymin and died at Suez, Egypt, as David Seymour. Ethnically a Polish Jew, he started his life as a Russian subject and ended it as a US citizen. A sensitive man who abhorred violence, he spent most of his life on the battlefield. He never found the rest he so much longed for. He was an eternal wanderer whose home was the world: Poland, France, Spain, the United States, the Middle East, wherever his assignments took him. He lived in hotel rooms, never married, had no children and yet his death, in a jeep blasted by an artillery shell into the waters of Suez, was mourned as that of a beloved son by families all over the world in whose homes he regularly appeared with his reports.
Chim, as he was called because of his real name, Szymin, had first wanted to be a concert pianist but soon found that he lacked the talent which distinguishes a good musician from a virtuoso and so he switched to graphics and photography. Disgusted by the political climate in Germany, where he studied, he went to Paris in 1931, where he became a photojournalist. France in the 1930s was also shaken by political conflict and progressive, anti-Fascist Frenchmen rallied under the banner of the Popular Front. 'Vive la commune! Vive le Front populaire!' chanted workers and intellectuals, united by their concern for democracy and opposing Fascism in Germany, Italy and Spain.

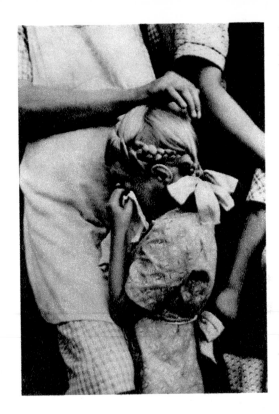

Seymour enthusiastically placed his abilities in the service of the movement, together with his close friends Robert Capa and Henri Cartier-Bresson.

He was among the first to go to Spain to report on the Civil War and also to join the army voluntarily when World War II broke out. When it was over, he had a medal for bravery, American citizenship and miles of memories on photographic strips. It was compassion that now took him all over war-devastated Europe, photographing children. It was compassion and also fear. When he reached Warsaw he knew that his premonition had been right: his parents' house was in ruins and his parents had been killed. Chim's speciality was not war although he practically never photographed anything but war. His pictures capture those who have the least in common with war but who invariably suffer most: children. A rally in Paris with a little girl almost asleep with fatigue on her father's shoulders, but with her little fist clenched defiantly; a Barcelona mother glancing anxiously at approaching planes, holding an infant to her breast, who is totally unaware of the imminent danger; Therese, a mentally disturbed Polish girl who even after several years spent in orphanages keeps drawing pictures of her lost home; a ragged Greek boy, triumphant and on the verge of tears, looking at his first pair of shoes. For Chim, war was a crime against childhood and his pictures have become an eternal memento, warning and accusing.

In the summer of 1956, he was on vacation in Greece, admiring the classical architecture.

Then the Suez crisis turned into an armed conflict. Within two hours he was airborne and the same day got himself accredited as a reporter. One of his last pictures shows a boy crossing a Port Said street, facing a tank. It was violence that dispossessed David Seymour and it was violence that killed this most non-violent of men.

# Henri Cartier-Bresson

/1908/

This inconspicuous, shy man, given to highly polished shoes, wearing rimless glasses over his quick-darting eyes, eventually became the most influential photographer of his generation. Today, he is an authority quoted by theorists, a yardstick for the efforts of several generations of photographers and his name defines the paradigm of 'Bressonian' photography. His opinion and method have become a part of the photographer's syllabus, for Henri Cartier-Bresson has the ability to tiptoe unobserved onto the stage, make a mental composition of the frame, recognize the key moment instinctively and snap it. H.C.B. is a legend, an institution.

His subjects are extraordinarily simple: a woman holding a comb, men at a fence, lovers at a café table, a boy carrying empty bottles photographed while crossing the street. But in all these pictures the ordinary aspects of everyday life suddenly touch upon the essentials of the human existence. 'There is one moment at which the elements in motion are in balance. Photography must seize upon this moment,' he says. Indeed, the fat Spanish lady is captured in the typically female posture, the inquisitive man at the moment when he starts turning away from the fence, the couple when their lips are about to meet, the boy with the empty bottles in the very

moment when his little face reflects the self-importance of his eight years. People in Cartier-Bresson's pictures are replaceable in the sense that it might be anyone in the picture, for Bresson's people are just representatives of the human race. Bresson has a unique instinct for the decisive moment in which the visible phenomenon reveals the naked inner truth about human existence inherent in the captured image. His art is governed by his profound sympathy with the human situation and a keen understanding of its significance. In this lies his greatest contribution to modern photography. Born in Chanteloup, France, he studied

152

When he was asked how he arrived at the now universally adopted term 'the decisive moment', he replied: 'I have nothing to do with it. I just once found the following sentence in the memories of Cardinal de Retz: "Everything in the world has its decisive moment..." and when we were discussing the title for my book with my publisher, he suddenly said: "How about *The Decisive Moment,* for instance?" It was a fitting title and now I am a plagiarizer so to speak... Naturally, the moment is a question of concentration. You must be concentrated, you must think, look, that's all... The difference between a mediocre and a good picture amounts to a few millimetres...'

literature and painting at Cambridge, England, where he also became interested in photography and film. In 1931 he discovered the Leica camera, which became an extension of his eye and to which he has remained faithful ever since. 'I kept walking the streets, high-strung, and eager to snap scenes of convincing reality, but mainly I wanted to capture the quintessence of the phenomenon in a single image.' His photography was an instant success and he started travelling all over the world on assignments for various magazines but also taking pictures just for himself. Right after the war he had a large exhibition in the Museum of Modern Art in New York. He was extremely interested in Surrealism then but his friend Robert Capa told him: 'You will have an exhibition once in a while and your work will become precious and confidential. Keep on doing what you want, but use the name "photojournalism" which will put you in direct contact with what is going on in the world.'

A human look — such was the creed of the Magnum Photos association which he founded with his friends Capa and Seymour. It was for Magnum that he produced his famous essays but his work has primarily formed that type of photography which relies on the method of photojournalism but unlike photojournalism is not a record of a particular event in a particular place and at a particular time, for his kind of photography adopts a more general approach to express situations that are universally human. To be able to do this, the photographer must have a philosophy of his own. 'Some photographers are great, other just gather facts,' he says. 'But facts alone are not interesting. What is interesting is the approach.'

# William Eugene Smith

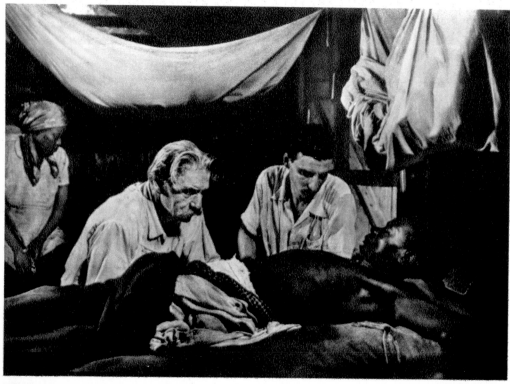

William Eugene Smith was obsessed with the idea that the photographer was responsible not only for his work but also for its impact and that if he distorted the truth for whatever reason, he committed a crime against the public. 'I would have my accomplished image transcend literal truth by intensifying its truthful accuracy, indicating even of the spirit and symbolizing more. And my only editor would be my conscience and my conscience would be of my responsibility...' In this he knew no compromise and therefore his relations with some of the magazines for which he worked were often strained. His stance, however, has been vindicated by his work.

Even as a young man he became intoxicated with journalism. He started photographing for the Wichita, Kansas, press but at the first chance left for New York City. He was almost immediately hired by *Newsweek* and two years later was offered a contract by *Life,* the most prestigious of picture magazines. But his great moment came during World War II, a moment for which he ultimately had to pay. From 1942 to 1945 he worked as a war reporter, covering thirteen invasions in the Pacific and Europe and participating in more than twenty air sorties. He was so famous for his courage and his dramatic reports were so honest that they were carried not only by the US press but also by Japanese magazines. Then on May 22, 1945, during the invasion of Okinawa, he was hit in the face and hand by grenade fragments. For two and half years his life was in the balance. Even after thirty operations he could not be sure whether he would be able to take up the camera again. 'The day I again tried for the first time to make a photograph, I could barely load the roll of film into the camera. Yet I was determined that the first photograph would be a contrast to the war photographs and that it would speak an affirmation of life...' Thus a picture of two children, his own two children, was taken. And the image of two children emerging from a dark forest into the sun was selected by Edward Steichen to close the famous exhibition *The Family of Man.* The post-war years brought periods of fame and success alternating with years of difficulties and uncertainty for Smith. His passionate insistence on truth as he saw it, his

undying feeling of moral responsibility were his rise and fall, a source of conflict, stress and depression but also of a lifetimes work. His essays *The Spanish Village, Country Doctor, Man of Mercy Albert Schweitzer* or *Pittsburgh* are now legendary and perhaps the biggest single success of photojournalism.

In 1956 Smith resigned from *Life* in protest against their treatment of his essay on Albert Schweitzer and joined Magnum Photos for which he was predestined by his humanist philosophy. He continued photographing, writing and teaching. 'The journalistic field must find men of integrity, openminded and sincere in purpose, with the intelligence and insight to penetrate to the vital core of human relationships — and with the very rare ability to give full measure of their unbiased findings to the world.'

In 1970 the uncompromising journalist settled in Minimata, Japan, where he produced yet another of his immortal essays. It was a story on sea life killed by the poisonous effluents of the Chisso company plant, a report on people paralyzed by 'Minimata Disease' from the poisoned fish they ate, about children born with serious defects. Smith and his Japanese wife, Aileen, decided to stay in Minimata until the industrial company was sentenced to pay at least partially the damages of the victims and he kept his promise.

233   From the essay *The Spanish Village*, 1951
234   From the essay *Man of Mercy Albert Schweitzer*, 1954
235   From the essay *Minamata*, Japan, 1972
236   From the essay *Minamata*, Japan, 1972

# Elliott Erwitt

/1928/

photography and using a Rolleiflex bought with money from odd jobs he started taking pictures of friends, weddings and funerals. When he enrolled at the university where he signed up for photography, he had already had some experience with advertising. He moved into a house shared by students interested in film, literature and art. It was a sort of commune where work was shared and the evenings were spent in endless discussions. Like others, he had to work to pay his way through the school. He is said to have been able to print 25 thousand signed photographs of Ingrid Bergman and other movie stars in a single week.

At twenty-three, while doing his stint in the army, serving in a reconnaissance unit, he entered his photographic essay *Bed and Bored* in a *Life* contest, winning the first prize. He used the prize money to buy a car, naming it with his peculiar brand of humour 'Thank you Henry' in honour of *Life*'s founder and owner, Henry Luce. Success gave him much needed self-confidence. One day he showed his work

'Personal photographs' is the term Elliott Erwitt used to characterize the pictures he produced on compulsion rather than commission. These pictures show ordinary life yet they are anything but ordinary. They are whimsical, casual and unusual, because they represent the world in two contrasting plans whose parallel or contradicting action can imply a conflict, tension or harmony. Erwitt's photography, although seemingly simple, is highly sophisticated because the message is never straight-forward and the simplicity only superficial. Erwitt is a master of fine nuances and is able to communicate the incommunicable. Thus his photographs, sometimes benevolent and understanding, often biting, ironic and bitter, are speculations on the meaning of life rather than straight reports.

Erwitt was born of Russian parents in Paris but spent his early years in Italy and Los Angeles. High school did not mean much to him but he was able to speak Russian, Italian, French and English. He did not enjoy books much but spent his time reading magazines and newspapers, seeing film, theatre and other visual media. Soon he discovered

to Robert Capa, the 'benevolent dictator' of Magnum and Capa liked it. When Elliott received his discharge, he joined Magnum which was independent of the policies of picture magazines and enabled its associates to place their talent in the service of humanity. Erwitt produced a number of large series and advertisement campaigns. He photographed John F. Kennedy's inauguration as well as his funeral, and made a promotion trip around the world, publishing material from it in various magazines. When Russia was celebrating the

fortieth anniversary of the October Revolution, he travelled to the USSR, bringing back a fine report. He contributed to Steichen's *The Family of Man,* to a book on the Kennedy administration *Let us Begin,* and published a few books on his own. Whatever he did, he always looked for material for his open series of 'personal photographs',

reflecting his personal experience and insight, a humorous, yet deeply involved comment on life. These pictures reveal the truth about humanity and are governed by compassion so genuine that the photographer can afford to be brutally honest.

A reviewer of his book *Photographs and Antiphotographs* wrote that 'Erwitt's

photography makes the "human comedy" more bearable.' This, in fact, seems an apt description of Erwitt's entire work.

# Bruce Davidson

/1933/

'What you call a ghetto I call my home,' Bruce Davidson was told by a resident on his first visit to New York's Harlem. The words haunted him for the two years he spent photographing the people of a single block on East 100th Street. Home was an old man growing grass in the rubbish of a tenement backyard; children behind wire-screened windows; walls of dark rooms decorated with pictures of Christ, John F. Kennedy and American flags. Home was a black boy wearing an African amulet on his neck who did not want him to photograph the pigeons he kept on the roof of his house because he wanted them to remain free. 'I entered a life style, and, like the people who live on the block, I love and hate it and I keep going back.'

Davidson's sociological study of ghetto life was published as a book in 1970 and was hailed as a major photographic and sociological feat. It took the spectator into the foul-smelling alleys and dark tenements, a world of poverty and crime, yet a world where tenderness, compassion and a sense of belonging prevailed. It is a highly personal, painful and caustic essay and Davidson put his whole heart into it.

Bruce Davidson has been always sensitive to loneliness, injustice and oppression and his subjects have always been people in critical situations. He has photographed civil rights marches, Brooklyn street gangs, Welsh miners, the story of Jimmy the Clown. At first he tried to remain unseen and enter unobserved into people's lives to make reports. Then he realized that although 35 mm cameras enable the photographer to catch people off guard in the flash of a second, they exclude personal communication and rapport with the subject. In 1966 he therefore switched to a large format camera. 'The photographer is seen, he is overt. He does not hide behind the lens to capture things on the sly and then leave unobserved. The fact that I erect a tripod and mount a large camera on it and ask people whether I may photograph them establishes an open, honest eye-to-eye communication between the photographer and his subject. A photograph is cooperation — and celebration. And when the meticulously prepared image is finished you feel that the

moment is something very special.' This was precisely the way he photographed *East 100th Street*, the essay that won him fame and respect.

He was born in a Chicago suburb in 1933 but in his eyes his real life started some ten years later when he discovered photography. He kept photographing throughout his school years and says he must have done more photography than work. Photography was his surrogate education and when he decided to go to university, the only school he recognized was the Rochester Institute of Technology and its photographic course. After two years in Rochester he got a job with the Eastman Kodak studios but the dreary sterility of the nine-to-five routine made him feel that it was a tedious existence. He went back to school 'to find out if I was able to become alive again'. Apparently his stay at Yale where he studied philosophy, painting and photography revitalized him enough, for he soon started selling work to big picture magazines. In 1959 he joined Magnum Photos. 'I use my camera to look at people but also to express what's inside myself, the emotion, struggle and subconscious, revealing the author of the picture,' wrote Bruce Davidson.

241   East 100th Street, 1970
242   East 100th Street, 1970
243   New York City, 1970

# Donald McCullin

/1935/

'I have got to make people aware, I have got to get people into the picture. They've got into it, so they're part of the situation,' said Don McCullin.

Destruction, anguish, hunger, pain, cruelty, war — these are McCullin's most frequent subjects. He does not photograph them out of curiosity but because he wants to give these abstractions a concrete form and to protest against them in the name of humanity. He has photographed in Biafra, Vietnam, Kampuchea, Northern Ireland, Congo, India, Benghal and the Middle East and his reports have received much space in magazines and on television. *Is Anyone Taking Notice?* is the title of the best-known of his books. This pressing question is inherent in all his pictures yet it is not calculated to arouse emotions; it is not sensationalist, for Don McCullin has no easy time getting his pictures to the viewer.

McCullin was born in the East End of London in 1935; his father was a street vendor but spent most of the time on the dole and his mother was a household helper. As so many other children of his background, Donald grew up on the street.

His luck was his talent for drawing. In fact he

160

was so good that at thirteen he received a scholarship from the Hammersmith School of Arts and Crafts but two years later his father died and Don had to leave the school, moving from job to job, making toys, waiting on tables in dining cars on the London—Manchester railway line, decorating shop windows, and so on. Then the big break of his life occurred — ironically, it was national service. As a reconnaissance platoon photographer's assistant he saw Egypt, East Africa and Cyprus, slowly becoming aware of the potentials of the medium and its power. He struggled to save £ 32 to buy his first camera, a Rolleicord. He was lucky: his pictures of a policeman killed by street thugs were bought by *The Observer* and McCullin started working for the press. In 1964 *The Observer* dispatched him to Cyprus to cover the conflict there and his pictures won him the World Press Prize. Don McCullin was now a star, travelling all over the world, wherever there was news.

From the very beginning his photographs were thought sensational because they left the viewer speechless, horrified and tearful. Don McCullin has never been merciful or considerate to the public, never tried to hide anything, be it death, brutality or suffering. Some of his colleagues think that the press may be overtly exploiting him sending him as often as three times each year to some corner of the globe to risk his life, but McCullin himself does not think this way. In his mind, photography's mission is not to show the beautiful and the placid but rather the injustice and inhumanity committed often in the name of progress and humanity. 'I find beauty a bit of a bore to photograph,' he says. 'I get most interest somehow out of ugliness.'

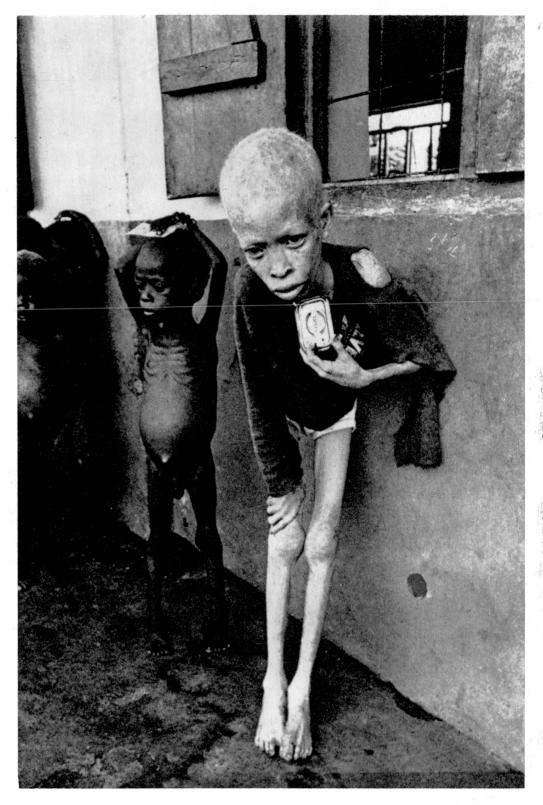

244  Hue, Vietnam, 1968
245  Vietnam, 1968
246  Albino Boy, Biafra, 1970

# Kishor Parekh

/1930/

Originally, Kishor Parekh wanted to report on life, its meaning and values, but life itself forced him to photograph destruction, death and destitution. 'I have seen and photographed things which will never allow me to be happy,' he said after his coverage of the bloody emergence of an independent Bangladesh. 'I saw hordes of homeless people fleeing through devastated countryside. I saw the face of a mother whose child had been killed in front of her own eyes, I saw human skeletons half buried in mud, with hangman's nooses still tight around their necks. I saw a little boy tenderly feeding his dying mother with one grain of rice after another. I saw a girl of ten in the street who in front of my eyes turned adult from all the horror. The eyes of these people haunt me wherever I go.' Born in Bombay, he was of the age when Third World countries had just rid themselves of colonialism, a time of determined but painful transition. He was barely nineteen when one of his first pictures appeared on the cover of his school magazine. His university studies of chemistry and botany left him with a feeling of discontent. Today he says that he lacked any emotional involvement at that time. He went to the United States and after three years of photographical and cinematographical studies he received his MA. The title of his thesis was *Documentary and Life Photography in Theory and Practice*. By this time he had already won the first prize in a competition organized by the National Press Photographers' Association and *Life* magazine. Big illustrated magazines now started vying with each other to offer him a job but he refused all because he did not want to feel restricted by their house policies.

Instead he returned home to Asia to the people to whom he felt closest because he understood them and was one of them. Besides, things were then happening in Asia which deserved to be covered. Kishor Parekh became chief reporter for *The Hindustan Times* but his photography was also printed regularly by *Paris Match, Life, Stern, The Sunday Times* and other magazines. Later he joined the *Asia Magazine* in Singapore, the biggest Asian publication with a circulation of 6 million. Still he was not completely content: 'Big magazines strip you of your individuality. I've got to work the way I feel, not the way somebody wants me to.' So in 1972 he decided to quit and went home to Bombay to be a free-lance photographer.

His reports on the famine in Bihar and his coverage of the Indo-Pakistani and Sino-Indian wars made him world-famous. He devoted a whole book to the emergence of Bangladesh. The book entitled *Bangladesh,*

*a Brutal Birth* is about life and death, faith and desperation, it is a book about man's innate desire to have a home and to raise and feed his family. 'I want my pictures to help people understand life. And to do this, I must first grasp it myself, I must not only understand and be interested in things around me but I must be deeply involved myself, I must get the taste.'

Kishor Parekh is not a hard-boiled reporter feeding his paper news without being really interested in what he photographs. Perhaps one of the reasons why he *is* involved is that he works on his own homeground and feels responsible for ensuring his work is genuine. In fact he describes photography as a historic mission because it is a medium capable of authentically expressing things that defy words. His pictures make the viewer on the other side of the world live them too: 'We all belong to a single human family,' he says, 'and what concerns me must concern all.'

Guided by his personal philosophy, Kishor Parekh, a sensitive Indian photographer, has become a humanist chronicler of the Asian continent.

Today, Tim Page is more a superhero of various memoirs, books, television shows and Hollywood superfilms than a photographer. Yet whenever he is quoted or portrayed on the screen by an actor he is always presented as a journalist with a camera for whom nothing is impossible or too dangerous, a man willing to cross a mine field, crouch in heavy fire, lie in mud for days on end or be a live target suspended from a helicopter, a man willing to do almost anything to get his picture.

'I'm a war baby. I was born in 1944 and grew up on Hotspur comics and books like Biggles. I loved to read war books and I still do. It seems a very relevant subject in terms of where the world is — Vietnam seems to have caused where we are in the world today economically and politically . . .' When he was seventeen he left his comfortable home in Kent, England and two years later, in 1964, he was already in Vietnam as a *Time-Life* reporter. During the next five years this 'crazy kid', as he was called by Michael Herr in his book *Dispatches,* managed something almost unparalleled in history: besides selling work to services like UPI and Associated Press and big magazines, *Time* and *Life* between them printed eighty pages of his colour photography. Tim Page was in fact the most printed photographer of the Vietnam war.

'I was twice in Vietnam, the first time for two and half years. After having been wounded three times and after I had seen too many risky actions the editorial office forced me to leave. "You're becoming too dangerous," they told me, but in less than a year I was back . . .' He was one of the few who travelled with the ARVN rather than journalists and public relations officers, spending at least half of his tour with the Vietnamese. He has summed up his opinion on photographing war in the following way. 'Once you start thinking of it all, you won't take a single picture. In the very beginning, during the second action, the GIs caught an enemy scout and tried to get information out of him. They slowly opened him with an assault knife. I had to leave because I was sick, but Eddie Adams from Associated Press kept taking pictures. Next day I found a wire in my pigeonhole at the hotel asking me for pictures of the event. I know that my duty was to take those

pictures and show the people the truth about the goddamn war. But once you are in action and become involved, thinking of morality and humanity, you won't be able to release the shutter. You can only hit the ground and be very very sad and then get up and get drunk or smoke a lot of opium ... No, I belonged to a generation of young photographers who were more into being cool than into compassion. Otherwise we would not have been able to record all the horror. But the way the pictures are used, that's a different story altogether ...'

Throughout his tours in Vietnam he did not care how much he was being paid: he was fed by the army and the best camera on the market could be had for ninety dollars at the PX, the lenses for fifty. He destroyed a dozen Leicas and Nikons of the best models but he never gave them a second thought because the cameras were just his tools.

His tour ended in 1969 when he was wounded for the fourth time and a shrapnel fragment that lodged in his brain was almost fatal. His memories of his last moments in action are highly characteristic of his whole approach: 'My brain and my eyes were bleeding and my guts were all over the place. I don't know how I did it but I managed to put the right lens on my Nikon, snap four or five pictures and crawl back to the chopper. Afterwards everything is blank. The next thing I remember is that I was in the surgery room dictating captions to my bureau chief.' Tim Page spent some thirteen months in hospital. His health has been badly affected by his wounds. Still, he would do the same again. 'Thanks to what I've been through, I'm stronger and more sensitive ...'

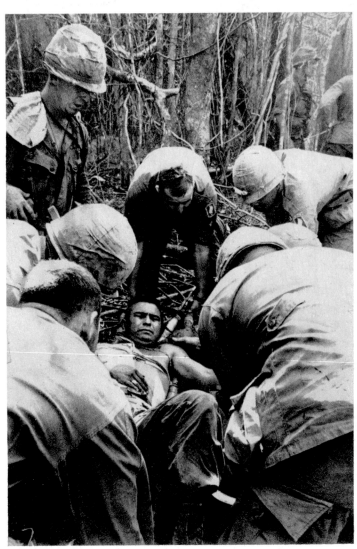

# Abbas /1943/

must be changed. Only rarely will photography influence the situation immediately... In 1973 famine struck Ethiopia but the government naturally tried to hide the fact from the press. I was there first and my pictures of Ethiopia mobilized her troops. But this is not common; usually it's a long process which photographers can only accelerate.'
He has photographed wars, famines and social upheavals in Biafra, Bangladesh, Vietnam, India, Pakistan, Nigeria, Ethiopia, Iran and other places. His courage to present things as they are has won him international acclaim. Until 1981 he worked for the Gamma service but their assignments always forced him to do short 'hot' reports to make the deadline. Then he joined Magnum Photos where he appreciated the chance to work on longterm in-depth projects.
In 1978—9 he worked almost exclusively in his native Iran. Nothing would have stopped him from covering the revolution of his nation. However, his being an Iranian was no asset in Iran at that time, for both sides in the

At the age of ten Abbas already knew he wanted to be a journalist. He was born in Iran but considers himself a citizen of the Third World because he understands its people and the events taking place and because he wants to show why things must be changed there. His opinion of the work of a photojournalist is summed up in the following way:
'Photojournalism is not neutral, it is a highly political matter.' He resents that he often has no control over the use of his pictures.
'Naturally I provide captions for my photographs but the editors may not use them in the end but make their own which may turn the meaning of the pictures upside down...
Once it happened that *Paris Match* completely changed my captions and even supplemented them with their own commentary. I told them then that I had nothing against their opinion on the situation in Iran but that I didn't want them to assert it with my pictures... I don't want to lie.
'Some people think that photojournalists can change the world with their pictures but the only thing we can do is to show why the world

166

conflict thought him a spy at one time or another and often only sheer luck saved his life. The result was a book entitled *Iran — La Révolution Confisquée* which aptly captured all the hopes and disappointments of that period.

'I like to be in places where there are things happening because it is in places like that one has the chance to see the best and the worst in man within a very short period. What could otherwise take years to learn will be suddenly revealed right in front of one's eyes.'

He is fascinated by wars and revolutions because he sees them as 'social phenomena'. Like Tim Page, he is ready to admit: 'If I allow myself to become emotionally involved in the thing, my hands start shaking and my pictures are not sharp. But I want to make sharp pictures because otherwise they would not have the impact they should.' He is not ashamed to photograph people dying in front of his eyes but this does not mean that he is unconcerned. Vietnam was his nightmare for three years and memories of Iran still haunt him.

253   South Vietnamese Soldier, 1972
254   At School, Somalia, 1974
255   South African Police in Training, 1978

# Susan Meiselas

/1948/

When Susan Meiselas landed in Managua, Nicaragua, in June 1978, she stepped right into the middle of a revolution, for the once small and isolated groups of Sandinista guerilla fighters had grown into a people's army. The young photographer found herself in the eye of a gathering hurricane. She had no accreditation, was poorly equipped, knew no Spanish and had no idea how to behave in the combat zone. She went there because she had read newspaper accounts of the execution of the editor-in-chief of the Nicaraguan opposition daily *La Prensa* and thought that a visit to the country would be the right start for the photojournalist she wanted to become. Three months later her pictures of the Sandinista movement and the street fighting were bought by newspapers and magazines all over the world. The young, unknown photographer working on her own became the centre of international professional interest, won the prestigious Robert Capa Prize, joined Magnum Photos and published

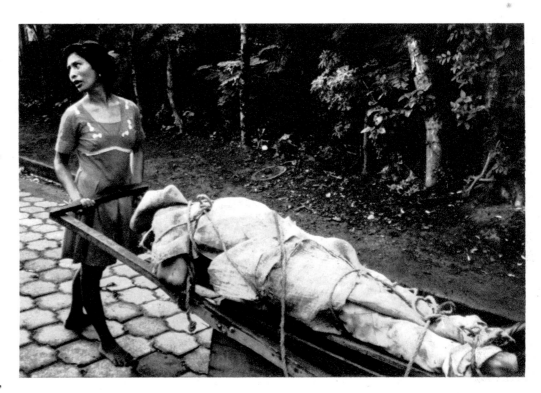

her colour photography from Nicaragua as a book.

Was her success caused by the simple fact that chance took her to the right place at the right time? The answer is yes — but only partially. The main reason is that her pictures captured something which has been recorded only rarely by war photography. She showed a revolution in the making, the transition of a longsuffering people from passive resistance to open armed revolt. Everything in her pictures — arrests, jail sentences, murder, anguish, violence — brims with hope, for her subject is a nation making its own history.

In 1980 she went back to the South American region. This time she had accreditation and her destination was El Salvador. This assignment turned out to be even more hazardous than her previous work in Nicaragua because the government had banned journalists from sensitive areas. Yet this did not matter, for her Salvadoran pictures reveal the same personal approach to her work as that from Nicaragua: a man lighting a cigarette while closing a coffin; a dead body in a brightly coloured sports shirt, lying face down. Violence and ordinary life are but two aspects of her Salvadoran experience, but she views violence without emotion because in El Salvador it has become an everyday reality.

'I could never view the things that were happening around me there as war in the usual sense of the word,' says Susan Meiselas, 'because one couldn't remain unaffected by the optimism of people fighting for a future they believed in. What I photographed was not war but a people in revolt.'

Everything that Susan Meiselas has done since she first went to Nicaragua is far removed from her very ordinary early life.

She knows what she wants to make her photographs and knows she might pay for this quest with her life. 'When you are with people facing the same danger as you and they still don't give up, you can't start thinking of yourself,' she explains. Recently in El Salvador the car she was driving tripped a mine. Her colleague was killed but she escaped with only wounds. 'I was lying by the roadside and two peasants armed with machetes were approaching me. I thought they were coming to finish me off but in a while they brought a stretcher. During those seconds of misgivings I felt neither fear nor anger. After all, they were fully justified to be distrustful of a journalist ...'

# IX PHOTOGRAPHY AND LIFE STYLE

Photographers reflect the world in their photographs and in doing so affect the world they reflect. In this sense, the story of photography is a living chronicle of our world, a stimulus, a testimony, a reflection. However, sometimes the reflection may be too advanced to be generally understood and in such cases photography is an anticipation of future developments in the art.

Such was the case of the American photographer Weegee when he published his *Naked City* in 1945. He was unlucky in being the first to show the city as a nightmare in which viciousness, cruelty, crime and debasement ruled. None of his New Yorkers — con men, thieves, extortionists, arsonists, hookers, seedy characters, candidates for the electric chair and members of the anonymous crowd — corresponded to the image of human goodness and the happy future promoted by photography in the early postwar era of optimism and faith. Weegee's view was a realistic one but people preferred the celluloid dreamworld in which neon lights and colourful billboards seemed to shine with the promise of a good future.

Twelve years later a photographer named Robert Frank travelled widely through the United States and brought back a unique pictorial document. America as he saw it was much different from Hollywood and television soap opera myths: in Frank's pictures the superman was a human ruin and the cheerful, happy, successful Americans were portrayed as ridiculous ants toiling to add more junk to their pathetic pile of possessions. He saw this great land of plenty being reduced to a pitiful consumer cornucopia where life neurotically revolved around banalities. Although Frank did not intend to be ironic, he created a travesty that shattered the American Dream. A scandal followed and his book *The Americans* was banned from publication. This was in the period when humanistic photography was at its peak and the optimistic creed of *The Family of Man* that life and people were essentially good and photography could become a universal vehicle of understanding was widely accepted. Frank's view, however, did not reflect such optimism, for its intelligent analysis anticipated changes for which the public were not psychologically ready. *The Americans* was therefore first

published in France in 1958. However, it was such a sensation that an American edition followed a year later. Observant Americans realized that Frank's view of America was akin in spirit to the message of the rapidly developing youth culture.

Robert Frank did not remain isolated in his view, for there came also other American and European photographers like Diane Arbus, Lisette Model, Charlie Harbutt, Leslie Krims, Leonard Freed and Leo Friedlander who have since helped photography shake off the idealism of the 1950s and 1960s.

Interestingly, it has been up to women photographers to express the tragedy of the social and psychological setup of the consumer society and to become its visualized consciousness. Lisette Model and Diane Arbus unmercifully attacked the snug indifference, intellectual and emotional blandness and cheap existential clichés. Their photographs shocked many and even provoked some critics to accuse them of depravity and deviation. For most, however, their pictures were food for thought because in their work socially concerned photography whose history had been started by social documentarists of the late 19th century and developed by humanist photography received a new dimension.

On the surface their photographs lack drama. They are just statements. 'Bomb Hanoi,' urges the badge in the lapel of a young man staring stolidly in the camera. The absurdity of the scene is highlighted by the badge in his other lapel proclaiming: 'God Bless America. Support Our Boys in Vietnam.' The picture by Diane Arbus does not show anything dramatic, for it is drama in itself, it is reality speaking for itself.

In the mid-1960s, photography started to turn more towards studying human thought, life style, the living conditions of various strata of society, interpersonal relationships and the causes of the inner conflicts of our world, becoming a sensitive probe raising questions rather than providing answers. This analytical approach is much more akin to that of a sober-minded scholar, physician, sociologist or political scientist than to the emotional view of the publicist or artist. In other words, in-depth photography has turned again to documentarism and socially and sociologically motivated reportage. The authors need not always be so shockingly brutal or screaming in protest as Diane Arbus. Often they are just quiet close observers with a sense of humour and irony, like Patrick Ward of England, Mikola Gnisyuk of Ukraine or Aleksandras Macijauskas of Lithuania. Observations of those like Markéta Luskačová, a Czech, Chris Killip, an Englishman, or another Lithuanian, Antanas Sutkus, are marked by deep sympathy, while the work of Martine Franck of France reveals sober refinement and that of the Russians Anatoli Garanin and Igor Gnevashev is infused with oversensitive tenderness. All these photographers confront us with life. The individual views may be marked by different social or political backgrounds, beliefs or creeds but all together these pictures constitute the image of the life style of our age. In these pictures we see how we think and act, what we are interested in and what leaves us dispassionate. This photography shows us everything in one form, which once constituted the separate domains of documentary, snapshot, reportage, fashion, advertisement and portrait photography. Photography has become not only the expression and creator of the life style but to a great extent also the most distinctive feature of that life style. It seems that whereas the spokesmen of our fathers' and grandfathers' generations was the writer or the poet, ours — besides the pop singer — is the photographer. It is the photographer who is best equipped to handle the most exciting attribute of our times, the fact visualized, for it is the image that has become the ruler of our thinking. Yet however strange it may seem, some of photography's functions as they exist today are only vaguely understood. One can but agree with Susan Sontag who — in contradiction to earlier tradition of speculation about the aesthetic and cognitive functions of photography — interprets the medium psychologically, holding that 'the grandest result of photographic activity is the fact that it enables us to feel that we can grasp the world as a set of images'. And thus although 'photography remains an interpretation of the world just as any work of art, it is a *part* of the world rather than a message about it: it is a miniature of reality . . .' because 'it puts man into a special relation to the world: to photograph means to appropriate the photographed'.

But regardless of interpretation, the fact remains that the essential character of photography today lies in its endeavour to see the invisible quintessence — to grasp the meaning. Therefore today's portrait photography is not so much after the likeness as the character behind the face, while fashion photography is less concerned with fashion than with the woman who is to wear it. Similarly, life photography is no more interested only in the external world but in our inner worlds as well. Reality captured by photography usually represents merely the first plane under which other levels, the true meaning, lie submerged. Only photography is perhaps capable of discovering what truly interests us today: to see what makes us tick, why we live the way we do.

# Weegee

/1899—1968/

family settled on Lower East Side, New York, which had improved somewhat thanks to the photographic exposé of Jacob Riis but which was still crammed with people. Usher grew up in the streets. He worked as a butcher and a dishwasher and then became a street photographer. It took six years of a hand-to-mouth existence before he was hired as laboratory technician by the Acme Newspictures, later UPI, for twenty dollars a week. It was here that Weegee the newspaper photographer was born. He did not want to become a news service photographer at the price of having to put on a tie, he preferred to remain holed up in the laboratory, venturing outside at night and photographing what usually remained hidden under the cover of the dark. When he did not photograph, he accompanied silent movies on violin in a Third Avenue moviehouse. He needed little, kept moving from one furnished room to the next or slept on his desk in the laboratory.

In 1935 he became a free-lancer, for by now he had learned more about the city at night than anybody else in New York and knew where and how to get pictures that editors would be willing to buy in the morning. He rented a room with a phone and used his

Weegee had long unkempt hair, a preoccupied look and his zippered pockets were bulging with films. His Speed Graphic ever ready, a lit cigarette hanging from his lips, he was always in a hurry to get somewhere. He was a local news reporter, recording petty crime, traffic accidents, murders, fires and social events. He never cared much for technique or composition because the only thing he was interested in was to get to the scene and take his pictures for the papers to buy.

Usher Fellig, later known as Weegee, was born in the province of Złoczew, which then belonged to Austria. When he was ten his mother took him and his three brothers to America to join their father who had gone there earlier with so many other thousands of poor Europeans to make money to provide a decent living for his family. At Ellis Island where Lewis Hines photographed immigrants at that time, an immigration officer changed his name from Usher to Arthur. The Fellig

172

woman, insensitive crowds gaping at a mutilated body and other dark, seemy aspects of life in New York.

But he could never deny his background, for he could never look at the rich without seeing them as funny and useless as shown by the most famous of his pictures, *Critic*: two old ugly jewelled and minked women going to a first night at the Metropolitan Opera House, stared at by an ordinary woman with her mouth open wide in astonishment. When Weegee died of a brain tumour in 1968, he left behind five thousand negatives and some fifteen hundred prints. None of them showed any great events: all were snaps of everyday, ordinary life, yet each of them casts a sharp light on humanity.

connections with the police department to install a police radio in his battered car. This enabled him to reach the scene of a crime or accident right on the heels of New York's police, snap a few pictures and rush back to his darkroom to develop them. In the morning he sold his pictures at five dollars a print. Legend has it that his *nom de guerre*, Weegee, comes from a term for the Weegee board because his contemporaries could not understand how he could sense that something was going to happen. The backs of his photographs were stamped with the slogan 'Credit Weegee the Famous'. Perhaps no other photographer has ever seen so much blood and gore in peacetime as he. 'Sometimes I even used Rembrandt's side lighting, not letting too much blood show! And I made the stiff look real cozy, as if he were taking a short nap,' he wrote in one of his books. He became the photographer of a naked city and turned his lens not only on crime but also drunks, passionate lovers in the crowd, passers-by staring as a wounded fat

# Robert Frank

/1924/

Mason-Dixon line, met the stars of Hollywood, admired the leather-necked stockmen at a rodeo, walked the streets of downtown Chicago, Detroit and Los Angeles. The locations differed but the situation was same everywhere: grey blocks and grey streets overcrowded with grey people. Even places like Chattanooga, Washington, Santa Fé or Lincoln, places whose names ring with America's past, her political, national and religious ideals, came out differently in Frank's pictures, as confrontations of myths and reality.

'Swiss, unobtrusive, nice, with that little camera that he raises and snaps with one hand he sucks a sad poem right out of America onto film, taking rank among the tragic poets of the world.' Thus the spokesman of the beat generation, Jack Kerouac, characterized Robert Frank. Yet Frank's intention is not to make people sad or to shock with his pictures. He does not subscribe to the Bressonian theory of the 'decisive moment'. So he photographs the most banal scenes around him. He does not wait for them to culminate because banalities never culminate, they only persist. His pictures feel as if they were taken just at random, evoking a feeling of mediocrity. But it was this European who discovered America for the Americans.
In the mid-fifties he came to America — the land of unlimited possibilities and technological wizardry, the land of the American Dream. He followed the classical pattern of the foreign tourist: he looked up at the face of the Statue of Liberty, visited Las Vegas, saw the Blacks south of the

The focus of Frank's photographic interest were objects: plastic bags and paper plates, refrigerators and transistor radios, engines, television sets, highways, cars, toasters, express trains, Coke bottles, poolrooms, neon lights, billboards and other symbols of an affluent technocracy. They made up an image of a place and a period, yet only a few noticed at that time that Frank's pictures lacked 'real people', for the people shown by Frank's vision were just cogs in the huge machine of the consumer society.

The result of Frank's great American journey was a shocking essay published under the simple title *The Americans* in 1958. The age-old American myths were suddenly shattered: the heroic cowboy became just a nobody in western clothes; the country of miraculous know-how, a dehumanized society full of futility, a land of the 'lonely crowd', of people unable to communicate or enjoy life, distrustful individuals caught in the impersonal world of impersonal things and relations.

Frank did not only 'discover' America for the Americans. He has also photographed fashion for *Harper's Bazaar,* travelled widely, publishing his pictures in *Life, Look* and *McCall's.* His most important essays besides *The Americans* are devoted to the Welsh miners and Londoners.

# Lisette Model

the more specific you are, the better you are able to make a generalization. Using specifics, she performs a psychological and sociological analysis of a world in which she sees consumer insatiability as wed to frustration and alienation. It may be significant that Diane Arbus studied with Lisette Model, since both artists raise this same view and both protest by being critical. But whereas Diane Arbus' criticism is maximalist and sometimes even hysterical in its desperation, Model's vision is less tragic as if she can still see some hope, as if she still nurtures at least the slimmest hope in humanity.

From the beginnings of her photographic work Lisette Model concentrated on the content of her pictures because she believed that to concentrate on art means to lose one's subject while to concentrate fully on the subject enables one to find art. 'Don't shoot till the subject hits you in the pit of your stomach,' she said.

'Why is it that the Americans seldom admire their skyscrapers? Why is it that they don't admire glamour as well? Is it because they are so close to both? They live them and breathe them day in and day out. But the Oxford Dictionary calls glamour a magic, an enchantment, a spell, and Webster says it is a bewitching, intangible, irresistibly magnetic charm. We are surrounded by glamour. Anyone can buy it everywhere and anywhere but no one can be sure of it. It is both artificial and profound. It is our most precious export: the real American Dream. You cannot have beauty, success and happiness without it. Its origins are sacred and no one is immune. Marilyn Monroe died of it. A Christmas tree in the landscape shines with it. Costumes and decoration, fun and religion follow where it leads. I want to follow this Pied Piper too; to photograph America's self-portrait a million

times projected and reflected, to make the image of our image.'

Lisette Model was born in Vienna and lived in Paris for some time. Perhaps this is why she was able to see America, where she lived till her death, so clearly, with all her hard drive and vitality. Her pictures do not ridicule but offer a close look, so close you sometimes wonder why none of her subjects kicked the camera out of her hands.

Henry Miller once said about Brassaï that his eye was never blind to anything, be it beauty or ugliness. Lisette Model seems to remain permanently blind to conventional beauty. Her people are almost as a rule anything but beautiful: fat, small, emaciated, lacking all taste or simply comical. Lisette Model has consciously rejected all the usual standards of beauty, purposefully selecting people who are unique in their way, because she believes that

Lisette Model studied music, first in Vienna, then in Paris. She took to photography only as late as 1937 when she and her husband, the painter Evsa Model, moved to New York. Four years later she had an exhibition at the Museum of Modern Art. From then she exhibited all over the world. In 1947 she started lecturing on photography at the San Francisco Institute of Fine Arts and from the 1950s she taught at the New School of Social Research in New York until her death in 1983.

# Diane Arbus

/1923—1971/

Born into the family of a rich Fifth Avenue department store owner, Diane Arbus could have anything she wanted, yet her life lacked excitement and challenge. Overprotected by her background, she felt separated from the real world. She began to resent this artificial immunity and longed for independence, so at eighteen she became a fashion photographer and until thirty-five spent her time working for most of America's big picture magazines. Then, at a time when she had made it to the top of her profession, she left her well-paid job to become a private student of Lisette Model, a photographer of fellow spirit with an obsession for the analysis of the social and psychological make-up society.

From then on Arbus trained her lens on people who deviated from the norm in any way: twins, triplets, giants, dwarfs, homosexuals, pensioners, lonely widows. She is even said to have had a list of potential subjects scribbled on a board above her bed. She was irresistibly drawn to those who were different. Her intention was not to make fun of these people, to ridicule or seek sensation, she sought them out because they helped her best illustrate the normal life style. Even her pictures of 'normal' subjects were snapped in moments when they were outside the norm of their ordinary lives, in situations that gave some counterpoint to their routine existence. She was fascinated by competitions of all kind, beauty competitions, dance marathons and muscle-builders' contests but she also discovered similar exhibitionism and social ritual in wedding banquets, parties and fancy dress balls. She was like an anthropologist scrutinizing the mysteries of the ritual of a newly discovered race.

Troughout her life she was depressive and could not accept the existing patterns of life. Two months before her death she wrote: 'Once I dreamed I was on a gorgeous ocean liner, all pale, gilded, cupid-encrusted, rococo as a wedding cake. There was smoke in the air, people were drinking and gambling. I knew the ship was on fire and we were sinking, slowly. They knew it too but they were very gay, dancing and singing and kissing, a little delirious. There was no hope.' At first sight, her photographs are static shots of abnormal people and an abnormal reality. The subjects stare directly into the camera and the frontal lighting is mercilessly stripping. Under the seemingly exotic exterior hides tragedy, under the apparent affluence is nothing but total emptiness. Hers are pictures

178

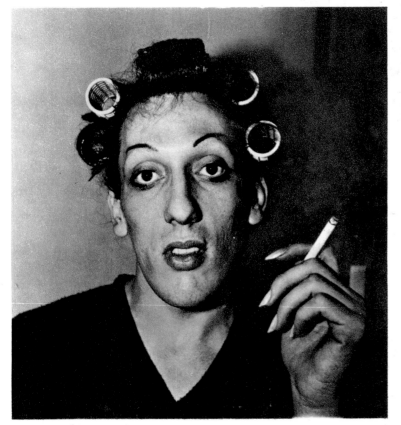

of a sick society, a world sick not from want but from gluttony. They are a reminder to man, warning him of the after-effects of the affluence he is not ready to use creatively. When Diane Arbus committed suicide in 1971, many saw it as a proof of her abnormality. Nothing could be less true. Her death merely vindicated her protest against the inhuman world in which people like her who still had not lost all sense for goodness and beauty could not live. When she died she was forty-eight and yet she was an idol of the young.

# Antanas Sutkus

/1939/

way of life. His great passion was for photographing children, particularly children in the moody, flat countryside sandwiched between the earth and the sky. These pictures constituted a new wave of photography that was optimistic yet with a human dimension, a photography that was unique and pure, full of refreshing simplicity and positive vision. *People of Lithuania* is the title of Sutkus' never-ending loose photographic cycle, a cycle unrestricted by partial themes illuminating the main subject from different angles of view. Sutkus' photography stems from the reportage approach although it is not governed by socio-critical considerations. Sutkus was born in Kluoniskiai, a village on the banks of the river Neman. His childhood and youth were marked by tragedy, for his father, a worker in a Kaunas factory and an important Communist functionary, committed suicide when Antanas was only one year old. His mother married again but her second husband was killed at the front when Antanas was three. At the age of sixteen he fell seriously ill and spent months in a sanatorium with tuberculosis of the kidneys. Here, at this sanatorium, he first became interested in photography.

It has been the closeness of his village life that has prevented him from growing bitter about his life's misfortunes. The trials he has endured and the tragedy that he has witnessed have only sharpened his view of the fundamentals of existence and enabled him to appreciate more life and its values.

In 1969 the Art Photography Society of the Lithuanian SSR was founded in Vilnius, Lithuania's capital. After several decades, in fact since the abolishment of the *Oktyabr* group, it was the first creative photographic association which united professionals and amateurs alike. Its spiritual father and first chairman was Antanas Sutkus, a promoter of modern concepts of education and development of young talents, tireless organizer of exhibitions, creative workshops and other things that have since constituted the national school of Lithuanian photography. Only thirty years old then,

Sutkus was the embodiment of things that had been fermenting in this tiny Soviet republic since practically the end of the Stalin era. Sutkus had started photography at university where he studied history and languages and became a representative of a new trend which rejuvenated the official stiff Soviet photography of the 1950s with young blood and new ideas. He photographed fragments and scenes of real life — people laughing, excited, meditating, in all kinds of moods; old men and women, lovers, young villagers, geese, ducks, almost anything he could capture of the traditional Lithuanian peasant

During his lifetime his kind of photography has been produced by only a few photographers in the USSR outside the Baltic republics, but Sutkus has been lucky enough to meet young people with a spirit akin to his, photographers like Romualdas Rakauskas, Algimantas Kunchius, Aleksandras Macijauskas and others whose work has since found a place in photographic collections all over the world.

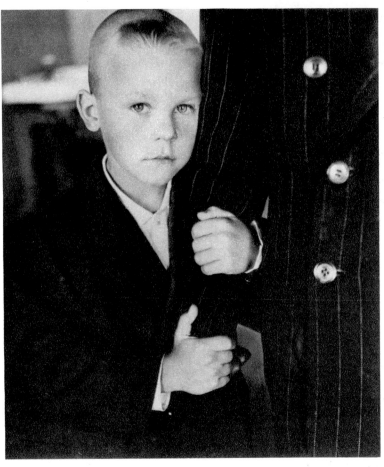

# Mikola Gnisyuk

/1944/

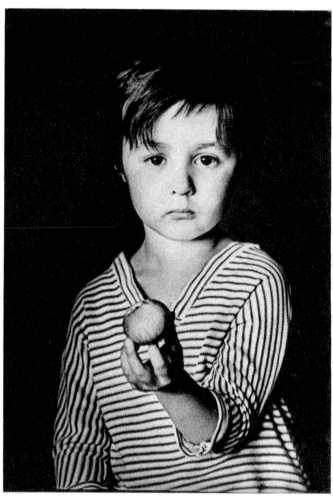

As a boy Mikola Gnisyuk tended cows in his native Ukrainian village of Perekorenka and greatly envied his elder brother who lived in the town. His brother was an amateur photographer and the little Mikola managed to persuade his mother to buy him a camera, too. By the time he was thirteen he was a trumpet player in a military band in Latvia's capital, Riga. It was here in Riga among film

and photography enthusiasts that he really took to photography. In time, he became a professional photographer working as a newsreel cameraman and in 1968 he won through tough competition the job of staff photographer of the prestigious film magazine *Sovetski ekran (Soviet Screen)* and moved to Moscow. However, the intellectual milieu of Baltic photography and his

memories of the village life of his boyhood marked his photographic style forever. His photographs are whimsical and humorous. When Gnisyuk photographs a truly great personality he is a little disrespectful in order to emphasize his subject's eminence; he maintains that the more frivolous the presentation, the greater is the impact of a profound idea. He always looks for something more than just the character, the place of the moment, and his pictures relate an acute and wise message about contemporary man. His propitious, understanding, all-encompassing philosophy rings not only with the amusing naiveté of folk painting or the moody village music, but also with the hearty Gogolian laughter to which nothing is sacred.

It is thanks to his philosophy that Gnisyuk is able to portrait the somewhat exclusive world of artists with whom he congregates, capitalizing photographically on his innocent trickery and irony. This whimsicality and sense for calculated ridicule is partly inborn, partly the product of the fascinating artistic milieu of Riga, the home of Gnisyuk's onetime photographic idol, Gunar Binde, who experimented there with post-Surrealist approaches to the medium. It was in Riga that Gnisyuk realized that the provoking simplicity of a 'naive Ukrainian cow herd boy' is as valuable an image for a photographer as the oversize shoes for Charlie Chaplin. Gnisyuk, an astute psychologist by intuition and an expert on human nature is at home as in the Ukrainian village common as in film studios, on location or Moscow's film-makers' cafés and clubs.

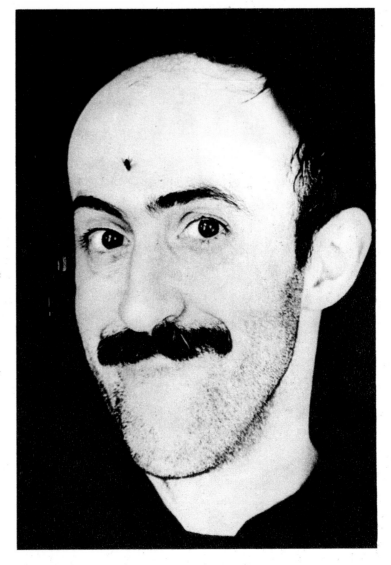

Gnisyuk loves to arrange and stylize: his photographs clearly reveal that he consciously strives for an expression. His pictures usually fuse a Gogolian persiflage and Surrealist mannerism so that one may not even be able to tell whether he is being serious or sneering. for example when he has a colleague and his wife, pose dressed as peasants in the window of a traditional Russian country cottage or when he adds a fly on the forehead of a wellknown film director. His subjects invariably look straight in the camera as if they were placing themselves at the mercy of his ironic, yet rather good humour. Gnisyuk's work for the film industry tries to offer a new view which will make the spectator stop and think.

# Aleksandras Macijauskas

/1938/

For ten years Aleksandras Macijauskas photographed nothing but village markets. He obstinately kept at it although he was criticized for being divorced from contemporary life and for idealizing the past. He persisted even though his job as a photographer for a daily newspaper made his freelance work extremely difficult. The result, however, is a great report on the ancient traditions of the Lithuanian village and its inhabitants who since time immemorial have been coming to the marketplace after the harvest to take part in that theatre in which everybody is an actor as well as spectator: horses, geese, ducks, cows, chickens, piles of potatoes, heaps of home-made products, people gathering, selling, buying, shouting, pigs quealing, geese cackling, excited children running from stall to stall. All this, however, is merely the setting because what interests Macijauskas the photographer most are human passions and relationships. His

village market is a place where people drive hard bargains, compete with each other, look sad or vengeful, grin happily, joke and gossip. Under the lens of Macijauskas' camera this 'folk theatre' becomes very much magnified: a close shot makes a pig's head supernaturally large, people taken by a ground angle shot acquire an unreal weightiness while the steeply convergent perspective of the wide-angle lens lends their ordinary activities and gestures an unusual dynamism. Macijauskas avoids the danger of being nostalgic, for his vision of the age-old rural world represents a link to our roots of which we must be reminded ever so often to avoid alienation, the predominant malaise of the contemporary world. Macijauskas' work is much more than just heaps of vegetables and other farm produce, it is more than a mere fascination with the simple joys of a country fair or excitement with primitive barter which serves not only purely utilitarian purposes but also a fulfilment of a need for fun, relaxation and social communication.

Macijauskas' large photographic essay is an analysis of human types, of a national mentality. It raises questions as well as provides answers to essential problems which worry every generation: where are we, what do we want and where do we go? These philosophical questions which in fact underline much other photography are discernible in Macijauskas' other cycles, the most recent being a study titled *The Veterinary Clinic*, on which the author worked from 1979. Still, Macijauskas has expressed his philosophy best in the sequence *Village Markets*, perhaps because the essay captured the quintessence of existence of the greater part of this still predominantly rural nation and because he himself was born and raised in the country and has been constantly returning to the village, the first and deep love of his life.

Aleksandras Macijauskas, one of the founding fathers of modern Lithuanian photography, is also a co-organizer of the Art Photography Society of the Lithuanian SSR. Like his colleagues who share his philosophy, he is highly expressive in his work. His imagery utilizes the potentials of modulation afforded by the wide-angle lens although it is no fancy trick but a strictly functional thing with him. He uses the wide-angle lens to heroize, poetize and even ironize the subjects which lends his essentially documentary photography a metaphorical value. It has been Macijauskas' fascinating example which paved the way for life photography in the Soviet Union. His work is represented in collections of the Bibliothèque Nationale, Paris; Reattu Museum in Arles, France; and the Museum of Modern Art, San Francisco.

# Igor Gnevashev

/1941/

Like his contemporary Mikola Gnisyuk, Gnevashev is distinctly national in his outlook, but whereas Gnisyuk, a Ukrainian, is a Chekhovian ironist and Gogolian teaser, Gnevashev, who is Russian by birth, is a sensitive intellectual who revolts against modern civilization by seeking refuge in the meadows and fields of a dreamy Turgenevian landscape. His work is marked by nostalgia stemming from an awareness that the traditional life has lost its distinct character and the new life still lacks one. It is as if Gnevashev yearns for the peasant Russia of old, for the wide stretches of the fertile land

Igor Gnevashev's refined work reflects the spiritual heritage of Russian drama, psychological novels and modern Russian avant-garde poetry which in the first decades of this century became a melting pot of ideas for modern European art, Soviet revolution and the Russian soul. Gnevashev's photography rings with the echoes of Tolstoi, Turgenev, Dostoevski, Esenin, Tsvetaeva, Balmont, Khlebnikov, but also his contemporary Vasili Shukshin and his simple but wise philosophy of today's informed man. Gnevashev is a major representative of that part of young Soviet photography which relies on the inner rather than outer reality to be free to work with the symbolism of signs and meanings. He is a staff photographer of the Soviet film magazine *Sovetski film* but his freelance work philosophizes on the basic values of life and man's place in nature. This takes him outdoors into the country where the traditional village life is still simple and unaffected by the 20th century.

and its traditional isolation as well as the invigorating intimacy of people and nature. While Gnisyuk's vision is often a reality arranged or even manipulated, Gnevashev's is a reality discovered: he is a pilgrim in quest of his ethnic roots.

Gnevashev belongs to a generation that entered photography in the early 1960s, unburdened by the schematism of the earlier periods but also marked by ignorance of the early Russian and Soviet photography. It was a photographical *tabula rasa* that Gnevashev discovered, armed with the cheap popular *Lyubitel* camera. His favourite pastime was painting, especially of genre street scenes but as Talbot before him, he decided that drawing by light was quicker, easier, more accurate and credible. He was fascinated by the truthfulness of life as portrayed in photographs, a truthfulness which he absorbed through every pore when he used to rush out from the printing shop where he was apprenticed to photograph during his lunch breaks. Eventually he signed for the night shift to be able to pursue his passionate hobby during the day. It must have been then that his somewhat naive feeling of creative freedom produced a distaste for the prefabricated topics and slogan imagery of period Soviet photography.

Ten years later he became a film photographer, 'strong enough and ready to defend his ideas'. He now knew that nobody could manipulate or influence him, that he was strong enough to retain his own spontaneous approach to photography, that he 'would not lie photographically'. His work offers a message about the existential feeling of contemporary man stigmatized by separation from his rural past but also constitutes a testimony about the eternally wounded and ever passionate Russian soul.

# Chris Killip

Chris Killip has never been just one of a crowd or taken part in group exhibitions. He has likewise never subscribed to anything which would conflict with his convictions. He would rather wait for his chance to do what he wanted. And thus he would patiently work as an advertisement photographer to be able to 'walk through the country', or work on commission as an industrial photographer to come back to the same places and see the landscape and the people in his own way. Commercial commissions earned him a living and gave him professionalism while his freelance work gave him self-realization. His unbending character has not made his life any easier. Killip was born on the Isle of Man, where he finished his secondary education and started working, first as a field hand, then a cook and casual labourer. In the end he became a beach photographer, scraping enough money to go to London. He was assistant to various commercial photographers but he was so good that he often earned commissions of his own. Slowly he built up his reputation, working for such prestigious magazines as *Vogue* and *Harper's Bazaar.* Four years later he quit and returned to his native island in the Irish Sea. He started photographing it systematically, capturing the intimately familiar countryside and its melancholic, ragged beauty, its fishermen, shepherds, farmers and their homes. Such were the origins of a photographic cycle about man's place on the earth and the symbiosis of the two.

His essay on the Isle of Man is in fact an essay on life. But unlike other photographers of his and younger generations, for whom sociologically oriented photography is a mode of learning and communication, Killip astonishes by the aesthetic qualities of his imagery. His pictures are characterized by a formally perfect composition as if the author had to wait for weeks on end for things to assume a balance fitting a preconceived idea. His pictures are indeed perfect portraits of people, landscapes and homes.

His photographic series on the Isle of Man was successful and was even published in book form although the author had to argue

at length with the editors before the book was produced how he wished. Exhibitions in London and New York soon followed and in 1974 Killip won the British Arts Council Prize. Unfortunately, all this did not give him a living and Killip therefore took the job of a documentary photographer for a gasline project in northern England. In Newcastle he met a group of young photographers and film-makers who wanted to work unharrassed by the pressures of commercialism. Together they tried to win the support of authorities and corporations and in the end they bought a warehouse in Newcastle which they adapted into a complex of photographic and film studios containing a cinema, a film club, a library and a large three-storeyed exhibition room known as the Side Gallery. Chris Killip became its director and devoted all his time to its management until he found that he had no time left for photography. He left in 1979 and accepted the position of a lecturer on photography at the university of Wales which gave him more time to spend on his photographic essays on life.

# Markéta Luskačová

/1944/

Markéta Luskačová turned to photography because she wanted to capture what defied verbal description. She was then a sociology student at Prague's Charles University and she wanted to be as precise as possible in her sociological studies, so she enrolled in the department of photography of Prague's FAMU (Film Academy). This gave her a sound knowledge of photographic techniques which enabled her to present her sociological theses entitled *Fairs of Eastern Slovakia* in the form of a photographic essay. It is a strong, mature work which is not only sociologically sound but offers an imagery characterized by perfect composition. The work immediately placed the young author in the vanguard of that part of young contemporary Czech photography whose programme was to probe the essentials of social phenomena.

What had originally started as sociological documentation revealed to the author the possibilities of pictorial expression and Markéta Luskačová's interest switched exclusively to photography. The picturesque village of Šumiac lost in the mountains of Slovakia where she had first tried her hand at the medium, totally spellbound her, becoming her second home. It was here that she discovered the age-old symbiosis of man and nature lending sense to existence. She found good friends here and pure human relations, the roots of her faith in life and its basic values. It was here that she first tried to understand the ceaseless flow of time and was able to look anew at human existence.

Since then, she has been going back two or three times each year although her work has taken her to Switzerland and England.

293   From the cycle *Šumiac,* 1970
294   From the cycle *Šumiac,* 1971
295   From the cycle *Šumiac,* 1980

are a quest for humanity, a closely-knit community of relatively free people unaffected by the complex system of material bonds of the highly structured Western consumer society. Yet the situation of these people does not serve the photographer as a soap box for moral indignation. Luskačová seems to appreciate the burden that these people have to bear. In this sense her photography is a positive affirmation of life, a tribute to human dignity, an acknowledgement of the ceaseless struggle for existence. Luskačová's photography is a social phenomenon and also a passionate personal message reflecting universal human experience and provoking thought. Each photograph is a part of a larger cycle and yet it constitutes an independent, self-contained and aesthetically valid message. Ever since her first independent show in the lobby of the now defunct Prague avant-garde theatre Behind the Gate (Za branou) in 1971, Markéta Luskačová has never lowered her personal standards, she has always known both her aims and limitations.

'I photograph people,' she says tersely and her photographs are as straightforward and simple as this statement. In the early 1970s she photographed the Irish in Ireland and the pictures ring with a distant echo of Slovak villagers at a country fair because these were also simply country people, albeit with a different cultural, national and mental determination. Even her later work, be it London street markets or street musicians; workers holidaying at the cold seaside of northeastern England; or London refuges for abused mothers and children, has a common denominator: a deep interest in the situation of people determined by their social environment. In Slovakia it was inhabitants of a remote mountain village practically untouched by civilization, in England it is social outcasts or people who are in some way socially handicapped or excommunicated. It may be asked whether these monothematical cycles represent sociological photography. Markéta Luskačová uses her material to raise some disturbing questions yet she is no dispassionate analyst, for her efforts

# Patrick Ward

/1937/

Patrick Ward was doing his national service when a friend sent him the catalogue of *The Family of Man.* He had never realized before that photography could be so subtle a means of expression and he immediately wanted to try his hand. He enrolled in a photographic course but soon quit because he considered it a waste of time for the instruction was concerned only with technique. Then he was lucky enough to meet Norman Hall, an important picture editor who got him a job of assistant to John Chillingworth who was then working for a number of leading British magazines. He belongs to a generation of British photographers who started working for the press at the turn of the 1960s. The pathos of *The Family of Man,* its grand ideas and emotions were already somewhat removed from their own expression because this was a generation that was tougher, more rational and matter-of-fact than those photographers who had brought life photography to its peak. Don McCullin and Philip J. Griffith turned to war photography while Ian Berry, David Hurn and Patrick Ward started photographing anything

which seemed to lack all drama or excitement. All these photographers, however, were looking for the same thing: a close, inquisitive look at the world rather than a record of specific events. They were more interested in an analysis of the human situation — both internal and external — rather than its mere representation.

Patrick Ward is gifted with a fine, dry, slightly mocking sense of humour so peculiar to the English. And since he is a photographer fascinated with people and their inclinations, follies and weaknesses, his is a good-natured humour. For years he photographed the English at play. 'You know, the Scots go to soccer games to see others play, the Welsh sing, the Irish fight, but anything that an Englishman does outside his work is fun, a play, including reading newspapers,' he said once to an interviewer. This was the aspect from which he viewed England's upper, middle and lower classes, producing a book which was a remarkable study of the national character, a book poking gentle fun at the English — including himself.

Patrick Ward is an intellectual, an intelligent observer and his pictorial epigrams are not concerned only with how people amuse themselves. His pictures also constitute a report on the class divisions of British society, proving that even dress, cars, hair styles, beards and leisure are class-determined in Britain: while the upper class fish for

trout and salmon, the lower class go for pike or perch. Yet Ward's look is not critical, it is only slightly ironic. The tone is even more evident in his series *Flags Flying* produced when Britain was celebrating the twenty-fifth anniversary of the coronation of Queen Elizabeth II. The cycle captures manifestations of British nationalism of which all Britons make fun but which they revere as just another ancient British tradition: the Union Jack in the mane of a horse, on a lady's hat, on

the clerical garb of a parson, in the trunk of an elephant, on the seat of blue jeans, the mouth of the Queen, pasted over with the slogan *God Save the Queen* — idols of a grand national past turned upside down, a national holiday perverted into a masquerade ball.

Ward is not a reporter but rather as essayist who can relate serious matters in a totally unserious manner, with an undertone ranging from a good-humoured smile to a bitter smirk.

# Martine
# Franck

/1938/

The wife of Henri Cartier-Bresson could probably capitalize on the fame of her husband to make a name for herself in photography. Yet Martine Franck has never done this. First, she is too independent-minded for such a thing and second, her approach to the medium has always been different from that of HCB.

For years she was just a part of a large photographic business, working in the *Life* laboratories where she applied her professional skill to finalize the ideas of others. Her constant contact with photography and the best talents in the business led her finally to try her hand at creative photography, since its potential fascinated her as a unique testimony of the times, a medium that may be authentic and convincing, yet highly personal. This, after all, was what *Life* had always dictated and Martine Franck absorbed this creative creed from the unique atmosphere prevailing in the magazine offices and studios.

However, she belongs to a different generation from her husband and other representatives of classical, candid or life photography. A different life experience forced a different expression. Like her husband's generation she has been spontaneously photographing life in all its manifestations, but unlike those who have been through the hell of World War II she has never felt an urge to take a proclamative stand for humanity, or to speculate emotionally about the human condition. Her expression is much more sober, less emotional but perhaps more attentive at that. This is demonstrated also by her subjects. She has photographed the life of a French family, recording how the French furnish their apartments, how they dress, take care of their children or spend their leisure time. She has trained her camera on ordinary scenes of life in Paris, snapping people at a Metro station, tourists in the Jardin des Tuileries, Louvre custodians leaving from work. Whereas the older generation emphasized action, her approach stresses non-action. Her pictures are almost static but they invariably have perfect composition. They capture just one of an endless series of ordinary moments: children at play at the beach in Beauville, tired tourists listening to their guide, blankly staring participants in the Veterans' Day festivities, deserted tables among the debris of a late afternoon in a garden restaurant. The dynamism of these pictures is in the inner content rather than action. Their aim is to record the life style of a time and place.

In 1972 Martine Franck joined a group of similarly minded young photographers and together they found the Viva service. The service has commercial objectives but accepts only such commissions that are in tune with the members' interests and philosophy. The aim of Martine Franck and other associates of the Viva service like Guy de Querrec, Hervé Gloaguen, Claude Raimond-Dityvon, Michel Delluc and others is to produce socially oriented photography that is inquisitive and

attractive due to its terse and unobtrusive authenticity. Their photographs seem to melt into the faceless crowd which they capture in trivial, yet relevant and revealing moments. What is new here is not the approach, for Viva has always credited its indebtedness to the tradition of American social photography of the 1930s, but the desire of these photographers to make their own contribution to the mapping of the contemporary life style.

Born in Belgium, Martine Franck has lived in Paris since 1958, where she studied art history at the École du Louvre. She has portraited many outstanding artists and scientists and proved her talent as a theatre photographer. Her essays have been printed by *Life, Vogue, The New York Times, The Sunday Times* and many other newspapers and magazines.

195.

# Yousuf Karsh

recording an interpretation of their character.' However, what has always been most important for Karsh is not so much the intimate detail but the mental rapport with the sitter because this is what enables him to produce a portrait of the sitter's soul.

He has always been fascinated by what makes man tick. Originally he wanted to be a physician and it was just chance that he started discovering man's inner make-up as a photographer. However, something of a physician's precision, perfectionism and total devotion to the profession is discernible in his photography. His portraits have become famous for their perfection and yet seemingly accidental nature, by character-lending light infusing the sitter with a reflection of their inner life, by the rich texture and deep blacks from which only the face and the hands seem to emerge. In many cases his works are the dream of every portraitist: a likeness synthetizing the quintessence of personality. He has photographed hundreds of famous men and women, politicians, millionaires, men of letters, actors, painters and many of these people have become famous because of the portraits of Karsh, a man with a special talent

'The human face is a great challenge to me and I am very curious,' he told a reporter when he was seventy. Fifty years earlier he would stop people in the street and ask them to sit for him because their faces were of interest. He has always subscribed to the belief that human physiognomy reveals charcter. 'Sometimes my subjects tell me intimate things they want me to know, assuming that it is important for your

196

to infuse in his pictures with the personal attributes and the public role of his subjects. Karsh's famous portraits include George Bernard Shaw, Ernest Hemingway, Joan Miró, Pablo Picasso, Winston Churchill, John F. Kennedy and most recently Queen Elizabeth II.

How did the Armenian-born Karsh become a photographer of the 'People Who Make Our World'? Early in his life his uncle, a photographer, took him from his home in Germany to Canada. The young Karsh had to make a living and he gave up his aspirations to become a physician and at the age of seventeen started working as an apprentice in the Boston studio of John H. Garo. The years spent with Garo were his best professional school, for Garo had numerous friends among artists, writers and scholars and his studio was a place for meetings and conversation.

After three years he left Garo and opened his own studio in Ottawa. He worked frequently for the big magazines, especially *Life,* and his commissions often paved the way for his own work. 'When I photographed André Malraux, he said, "Thank you for having finished me so promptly because I must go and receive Albert Schweitzer." I then photographed Schweitzer. Or, for example, I am in London and the person I am photographing is suddenly interrupted by a telephone call from Helsinki, it was Sibelius and my London host made it possible for me to photograph him. My work has always been simple . . .' The turning point in Karsh's career was 1941 when he became famous in both the West and East almost overnight. His historic portrait of Winston Churchill was produced in a manner which is almost anecdotal: Karsh snapped it at the very moment when he had just taken a freshly lit cigar from the Prime Minister's mouth because this was the only way to produce that slightly irritated but determined face so typical of Churchill. Since then Karsh's fame as a photographer has grown constantly and his portraits have become classics included in photography and historic textbooks. Karsh has the gift of a great diagnostician and it has been this gift that has always enabled him to recognize the most relevant feature of his model's character.

# Arnold Newman

'The portrait is a form of biography. Its purpose is to inform now and to record for history. We must record facts, not fiction or idealized images. The vital visual facts in today's magazine make up tomorrow's history textbook.' So said Arnold Newman at a time when others were experimenting with the specific potential of 35 mm cameras seeking rapidity and spontaneity. Newman was learning to use the time-tested qualities of the classical stand camera because it gave him time to think how to achieve perfect composition for his images.

Newman based his vision on the relation between man and his environment: 'The portrait of a personality must be as complete as we can make it. The physical image of the subject and the personality traits that the image reflects are the most important aspects, but alone they are not enough ... We must also show the subject's relationship to his world.' And thus in Newman's work Salvador Dali almost becomes a part of his own painting; Jean Cocteau is seen immersed in lofty ideas of his philosophical and literary thought; Alfred Krupp is a personification of

hard business drive, money and power, and Igor Stravinski shown at the bottom left corner of the huge black grand piano looks totally a part of his music.

Arnold Newman is a New Yorker by birth but he spent the greatest part of his childhood in Atlantic City and Miami Beach where his parents managed hotels for various owners. It is here where we can trace the beginnings of Newman's life-long fascination with human types, their features and fates. He had a distinct talent for art but the financial situation of the family barred him from

198

finishing his university studies and made him
accept the offer of one of his father's friends,
the photographer Leon Perskie, to become his
apprentice. He worked in a number of
Perskie's studios in Philadelphia, Baltimore
and Allentown, Pennsylvania, photographing
as many as seventy people a day for sixteen
dollars per week.

In the early 1940s Newman met several
people who had a decisive influence on his life
and career. Alfred Stieglitz provided him with
professional stimuli while the eminent
historian of photography Beaumont Newhall
offered him advice and encouragement and
arranged for him to meet important people in
photography which indirectly led to
Newman's first one-man show *Artists Look
Like This* at the Philadelphia Museum of Art.
The exhibition received good notices and
Newman became a photographer much
respected by critics, gallery directors and
photographers. It was at this time that he
decided to devote his career to portraiture.

In 1946 he received his first commission from
*Life* to photograph the great American
playwright Eugene O'Neill. *Harper's Bazaar*
soon followed suit, asking him to portrait Igor
Stravinski. Ironically, this portrait of the
famous composer and perhaps Newman's
best-known work was rejected by the editors
at that time. But other magazines were
already waiting in the wings and Newman
quickly received commissions to photograph
people like Lindon B. Johnson, John F.
Kennedy, Marcel Duchamp, Piet Mondrian,
Marilyn Monroe, Marc Chagall, Georg Grosz
and a number of other famous or important
people. Newman's house became a regular
*salon* frequented by painters, politicians,
writers, actors and journalists, many of whom
not only sat for him but became his close
friends.

Newman has always tried to establish rapport
with his model during the preliminary sittings,

studying his model during usual conversation,
selecting characteristic environment and
details. His photographic interpretation has
relied on intimate acquaintance as well as on
intuition. He has always admired Stieglitz's,
Steichen's and Man Ray's portraiture but
nurtured the same admiration also for the

social documentarists of the 1930s. This
affinity to two diametrically opposed modes
of expression has been a permanent mark of
his own work because he uses the aesthetic of
the former and the documentarism of the
latter to formulate his own vision which has
greatly contributed to the portraiture genre.

# Anatoli
# Garanin

/1912/

Although Anatoli Garanin has worked for the press throughout his life, he does not correspond to the public image of a photographer. He is impulsive and dazzles with split-second reactions but he remains unmoved by the external drama. His photographs are thoughtful, sensitive probes into the depths of the human soul, his main subject is the drama hidden under the exterior of the visible world.

He started his career as a combat photographer in World War II, the antithesis of his desire for the harmony bred in him by the intellectual atmosphere of his family and an intensive love of music. War was a denial of his life's basic values and brought about the kind of drama he had always avoided. Yet this sensitive, intellectual and fearful man produced photography of which at least one — his *Death of a Soldier* — ranks equal with Baltermants' *Grief* or Capa's *Death of a Loyalist Soldier.* Moreover, it is in a very different field where Garanin has left his mark.

Garanin's two lifetime loves are music and theatre. He likes majestic music, preferring that of the nineteenth to the eighteenth century. When he listens to music, he closes his eyes, an extatic expression in his face, totally in tune with the music. When Garanin goes to a concert, he does not photograph musicians but rather their music. He is a virtuoso of the tonal scales within a photograph, ranging from softest hazy greys to solid blacks, using any means of expression to relate the feelings evoked by the harmonic progression of musical tones. He uses lack of focus, distortion, motion and counter-motion coupled with his fine senses for the formal requirements of the image. As with music, his desire to relate profound ideas and emotions took him often to Moscow's theatres until he ended up as a photographer for the avant--garde like the *Sovremennik, Malaya Bronnaya* and *Taganka* theatres. Whenever a new piece is rehearsed in one of these theatres, Garanin almost becomes ill with work and cannot do anything but photograph, oblivious of the world around him.

The 'theory of noise' is how he expresses his methods of interference with the image to give it depth, emotional charge and space. To do this, he does not hesitate to use his fingers in front of the lens to produce magical effects or even to block off a considerable part of the image. This is why in his search for an expression he often relies on lack of focus or on minute detail which becomes the dominant motif of the picture. Garanin is a tireless experimenter, a magical virtuoso performing variations on a given theme, returning patiently again and again to his subject.

The same passion and dedication with which he photographs music and theatre go into his pictures of workers' meetings, the life of a long-distance haulage driver, the work of a librarian, the intellectual concentration of a researcher, or any other subject which his magazine *Sovetski Soyuz (Soviet Union)* assigns him. 'I shoot not only on location but also inside my head when I'm sitting at my desk at home,' he maintains. The result is almost invariably an in-depth report, usually composed of a number of pictures to bring home a universal message, but through man's individuality.

People in his pictures are usually solemn, concentrated on what they are doing, the results of their labour or creativity seeming to stem from a strong inner tension. Anatoli Garanin, a remarkable analyst of Russian soul and mentality, is today perhaps the most important figure of Soviet post-war photography.

# Cecil Beaton

/1904 — 1980/

For more than half a century Cecil Beaton was court photographer to the international jet set, royalty, famous men of letters, filmstars and the beautiful people on both sides of the Atlantic. He first captured the public interest during the Roaring Twenties. At that time he was a 'pathetic young man, an unusual self-conceited snob without any apparent talent but with a great desire to break out of anonymity and became somebody'. Despite this rather unflattering characterization of himself he was an instant success. He was not even twenty-four when he had his first independent exhibition in London's fashionable Bond Street in 1927. By this time, however, he had developed his own style which relied on an expert use of rather exotic props and which exuded finesse, superiority and affluence.

He started photographing during his years at Cambridge University. Later at home he developed his imagination by photographing his sisters and their friends. This images were a mixture of studio portraiture, pastoral scenes and theatrical posters all of which gave the young Beaton his own style.

The handsome, witty and sociable young photographer soon became a member of London's fashionable set. In 1929 he went to the United States where he went on to photograph scores of Hollywood stars.

He is remembered also as photographer to royalty, his picture of Queen Elizabeth II was a hitherto unprecendented official portrait: instead of having to make do with twenty minutes or so, he was able to make the Queen sit for him for hours. The result is a mixture of formality and informality: the regal magnificance transcended into elegant simplicity, the regalia presented with an air of casualness, the smile almost unroyal in its heartiness. All this made the official portrait a masterpiece of portrait photography.

The refined form, imagination, racy decorativism and wit of Beaton's portraits of magnates of the modern world are also characteristic of his fashion and war photography and even snapshots from the family album. Beaton was a man of diverse talents: besides photographing for magazines like *Harper's, Queen's, Vogue* and *Vanity Fair* he was also an accomplished painter and stage designer. His designs for the stage and film versions of *My Fair Lady* are still highly acclaimed.

When World War II broke out, Beaton the dapper dandy and photographer to royalty did not hesitate to work for the Ministry of Information, making pictures both at home in England and in the Middle East, India and China. His photography was carried by *Life* and even appeared on Red Cross posters. It was the war that made Cecil Beaton subdue his expressivity and curb his imagination. This was especially apparent from a retrospective exhibition of his work held in the National Portrait Gallery in London in 1968. Four years

later, Beaton was honoured like no other photographer before him: in recognition of his lifetime work he was knighted. 'Before me, photographers were nobodies hidden under the black cloth,' he once commented wryly.

# Sam Haskins

/1926/

 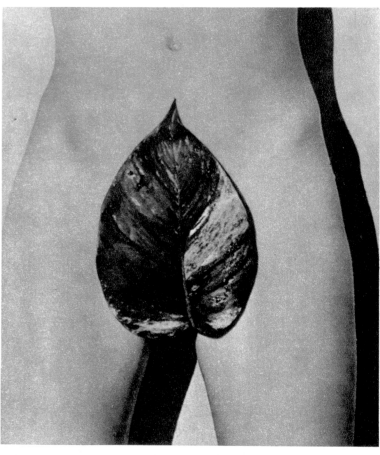

Sam Haskins' first book *Five Girls* created a sensation when it appeared in the early 1960s; it swept like a fresh breeze across the still waters of nude photography, for Haskins stripped the nude of cliché, stateliness, vulgarity and even a certain sacredness, making it a natural aspect of life. His second book, a story of a cute gun-slinging girl called *Cowboy Kate* became an instant international bestseller which crowned the author as the king of glamour photography.

Haskins' success was even more remarkable if we realize that his photographic stories were admired in countries as differing in tradition and taste as Japan, Italy, the United States and India. Perhaps the real reason was that Haskins' photography reflected the contemporary neo-Romantic ideal of life, offering excitement, amusement, freedom, fun, frivolity and beauty. Haskins' photographs simply came at the right time, filling a gap in the existing patterns of cultural life and leisure. Like the songs of the Beatles they voiced the sentiment of a generation.

Haskins was born in South Africa where he started his career as a commercial designer and graphic artist, also pursuing photography, taking pictures in gold mines, crocodile-infested rivers, on elephant trails, always honing his sharp, personal vision of a life full of paradox. At the age of twenty-one he decided to become a professional photographer.

After a stay in London where he gained technical erudition and professional experience he returned home in 1952 and opened his own commercial studio in Johannesburg. He recognized that advertisement photography was then a poor relation to wedding photography and Haskins spent the next fifteen years helping develop professional advertising photography in South Africa. In doing so, he managed to leave his personal mark on the world of advertising and glamour photography and did so in such a way that every photographer who has since ventured onto the same road has had to cope with Haskins' own unique contribution to the art.

Haskins' books were the product of the frustrations of a commercial photographer ever straight-jacketed by his commissions. He discovered that the most exciting thing about producing books was that he ceased to be a mere cogwheel in the big machine of advertising. The original idea, the script, the photography as well as selection of pictures, layout, the total book was his own work. Haskins' unlimited creativity thus produced novelties for the book market: pictorial books

that were not mere albums or collections of pictures but genuine pictorial stories including all the appropriate apparatus like exposition, plot, climax and denouement. Haskins' photographic stories are very exciting. His girl models look natural and his pictures are a well-balanced blend of motion, grace and playful sexuality.

Haskins is a virtuoso, a master of subtle, sophisticated associations and juxtaposition: an apple and the round female face or bottom; slimy fishes and the silky female skin; cold metal, the rough texture of bark and smooth nudity. He is a great expert at innuendo so typical of his recent advertisement work. His erotica constantly manages to maintain the extremely delicate balance between the aesthetic and the lewd and it is precisely this tightrope act that makes his imagery so exciting.

# David Bailey

321—3   Intimate pictures of Marie Helvin-Bailey from the late 1970s for David Bailey's *Trouble and Strife*, 1980

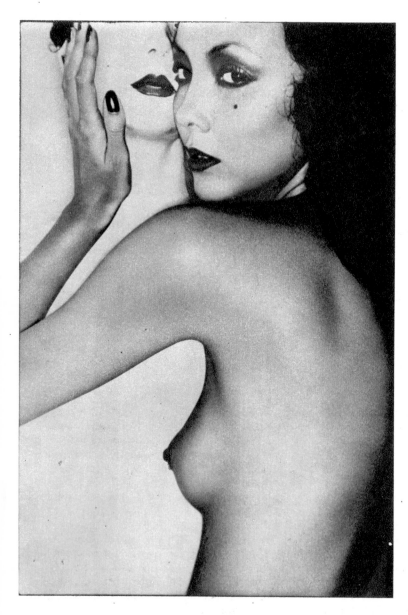

beach. In the early 1960s Richard Avedon started composing his fashion photography into self-contained stories and by the end of the decade models pictured in *Vogue*, *Elle*, *Marie Claire* and other fashion magazines became personalities themselves. The next stage of development came with the big fantasy of the period, playacting.

'I just photograph my own fantasies,' says David Bailey. He photographs his wife, Marie Helvin, as if he were playing games with

When fashion photography became established as a genre in the first decade of this century, it showed ladies of high society in magnificent robes posing in drawing rooms of patrician residences and boudoirs of aristocratic palaces. The result was that the models resembled figurines. Since then photographers have been trying hard to make the world of fashion photography lively and up-to-date. In the 1930s the photojournalist Martin Munkácsi took his models to the

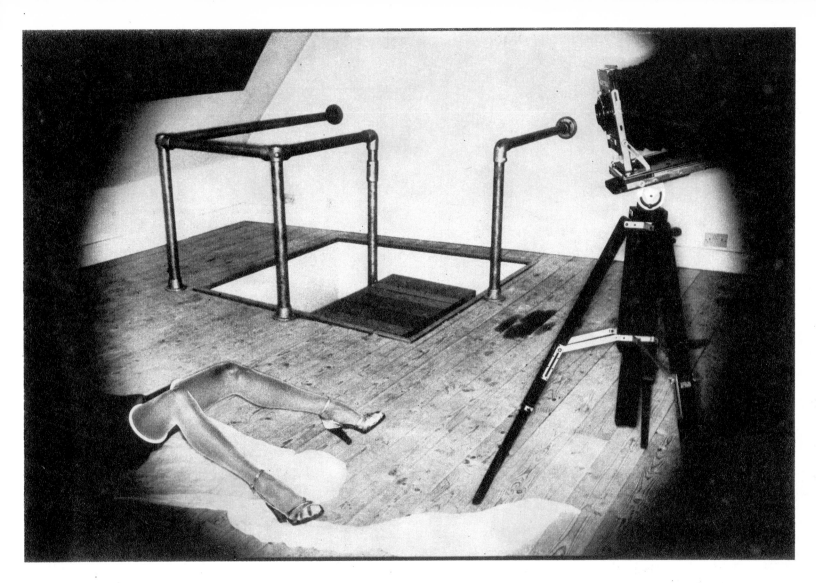

a beautiful, supple life-sized doll capable of being anything on command: a femme fatale, a vampire, a saint, an oriental or Victorian beauty or just an ordinary young woman. The pictorial fantasies of David Bailey are candidly erotic and dazzling with whimsical humour. Bailey always prepares and lays out his scenes in advance like a stage director, enhancing the suppleness of his model by using long focal lengths. Like other photographers of his own generation — Helmut Newton, Sarah Moon, Guy Bourdin, Deborah Turbeville and others — he is not after beautiful faces but personalities. His main interest is not fashion but interesting photography which in his opinion is doubly effective because it not only sells the product but also makes the spectator take a closer look at the picture. Bailey is one of those imaginative photographers who infuse fashion photography with fantasy, games, humour and sex, making it a less strictly utilitarian medium and more of a dreamworld. His pictures are in fact never concerned with the product, be it shoes, dresses or cosmetics but with the women who wear them. It has been this fine

distinction that has pushed Bailey to the top of world fashion photography today. Still, he seems somewhat annoyed: 'I've never been much interested in fashion, anyway. The English like to label everything and thus they like to think that if I've been working for *Vogue* for almost twenty years now, I must be a fashion photographer.'
He took up photography because he was an ardent bird-watcher, at school he even wanted to be an ornitologist. He drifted from job to job but the first one he got after his discharge from national service was sweeping the floors of a photographic studio. One day he went to see the well-known fashion photographer John French and was hired as one of his three assistants. After a year *Vogue* took notice of him and in this seemingly simple manner David Bailey became a fashion photographer. Talent? 'It's ninety per cent hard work and your personal philosophy, nine per cent luck and one per cent talent,' he admits honestly.
What of his method of work? He has three studio assistants, hiring extra help for larger projects. Whenever he shoots a film, he works with a staff of some thirty people. A hairstylist

and make-up artist must always be on call in the studio. Usually he works with five models of different ethnic origin. They are ready to fly in from Paris to New York or wherever they are if the pay is good. His equipment recalls that of a photojournalist relying on 35 mm cameras. The type? 'According to the job at hand. It's like automobiles. A Rolls is a magnificent car but it wouldn't help you much if you wanted to cross Africa by car. You'd rather take a Range Rover. But if you wanted to zoom really fast, you'd drive a Ferrari, right? The camera is but a tool, you simply select the correct one as you would a screwdriver.'

# Serge Lutens

/1942/

was only a short step to the stage, designing not only actors' make-up but even costumes and sets.

But his real meteoric rise came in 1968. Christian Dior was introducing a new line of cosmetics and asked Lutens to produce an original Dior Girl face. Ever since Lutens has been indispensable for the company image. Twice each year he creates a new cosmetic line which promotes a new fashion in make-up, a whole new image. During the spells between the collections he designs jewellery, thus when a new collection is

Serge Lutens was born in wartime Lille, France, and even as a young man he scandalized his native town by dressing completely in black, the deathly pale face fringed by long dark hair contrasting sharply with his clothes. He was regarded as strange and eccentric, especially when he became a hairstylist and started designing not only hair styles but also make-up for women. It was not long before he left his home town. At twenty he was in Paris, working as hairstylist and make-up artist for models in big fashion shows. His name soon became associated with Marc Bohan's creations and his top-line perfumes. He created a new style — a face style — supplementing the creations of the haute courturiers and establishing himself in the new profession of a 'visagist'. From here it

presented in Paris, Serge Lutens not only prepares his models completely by himself, making them up, dressing them and doing their hair but also designs their jewellery and the background for the shows.

Although Serge Lutens worked with top fashion photographers, he discovered that none was able to present the female face the way he wanted because every single photographer saw the models differently. He wanted to show his designs the way he wanted so had to take the camera into his own hands, becoming a professional photographer in the process.

His most interesting exhibition is entitled *Make-up Art.* During the mid 1970s it was exhibited in New York, Cologne, Moscow, London, Brussels, Milan, Oslo, Copenhagen, Amsterdam and Prague. Lutens' girl portraits are photographic paraphrases of various trends in modern painting. They are presented in two variants: the first is highly stylized and tries to resemble the individual styles of artists like Modigliani, Léger, Renoir, Seurat, Picasso, etc., while the second shows how the style in question can be used as an inspiration for practical everyday make-up.

'I create women,' says Lutens. 'No face is ugly. The face is an image and making it up is a holiday.' Thus, even though Serge Lutens uses a camera only to capture his art which would not last long without photography, he has made his personal mark on the art of fashion photography.

# Lucien Clergue

/1934/

Lucien Clergue was born in Arles, France, in the picturesque delta of the Rhône, known as the Camargue and famous for its beautiful white horses and as a place where Vincent van Gogh ended his tragic quest for colours radiant with the hot Mediterranean sun. Far from large cultural centres of the country, Lucien Clergue spent ten years selling wine and cheese but then after twenty years he made Arles the Cannes of photography. Photography helped him overcome the depressions he felt after the war which had ravaged his hometown, and after his mother died tragically. He photographed the miraculous world of shapes and structures of the Mediterranean landscape, the suspense of Provençal bull-fights as well as the dramatic encounters of bathers and the frothy surf. His precise, detailed vision became a romantic celebration of the unity of the human body and nature.

His meteoric rise as photographer and celebrity was undoubtedly boosted by his close friendship with many important people of French culture. At twenty he met Jean Renoir, the great French film director and son of the famous Impressionist painter, later he also met the poet, painter and playwright Jean Cocteau and Pablo Picasso, the genius of modern art. Countless other encounters followed, all motivated by his tireless efforts to make Arles one of the world's centres of photography. In the end his dream came true. Since the early 1970s famous photographers from all over the world have been coming to the photographic festival in Arles every year to meet colleagues, editors, critics, theorists and amateurs. In Arles lively discussions are held in exhibition rooms and at symposia, in the streets and during hikes and trips to the beautiful Camargue countryside, all unique workshops in which people share experience and learn from each other.

He was called a 'poet among photographers' by his friend Cocteau. He started photographing because he was fascinated by nature, its transformations and the variety of its structures and forms. However, even his

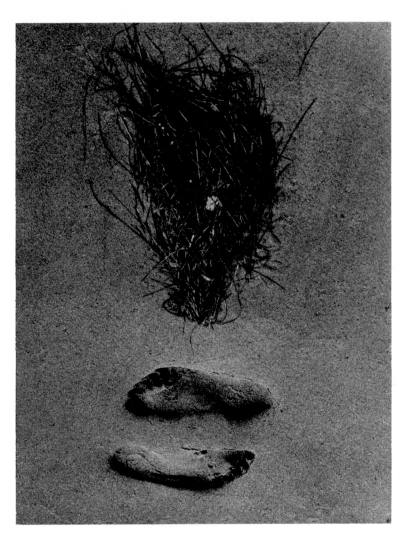

328   Nude, n. d.
*329*   From the cycle *Camargue,* 1939
*330*   From the cycle *Camargue,* 1940

beloved Camargue has not remained untouched by civilization and thus Lucien Clergue also records the marks man has left on the landscape. His pictures are no inimical rebuke to the despoiler of what should have remained untouched. On the contrary, Lucien Clergue always tries to see new poetry, he can often be harsh and ironic like so many of his contemporaries, but at heart he remains an irrepressible daydreamer and romantic, a poet. Lucien Clergue is not only a great photographer but also a teacher of photography and a tireless organizer even though he has now left the organization and management of the Arles festival to others. In recent years he has travelled, illustrated books and published his own photographic work. His photography has served as a basis for several ballet settings and his films have met with acclaim at major film festivals.

# X PHOTOGRAPHY AS MODERN LANGUAGE

Never before has man's visual perception been bombarded so heavily by visual imagery as today. Thousands of images appear in the daily press, thousands attack us from television and film screens, billboards, advertisements, packaging and almost everything we come into contact with: everyone seems to own a camera. Images and yet more images. Images have so flooded our lives that direct sensory perception of the world has been rapidly diminishing. Whether we want to or not, we view life through the prism of a ceaseless avalanche of images. Moreover, we have long learned to think of images as an active communication medium and thus often replace spoken or written communication by imagery. We no longer talk about the places we have been to, we show pictures instead: photographs, films, slides, picture postacards, brochures, even plane tickets, admission tickets and menus are now collected into more or less coherent presentations so that we become like the Dadaist artists who used to assemble their pictures from fragments of photographs. No wonder then that contemporary art draws on the specific potential of the new visual language, directly utilizing fragments of images from the 'street': shop windows, magazines and television screens. Reflecting reality, those images become the discordant symbols of our time: John F. Kennedy and a Coca Cola sign; Che Guevara and an anonymous buxom model; astronauts; the Pope blessing the crowds; the Statue of Liberty; and Charlie Chaplin smiling bitterly — our times *are* a collage.

As the poet Apollinaire once hurled the chaotic melange of his feelings and thoughts on to paper to give it a visible calligraphic order, so today's art strives for a new poetry which is not literature, or painting, or graphics, or photography, or sculpture, or any other traditional art discipline but merely life. It is a dream coming true, the embodiment of the aspirations of Czech Poetists of the 1920s who tore down the barriers between individual art disciplines to instate the rule of pure poetry whose matter would encompass everything, 'film and aviatics, radio, technical, optical and accoustical discoveries, sports, dance, circus and music-hall . . .', a poetry which would be a *modus vivendi*, a way of life.

The principle of associative montage and collage has become a natural responge of contemporary people to the complex world of today. These principles have become widely adopted not only in the visual arts but also in literature, music, theatre.

'A living work of art,' wrote Jan Mukařovský, an eminent Czech aesthetician and a major figure of the new aesthetics and theory of art of the 1920s and 1930s, 'always vaccilates between the past and the present aesthetic norms: the present . . . is always a violation of the past norm, a violation which is to become a legitimate usage or norm of the future . . . The aesthetic function . . . contributes to the determination how the individual and society relate to reality . . .' 'Quotations' from this reality with which today's artists invariably work, the 'photo-facts' taken directly from advertisements, magazines, film and television, indeed from the total environment, are not just fancy but have a profoundly logical social significance: they have become symbols of our era worshipping the image and the magic of reputation.

It is primarily photography that has been satisfying the contemporary need for document, the thirst for fact and its mass reproduction. It is photography that has become the integrator of artistic as well as non-artistic communication. Today, the traditional division of the arts into individual disciplines has become largely formal since the boundaries between the once 'pure' disciplines have grown indistinct. Today, painting is no longer just painting but shares a common ground with sculpture, photography and poetry while sculpture fuses with painting, photography, film and theatre; theatre and literature are now using methods long reserved to recordings of reality by purely technical means such as the camera or the microphone, and photography has incorporated intellectual stimuli which until recently were the supreme domain of literature.

In the early 1970s the fascination with 'photofacts' led to the establishment of a distinct trend in painting dubbed as photorealism, new realism or hyper-realism and based on so perfect a transposition of photography onto the canvas that it almost seems as if painters have turned the tables on photography and made it look imprecise and inexact. Photography and art in general has begun to move out of galleries and exhibition rooms into life. Art has rejected academic laurels and honours of officialdom. To be able to perceive such modern art, the spectator must participate actively in the creative process.

'The greatest potential source of photographic imagery is the mind,' says Leslie Krims, who produces pictures expressing his disgust with the conditions of our mechanized and mechanistic society and his fear of future developments. 'I can sit in my room and have the whole world inside my head,' states Duane Michals, whose photography involves us in his meditations and personal, intimate experience. 'I decided to analyze my own self so I started photographing myself,' states Linda Benedict-Jones, whose pictorial confession is entitled *On My Self*. The photography of these authors is but a vehicle helping the photographer to express his or her own feelings, experience and ideas.

Of major importance in today's creative photography is the relation between fiction and reality, this is why photographic pictures are carefully contrived, staged, directed and presented as situations or stories, often in whole series or cycles. Photography is no longer used as mere imagery but as a language or even a stream of consciousness. It is moving towards a theatre of life, of sorts, as proven by the figural compositions of erotic psychodrama of Jan Saudek of Czechoslovakia; absurd scenes by Leslie Krims of the United States; staged persiflages by Lorenzo Merlo in Italy; Henk Meyer and Paul de Nooijer of the Netherlands; and philosophical visions by Vilhelm Mikhailovski of Latvia. Each photograph is an independent, self-contained and richly plotted story. But contemporary photography is much more than that: the sensory experience of abstract time and the objective world can be expressed by a variety of means as shown by the imagery of Bernard Plossu of France and Ralph Gibson of the United States, or by the programmatic post-Surrealist 'interference in reality' of Charles Harbutt of the United States, whose reflections, insights and twisted speculation constitute his private dialogue with reality.

In the foreground of interest for contemporary photography is man's intellectual and emotional world and its reflection on himself and his society. The realm of this photography is a world of harsh reality and dream, visionary aspirations and destructive banalities, undying faith and debilitating frustrations, hope and disillusion, compassion and irony. It is also quite typical of this type of photography that its message is conveyed by series or sequences of images. In this respect photography is a medium which is gathering its still undiscovered potential and creating its own 'public images'. 'So far, photography has been giving us straight images of the world. But it is high time we started putting these images together to come up with a new interpretation of this world,' says the Polish photographer Zdisław Beksiński. Aware of the mosaic structure of our life experience expressed through a chaos of visual images, Beksiński and his colleagues have started producing images with several levels of meaning in which objective photographic facts constitute a personal vision of the world, a sort of personal reportage on one's own experience. Similarly, another Polish photographer, Andrzej Lachowicz, uses hundreds of offset-printed split-second reportage shots to compose a mosaic called *My Own World* while Leszek Szurkowski used details of landscapes, bodies or soil to produce his mosaic called *Penetrations*. Photography has gone beyond its traditional scope and is now becoming a composite feature of a modified reality. Its basic endeavour, typical for all contemporary art, is to break down the autonomy of the discipline and to fuse it with other spheres of artistic and non-artistic communication which would meet the needs of modern times. The photograph has now become rather a means of creation of a new poetry. In this respect a statement by John Szarkowski, curator of the Museum of Modern Art in New York, that 'one day great photographers might be those who have a totally different profession, say philosophy, physics, or agriculture', is indeed very illustrative of the present analytical and speculative trends in photography and of the integrating role of the medium as a universal language of modern civilization.

# Charles
# Harbutt

/1935/

sorrows, the difficulties of sustaining emotional relationships. The damage people do to each other and the delight they can and do give one another,' said Harbutt about his book *Travelog* which was published in 1974. The book, a deeply personal confession, represented a sharp turn in photographic thought and made Harbutt the founder of a modern school of American photography represented by authors who feel an urgent need for a dialogue with the world around them.

Charles Harbutt's photography resembles European Surrealism in the way it reflects the absurdity of a hypertrophic civilization as represented by the American way of life. His insights, reflections and haunting spectres created from ordinary

In the epilogue to his *Travelog*, Charles Harbutt says that he stopped writing because he was fed up with making things up. This was the time he began to be fascinated by 'photography's authenticity' and was driven by an urge to be 'at the scene' to photograph the event in the making. He began seeing photography as the only medium facilitating a direct dialogue with reality and thus he changed his career from a journalist and writer to that of a photographer.

Harbutt worked as a photojournalist at first but soon became dissatisfied again because his work had to reflect an editorial opinion which meant that it had to be unambiguous, and this he felt a restriction. He started searching for ways how to relate the complexity of our world, and to express reality through deeply personal experience, making the resulting images radiate tension. 'When you judge the quality of a photograph, you must always ask: "Is life really like this?"... My photographs are both real and surreal... They show the loneliness, alienation, and fears, the sexual

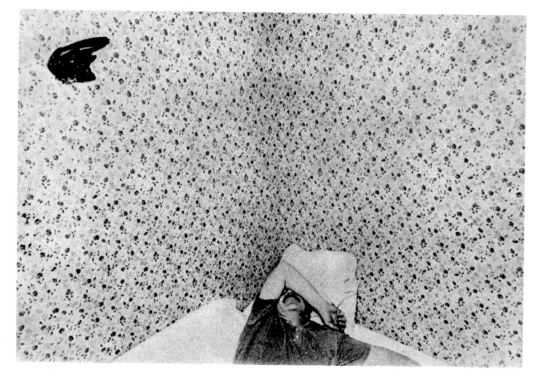

things are images whose vision penetrates under routinely perceived reality, lending it several visual planes, not least human disconsolation and confusion. The effect is achieved by unexpected juxtaposition, association or composition relying on unusual angles of view, lighting and other technical means. The resulting photographs transcend the bare reality, enriching it with a personal dimension of ambiguity, mystery and fantasy. Charles Harbutt was born in New Jersey. He studied philosophy and worked on the editorial staff of the *Jubilee* magazine. He took a deep interest in the agrarian question, desegregation and the peace movement. Before he realized that he could express himself best by photography, he used the medium only to accompany or illustrate his articles. In 1963 he joined Magnum Photos but even there he felt that photojournalism was not the perfect vehicle with which to express everything he felt. Eventually he arrived at a new photographic expression, a dialogue with reality which best reflects his life style and his thought.

*331—4* All selections from 1973—5

# Ralph Gibson

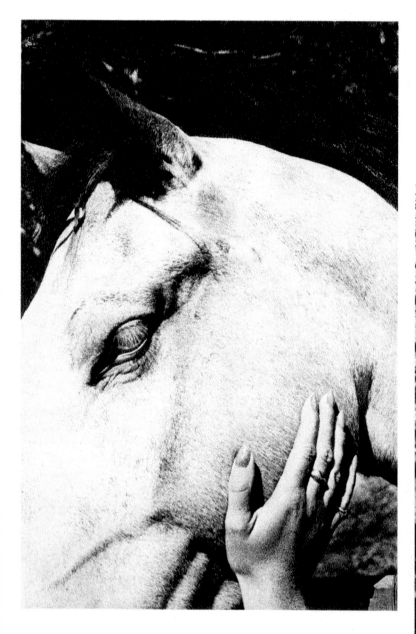

1966, the years spent working with Lange were his best asset. Before long he was working for the press but also producing advertising, fashion and technical documentation photography. The era of life photography was just at its peak and its humanist message had universal impact. He photographed all the things with which both the photographers and the spectators were concerned but soon he felt an urge to venture

'I used to be greatly interested in social problems. I believed that socially concerned photography was the noblest mission of the photographer.' Ralph Gibson's ideas are not surprising when we realize that he was assistant to Dorothea Lange, the legendary lady who produced with her camera a deeply emotional statement about the evils of our world. Thus, when he came to New York in

216

awareness of reality. For Ralph Gibson the visible world is merely a vehicle of meditation about the eternal variability of life. *Déjà vu, The Strip, The Somnabulist* and *Days at Sea* are typical titles of his books.

Ralph Gibson was born in Los Angeles and became an amateur photographer while serving in the US navy. In 1960 he started studying photography seriously at the San Francisco Art Institute, but soon dropped out and became assistant to Dorothea Lange, with whom he started photographing. His obstinate pursuit of things that interest him deeply has since been the major decisive factor in his life.

beyond the visible reality. He ceased to be excited by social problems or interested in commercial work, discarded Dorothea Lange's teachings and began searching for a more complex vision of the external world and the world within. He started performing a deep analysis of things around him. On the face of it they seemed to be the same as before yet they kept constantly changing, acquiring new dimensions and significance with each new experience. An instant just before a foot touches the ground; the moment before hands put glasses on the nose; the second the fingers gently touch the head of a horse; when a strand of blond hair sticks to the wet mouth; when a person makes an involuntary gesture to cover his or her face. Even totally static subjects like a row of buttons on a man's shirt, a brick wall, a glass of water on a table, a knotted necktie with a pin, all these objects acquire a new quality, a new uniqueness with each successive moment. The man wearing the shirt moves, the shadow of the drinking glass is shifted, the quality of the spectator's perception is changed. Although the flow of time is arrested by the image, we still feel it moving on. Ourselves and things around us in unspecified time and space, such are the subjects of most of Ralph Gibson's photographic meditations. Gibson never photographs things in their entirety, always in detail. His images are fragments of reality. It seems as if the author uses them to corroborate his own experience with reality, as if he were using them to express his admiration for reality. Before long Gibson found that individual pictures did not suffice to express his

intentions and started arranging them in series. He wanted to publish them as essays in book form but every publisher to whom he showed his dummies tried to change his concept. In the end Gibson established himself as his own publisher and Lustrum Books now publishes books created by himself and his friends. Despite the obstinacy — or perhaps because of it — Gibson has become one of the spokesmen for a generation of photographers whose work is governed by their own inner

He does not care in the least whether his art will make him a living. 'I can't do anything else but what I'm doing,' insists Ralph Gibson, a photographer whose intimately personal work has become a bestseller.

217

# Duane Michals

/1932/

'You don't have to travel across a half of the globe to photograph other people or extraordinary things. I can sit in my room and have the whole world inside my head.' Duane Michals is not interested in the outside world but rather in his own ideas, experience, meditation and dreams. In Michals' opinion, photography is justified only if it tells something new, if it relates something about the author himself. He is intrigued by everything which penetrates beyond the visible world and his photography absorbs the spectator in the mysterious realm of his own inner experience full of magical boxes, devils, split personalities and other surreal objects and events which so often occupy our subconscious.

The basic form of Michals' expression is a pictorial sequence, a series of images relating an extraordinary story, often accompanied by words included in the margins. The series are either a sort of literary pictorial story in which every successive image develops the story further, or involve methods resembling Surrealist vehicles, e.g. distorted images, or the use of the mirror-in-mirror or photograph-in-photograph principle, or may even constitute a series of pictures developing the dialogue in the comic strip style. Sometimes, however, Michals makes do with a single image, often banal at first sight, registering only the external appearance of a phenomenon but accompanied by a verbal expression of the author's experience or feeling in the margin. In such case the message is borne by the text while the image is delegated the corroborative function. Michals' pictures are intellectually preconceived and then meticulously arranged: the spirit slowly leaving the human body; an eerie box revealing its mystery; a woman stripping in front of a motionless man, the tension increasing as the man remains cool and impassive; constant metamorphoses of an Alice-in-Wonderland mirror until it is shattered. Michals also loves to make self-portraits, questioning his own identity. Using various disguises, he photographs himself as his own alter ego with whom he

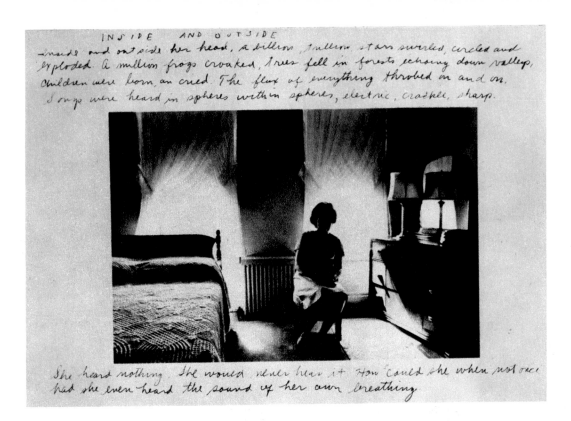

INSIDE AND OUTSIDE

*Inside and outside her head, a billion, trillion stars swirled, circled and exploded. A million frogs croaked, trees fell in forests echoing down valleys, children were born an cried. The flux of everything throbed on and on. Songs were heard in spheres within spheres, electric, crackle, sharp.*

*She heard nothing. She would never hear it. How could she when not once had she even heard the sound of her own breathing.*

can discuss himself. He often relies on montage, double exposure, reflection and personification of light to which he ascribes a philosophical significance.

Duane Michals was born in McKeesport, Pennsylvania. His grandparents came there from Slovakia at the end of the 19th century hoping to find work in the Pittsburgh steel industry. Just before he was born Duane's parents anglicized the Slovak Mihal to Michals. Duane himself was named after the son of the family where his mother worked as a domestic helper. Thus Michals' alter ego appearing under his Slovak name Mihal in his pictures is not a fiction but discloses something about his rootlessness and search for identity.

Duane Michals' childhood was not happy. He lived with his grandmother, his mother came home only on weekends and his father was constantly away on jobs. Duane used to spend long hours by himself, creating his own inner world completely independent of the things going on around him. He loved drawing castles, airplanes and comic strips, using paper which the neighbourhood baker used to wrap bread in. He dreamed of far-off lands where everything was different from home, and spent so much time in the local library poring over picture books that the librarian eventually started refusing to check them out for him. He was willing to pay any price to leave his native McKeesport; he first held a series of meaningless jobs, then his artistic talent helped him win a scholarship in a drawing contest and he started studying in Denver, Colorado. In 1958 he went on holiday

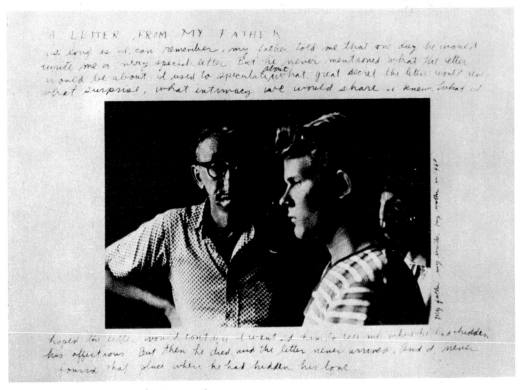

A LETTER FROM MY FATHER

*As long as I can remember, my father told me that one day he would write me a very special letter. But he never mentioned what the letter would be about. I used to speculate about what great secret the letter would reveal, what surprise, what intimacy we would share. I knew what I*

*hoped the letter would contain. I went for him to tell me where he had hidden his affections. But then he died and the letter never arrived. And I never found that place where he had hidden his love.*

to the Soviet Union. He took a camera borrowed from a friend and returned home with unusual portraits and a conviction that he was going to become a photographer. Today, he photographs fashion, advertisements and films and in his spare time investigates his private world: 'I use photography to help me explain my own experience to myself.'

# Leslie Krims

/1943/

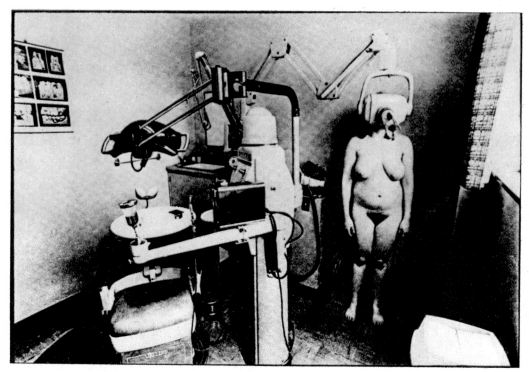

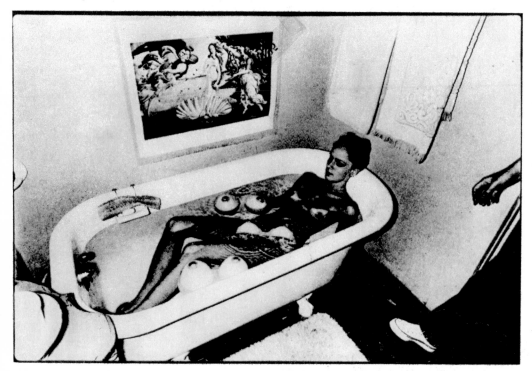

When the French monthly *Photo* printed a large portfolio of Leslie Krims' pictures in 1975, the public was shocked. The magazine was flooded with protest mail, many readers cancelled their subscriptions and a large French company stopped advertising in the magazine. Some people talked indignantly about sick extremism, others a bit pompously hailed the author as a Fellini or a Bergman of photography. The editors of *Photo* responded by polling aestheticians, art historians, sociologists, critics and even psychiatrists. As a result, Leslie Krims was proclaimed one of the greatest symbolists of our period. Krims was born in America in the first half of the 1940s, the right place and the right time to grow up in the post-war world of gadgetry and affluence. Everything around him felt unreal, unnatural, unacceptable and weird. His photographs are an exposé of a society where everything is mechanized and the individual is just a preprogrammed assembly with replaceable parts. This was the reason why Leslie Krims made shocking pictures like that of a dentist's X-ray apparatus eating up the head of a naked woman. This is the reason for his images of a naked body sown by a needle and suture, dentures, masks and diving suit helmets replacing the head. His pictures seem to tell us everything is artificial.

*Preparing Chicken Soup* is a series in which Krims used his own mother as a model. The chicken carcass cut up by a naked woman again elicits an irrepressible feeling that human beings have become senseless and emotionless, that human bodies are nothing but so much flesh, that we have all become just automatons. His photography is ironic, scathing and often even malicious but it is a result of a passionate protest against life becoming mechanized, against man's insensitivity to the environment and to himself. These pictures consciously tear down all taboos and shock in order not to be overlooked. Yet Leslie Krims' imagery is not a product of hatred or insanity but of anxiety and a strong sense of self-preservation, otherwise there would be no reason for Krims to capture a stiletto heel bearing down on the defenseless body of a white mouse. Why would he then want to photograph a mother whose body is totally covered by portraits of

her son? What Leslie Krims relates to us is a fear for humanity, a fear that human values are rapidly dying; his pictures reveal a desire for a reinstatement of ethics. Although Leslie Krim studies art and architecture and is a graduate of two New York universities, he remains a self-taught photographer. Immediately after graduation he was hired as assistant in photography at the Pratt Institute in Brooklyn and at the Rochester Institute of Technology. The uproar that his pictures caused, especially in conservative Europe, was quite considerable but has been since countered by positive reaction to his work. That the emotions provoked by Krims' work ran high is attested by an event in Memphis, Tennessee, where the child of a gallery custodian was kidnapped, the man refusing to release it unless the gallery reinstated four of Krims' photographs that had been taken down by the curators because they had been judged as potentially offensive. Needless to say, both the child and the photographs were returned where they belonged. *Diane Arbus Lives in Us* is the title of a series of four pictures in which Krims pays tribute to the photographer who has had the greatest influence on his work. 'Anything that comes to one's mind can be expressed photographically ... The greatest potential source of photographic imagery is the mind,' he says, adding: 'I'm no historian, I am a maker of history.'

# Bernard Plossu

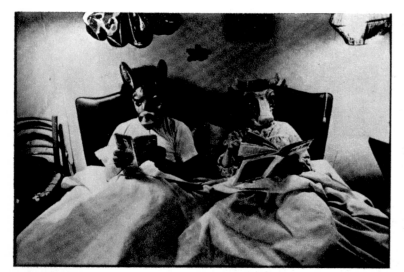 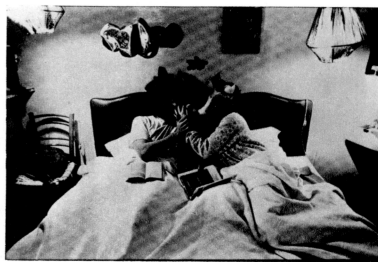

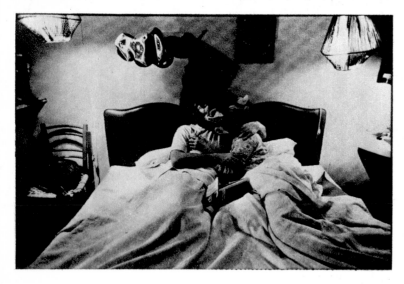 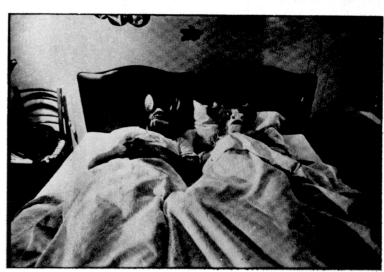

Bernard Plossu is one of those photographers who are fond of the most banal manifestations of ordinary life: a man in a hurry meeting another on a streetcorner, shaking his hand in passing, both rushing along; an empty room filled suddenly with the figure of a girl, the empty mirror reflecting the girl's face, the empty wall instantly enlivened by her silhouette, the presence of the human element lending space, the absence of such an element stripping things of all sense. In Plossu's pictures even time sometimes plays the main role: the passage of time conveyed by a shadow cast on a wall clock always showing the same time; or there are six identical pictures in which the only motion or dynamics are the titles representing the names of weekdays. At first sight these 'events' do not mean anything but when they are arranged into a series of four, six or more images, they become a speculation about the inherent laws of existence, human relationships, about the meaning and comicality of our lives and absurdity of things around us.

These sequences are not concerned with linear information but raise a question about the relevance of the human existence. 'Beautiful or aesthetic photography is no longer enough for me,' says Plossu, who tries to express his ideas by means of precisely arranged series of images as if he were grouping words into sentences or phrases. By writing out or spelling out his ideas he wants to make his spectators think and to experience the intimated events or phenomena. Some of his subjects are serious, other provoking, using fine humour to point out conventions and clichés of ordinary life, things that have become so 'normal' that we have long ceased

222

noticing them regardless of how comic or
absurd they may be. Plossu sometimes picks
seeming trivialities whose significance we
often overlook although they may be
important for us.

Plossu collected his images of everyday
banality into a book entitled *Surbanalisme*, the
title revealing that these 'super-banalities' go
beyond the mere banal as probes of our
subconscious.

Plossu did not arrive at his form of expression
by chance. It is a result of his experience as
a professional photographer. He was born in
South Vietnam but grew up in Paris, yet the
magnificent city of light disgusted him with its
incessant pursuit of status and money. He was
restless and so he went to Mexico where he
lived as a beach comber, subsisting on fish and
sharing the hard life of the native fishermen.
Then he was lucky enough to join a scientific
expedition as a photographer and went into
the depths of the tropical rain forests of the
Guatemalan frontier. After his return to Paris
he became totally absorbed by the magic of
photojournalism. His pictures from
Guatemala won him a reputation in
geographic exploration photography and
more expeditions soon followed to the
Mississippi, Ceylon and India.

After six years of travelling, producing scenic
pictures and manoeuvring in the maze of
intrigue and diplomacy of his profession he
began to feel tired of this itinerant life so he
gave up his well-paid job and started using
photography to meditate about the world and
himself. His meditations are smiling, sad,
humble and also ironic.

The 1970s were a great success for Plossu. His
magazine photography, books and exhibitions
were widely acclaimed and Bernard Plossu
was universally recognized as a major
representative of a generation of photographers who were using the medium to
convey their own feelings and experience,
a generation who offset their lost illusions by
an awareness that even the most banal things
of everyday life have a relevance for human
existence.

# Linda Benedict-Jones

'All those pictures are self-portraits. Naturally only in a broader sense of the word because not all show myself. I did them consciously at first. It was at a time when I was going through what until then had been the greatest crisis of my life, when my husband and I decided to separate...' This was how Linda Benedict-Jones once described the origins of her aptly titled cycle *On My Self*. The separation from her husband completely uprooted her life because until then she had lived in a traditional marriage in which the husband was the provider and the wife took care of the household. She had studied English and American literature, then followed her husband to Portugal where he trained the national basketball team and where she taught English. She did not have to worry in the least about making a living and could devote all her spare time to writing poetry and photography. Then she suddenly found herself alone and she turned to photography to express her anxiety, sorrow, loneliness and despair.

'I had been too much used to the idea I was a part of my husband and now I was unexpectedly faced with a number of problems: emotional, existential, professional... I decided to psychoanalyze myself. I wanted to think about myself and to understand myself and to find some solution.' Thus she started her private photographic diary, the diary of a woman feeling emptiness and an unfulfilled desire to live a normal life of a normal woman. It was the spring of 1975; in the summer, like so many other young photographers, she went to Arles in the south

224

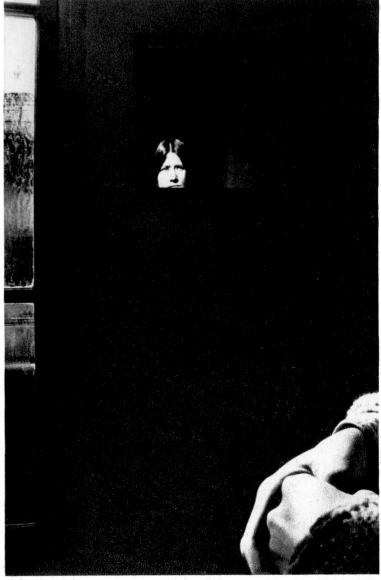

of France and enrolled in a photographic workshop conducted by Charles Harbutt. During discussions with Harbutt she showed him contact prints of her past work which included her self-portraits. For her they represented something she did for her own consolation, to fulfil her private need. She says she was afraid of what she had been doing, penetrating the most secret depths of her soul, but Harbutt managed to convince her that the pictures were of psychological and aesthetic value not only to herself but also to others. She returned to Paris and continued working on her cycle. Within a year her self-portraits were exhibited in the United States, Amsterdam and Milan. The Fiolet Gallery in Holland even published them as an exclusive portfolio.

The attraction of *On My Self* is probably a combination of the intimate expression of a woman's story and the fact that it is an original idea. A more philosophical reason for its success possibly lies in the photographs intimate lyricism, shocking with the candidness of Linda Benedict-Jones' photographic vision: a lonely figure walking down a deserted corridor; a naked female body crouching in the spiral of an endless staircase; two feet timidly peeking out of the bath into the emptiness of a bathroom; a shadow of a figure cast on the pavement: nobody before this had produced such a forthright, spontaneous and most intimate poetic self-confession. The exhibition was a testimony about the agony of her soul, about lonely wanderings through empty wastelands, about will for survival, independence of spirit and resolution to live rather than merely exist. The emotional profoundness and the perfect composition of her imagery have made Linda Benedict-Jones' private diary a remarkable work of subjective pictorial lyricism. Although the author intended to continue working in this intimate vein, the later cycles do not show the frankness of the emotional experience of *On My Self,* a work which will most probably remain a unique phenomenon in modern photography.

# Jan
# Saudek

/1935/

357    1980
358    1975
359    1980

Many things about Saudek are irritating or even provocative: his appearance, behaviour, manner of speech and dance-like walk, even his photography with its erotic highly exciting vision may provoke the same sentiments because Saudek seems in his photographs to reveal the female psychology and soul and to manipulate it easily. It seems as if Saudek constantly plays a theatrical character both in life and in his photography. His theatre is a make-believe world, a promised land of his vision where people can remain children, play games and act out their dreams, desires and sorrows; a country of gentle encounters and deep solitude; a realm devoid of indifference, inconsideration, nervousness or fear; a place where people still have time and zest to live fully without fear of being wounded by the great world outside. This is also one of the reasons why nothing is left to chance in his photography, why his images are invariably carefully staged and directed. Each of his photographs constitutes an intimate story and all together they are a passionate cry for close contact, for communication.

For all this manipulation Saudek's pictures look ordinary. The intellectual component is always in balance with an overpowering sensuality, the erudite is appropriately put down by earthiness. The spectator is almost willing to accept these stagings as reality. Saudek is fond of contrast which constitutes the cornerstone of the poetics of his imagery. A little girl in a womanly pose, a brazen teaser with a doll; the ripe body of a matron with a virginal gesture. In Saudek's pictures children behave like adults while adults retain something of their childhood. His imagery is a mixture of emotion and irony, sincerity and bizarre fantasy, reverence and irreverence. It is as if the author were afraid of being recognized, or even accused of being childishly sensitive. Thus he hides behind the camouflage of titilating contrasts to convey in code his message about humanity, its emotions and aspirations.

Saudek loves nudity but even this is a manifestation of his desire to relate the essential, 'what remains unchanged with time

226

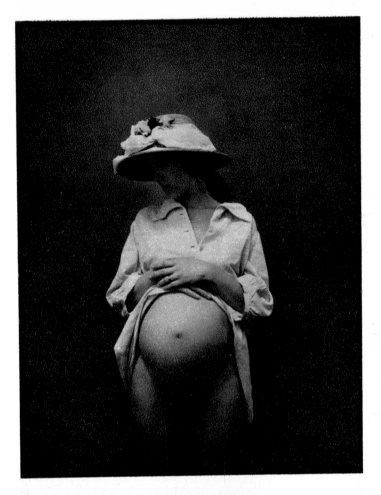

and place'. He says: 'Nudity is the most natural thing in the world; it makes men and women what they are, today as well as a century ago. I undress the woman to immortalize her.' For him, nudity rings with the promise of freedom. Costumes and sets, make-up, masks, props, marionettes, romantic hats, ballet slippers, parasols and other Saudekian paraphernalia are just vehicles of deliverance and release from inhibition. If you put on an unusual dress or surround yourself with sets, be they only walls with peeling paint; if you put on a clownish mask, you cease to be your old self and are free to become anybody you wish to be.

It is quite symptomatic that Saudek's photography was influenced by Steichen's *Family of Man* at first. In fact even today the main characters, actually the only characters of his 'theatre of life', are just the woman, the man and the child, the subjects, their relationship. Saudek's woman is always pressingly feminine, gentle and vivacious, sensual and maternal, wise and vain. But beautiful? 'Beauty is cheap; the real beauty lies in feminity,' says Saudek, who always manages to give un unconventional additional dimension of beauty to the image of any woman. On the other hand, his men do not have the plasticity of his women: they are unambiguous, sensed from the inner tension of the image rather than really depicted; they are what the author himself would like to be. Saudek is also haunted by childhood and adolescence, for these are the *leitmotifs* of his entire work. It is in childhood and adolescence that Saudek seeks security; security in an imaginary freedom but also in a return to full-bodied archetypal human relationships. This is why his photography is full of escapes and returns, solitude and encounters, security and mystery, comic pomp and timidity. His photography is an existential theatre, which is why it is so provocative.

# Lorenzo Merlo

/1935/

'We do not attempt to subdue reality. Quite the opposite is true: we are interested in making it more distinct, in making it more profound through inner experience and imagination,' Lorenzo Merlo wrote in the catalogue to the exhibition *Fantasy Photography in Europe* which he prepared for the 1976 International Festival of Photography in Arles, France. Three years later the collection, supplemented by work of Asian and American authors, appeared in book form, making Merlo a respected arbiter in things which concern that type of photography which conducts a dialogue between reality and imagination, consciousness, soul and spectator among familiar settings which blend strange elements to shock producing a mix of critique, irony,

good-humoured smile, sneer and dream. Merlo uses montage, solarization, tinting, grain, inversion and other technical vehicles of photography to create his artificial scenes representing modern life. He bases his work on the random association of mutually heterogeneous elements in a similar way to the work of the Surrealist painters. His thoroughly arranged montages purposely attempt to break down the boundary between reality and imagination and to fuse them into a single image: naked figures of men and women posing in city streets or at the edge of a desert; a motorcycle driving into a room where a girl sits on a chair; the reflection of a figure in a bathroom mirror is juxtaposed

228

with a painting installed in a window recess; a confusing labyrinth of reality and dreams. Merlo's philosophy is that of skepticism, an attitude produced by his experience of contemporary life. He wishes to believe in goodness, truth and beauty and therefore imagines them wherever he senses that discord, anxiety and horror have replaced the essential values of life. All events depicted in his pictorial scenes have an inherent potential of tragedy.

The authenticity of objects and ambiguity of their significance are in constant clash. Unlike Henk Meyer and Paul de Nooijer who are spiritually akin to Merlo — Meyer producing montages speculating about the limitations of contemporary existence and Nooijer being a witty satirist slashing with his ironic vision

— he relies mostly on absurd associations of utter banalities of ordinary life and on metaphysical scenes. His montages somewhat resemble the painting of Giorgio de Chirico or Paul Delvaux. In fact Merlo himself was originally a painter in the Surrealist vein. He was born in Turin, Italy, studied painting in San Francisco and photography in New York, married a Dutch girl and settled in Amsterdam. Faced with the northern placidity. his southern temperament found outlet in frenzied activity. Apart from photographing, Lorenzo Merlo organized exhibitions, edited photographic books and collected photographs. The Canon Gallery which he founded in Amsterdam has become a major centre of photography where authors from all over the world exhibit their work.

# Roman Cieslewicz

/1930/

Zoom
contre la pollution
de l'œil

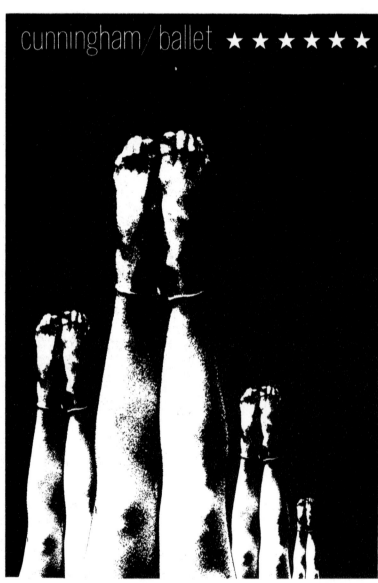

cunningham / ballet ★ ★ ★ ★ ★ ★

'Photography is now forever associated with civilization. It has become an integral part of civilization just as has electricity or the telephone. It has become a necessity of everyday life. It fascinates by its unlimited possibilities of utilization, its mass appeal, accuracy and the beauty of its authenticity.' This is no overstatement on Cieslewicz's part. Since the 1970s he has been one of the world's top graphic artists. His fame at least partially stems from the fact that his work has been principally based on photography.

Photography dominates his posters, book illustrations, advertising, typography and exhibition display designs. His is not a pure photography but one modified by other processes or methods of manipulation, be it special photographic techniques, various printing techniques or — and this is most important — by photomontage and collage. Cieslewicz's art is a blend of the imagination of a painter and verism of a photographer and his remarkable ability to fuse photomechanical processes with traditional

painting lends his work the charge of a dramatic conflict between reality and illusion: it is a Romanticism of the age of technology. His work appears mainly in magazines like *Opus International, Kitsch, Vogue* or *Elle* and his theatre and film poster art is characterized by great simplicity of expression and intellectual brevity. It is a representation of a part of modern civilization — the chaotic freakiness of the sideshow character of the world today. His art is aggressive and brash, leaving a lasting imprint in the spectator's mind even at first sight. In Cieslewicz's work photography is stripped of its narrative character and made more graphic in order to express the idea more succinetly.

Roman Cieslewicz was born in Lvov, Poland, studied at the Cracow Art Academy and came to Warsaw in 1955 to work as a graphic artist. During his studies in Paris, his art became attuned to the efforts of those artists who

james joyce
**bloomusalem**

teatr ateneum
warszawa

experimented with techniques obliterating boundaries between painting, graphics and photography. In Cieslewicz's own work photography has become an essential condition of all his art endeavour. He has travelled and exhibited all over the world and his posters and illustrations have won a number of prizes and awards and gained him professorship at the Académie des Beaux Arts in Paris.

Perhaps his greatest success so far has been

a series of symmetric serigraphies. The cycle, constituted by several scores of pictures, represents photographically registered figures and faces distorted by mirror effects. This was the technique used for the double images of his famous posters like *Zoom, Guernica* and *Bloomusalem*. Original photographs are here stripped of their realism in order to make the resulting unusual stylization, a sort of hint at a new realism, attract the spectator's attention more effectively than an image produced by

means of conventional techniques. Cieslewicz's colour collages are also famous; here photography is integrated into painting and vice versa. It is the shift of Cieslewicz's interest away from the stern simplicity of his photographic posters, mostly black-and-white and characterized by harsh contrasts, towards the fine filigree ornamentalism and colourful fantasy of meaning of his colour collage illustrations that serve as the best proof of what Cieslewicz sees as a logical continuation of the onetime efforts of the Surrealists to paint and draw photographically. 'Today, photography is an integral part of the work of the painter, graphic artist and even the sculptor. For me personally it constitutes a vehicle of imagination rather than a representation of reality. I think it is almost scandalous that the Nobel Prize committee has so far ignored its importance. The committee members must be very tired and sad gentlemen,' says Cieslewicz, one of the protagonists of photography's invasion into painting and graphics. You may perhaps ask whether he is basically a photographer or a graphic artist but in the context of his work such questions seem irrelevant.

# Vilhelm Mikhailovski

/1942/

Although Vilhelm Mikhailovski's official nationality makes him a Latvian, he is half German and half Russian by birth. Regardless of his ethnic background he remains a leading representative of modern Latvian photography because it is in its aesthetic vision and sensibility that the roots of his own expression lie. Like his friends Gunar Binde, Egons Spuris, Leon Balodis, Gunar Janaitis, Janis Kreitsberg and Janis Gleizds, he grew up in the Riga Photo Club and like them he started as an enthusiastic amateur. His success has been the result of the teamwork in the club where amiable competition among the

club members has always been a powerful stimulus for both collective and individual work.

Although his main interests remain reportage — stimulated by his work for the press — landscape and montage, his creative talent has found its greatest outlet in his pictorial visions, montages of complex composition provoking thought about the essential values of life. Mikhailovski's art makes these values more topical than ever, urging us to confront them with our life style. Mikhailovski's older pictorial structures had their philosophical premise in speculation about the mystery of

wider cycles whose titles aptly delimit the subjects of his speculation: *Origin, Sources, Reconstruction, Humanus, Sensibility, Renaissance*, etc. The scene of his symbolic imagery is the world in the widest sense of the word, man being its reflection.

Unlike other authors discussed in this chapter, Mikhailovski produces photography whose symbolics are less intimate and intensive because his art largely represents a philosophical position somewhat removed from the immediate everyday experience. Nevertheless, it is an art which provokes thought.

origins and preservation of life while his most recent work is characterized by speculation about the conflicts of the traditional way of life and the encroaching civilization.

In the late 1970s, Mikhailovski's photography constituted a sort of pictorial cosmology dealing with the problems of man's existence on our Earth and even with his potential cosmopolitan citizenship of the universe. Even here the technique of photomontage allowed him to enhance at will the expressivity of extatically suggestive compositions. The resulting vision, less ambiguous in meaning and more restrained in expression, does not deliver man from the troubles of ordinary existence nor does it strip everyday life of its human dimension but constitutes a dramatic message of what is trivial and insignificant in our daily routine compared with the hierarchy of limitless space.

Mikhailovski has replaced the mystery of natural life on the Earth by a vision of the mystery of the universe. However, he has not done so in order to express a desire for a greater justice of a higher, perfectly organized order but because by postulating the dialectical problems of the terrestrial existence within the wider, yet-to-be-discovered limits of space he celebrates the eternal continuity of life. His is a personal programme of associative photography conveying the sensibility and imagination of contemporary man regardless of his national origin.

Mikhailovski composes his photographs into

367  Reconstruction III, 1975—7
368  Passage, 1975—7
369  Humanus, 1975—7
370  Sources, 1975—7

233

# Leszek Szurkowski

/1949/

'An imaginary world of monstrous palms, fingers, feet and lips filling up extremely veristic pictures: this is no attempt on the part of the author to astonish the spectator with Brobdingnagianism but rather a result of a special method of analysis, a search for a way to grasp the limitations of photography as a medium and a mode of observation of reality.' So said Jerzy Olek, director of the Foto-Medium-Art Gallery in Wrocław, Poland, about Leszek Szurkowski's photography. The giant magnification of tiny items and traces left on things by human fingers, as well as the photographer's effort to venture beyond the framework of the photographic blow-up are a logical development of Szurkowski's earlier work on biological macrophotography.

Every day man is faced with an ever more complex reality which he must absorb *ad hoc,* and photography — like all modern art — has itself the necessity of finding an adequate expression for this variform phenomenon. The material is quite naturally sought both within the realm of art and without. Szurkowski's mosaic pictorial cycles are his favourite forms of expression in which photography functions as a means of cognitive insight in complex reality. This is why a number of his images bear the title *Penetration* in which the pictorial mosaic is a never-ending 'stream of ideas' making up a maze of meanings whose role is to provoke the spectator to an active participation. The approach, also typical for conceptual art in other media, obliterates *a priori* the one-time strict delimitations of boundaries between rational and aesthetic cognizance.

*371*   1975
*372*   1974
*373*   1976

Szurkowski's progressive magnification of objects with which he cunningly attempts to explain reality as if forcing us to press our eye against the eyepiece of a microscope is far removed from the systematic approach of a scholar. What Szurkowski is rather obviously looking for is a random rather than orderly character of cognition because although the exciting unexpected element may be attractive to the scholar, it is absolutely vital for the artist. 'What we must discover is not an expression of an imagination brimmimg with meanings but a possibility to enhance our sensibility because we must be able to absorb and utilize an ever-growing treasury of visual material,' he wrote in the catalogue to one of his exhibitions. Szurkowski's applied photography specializing in advertising is an example of a blend of the rational and emotional aspects of contemporary life. Like his fellow Polish experimenters in photography, Szurkowski is mainly interested in making his message open doors for us into an entirely new realm of meaning and symbols which attempt to meet the needs of mass communication today.

# Masaki Nakayama

/1945/

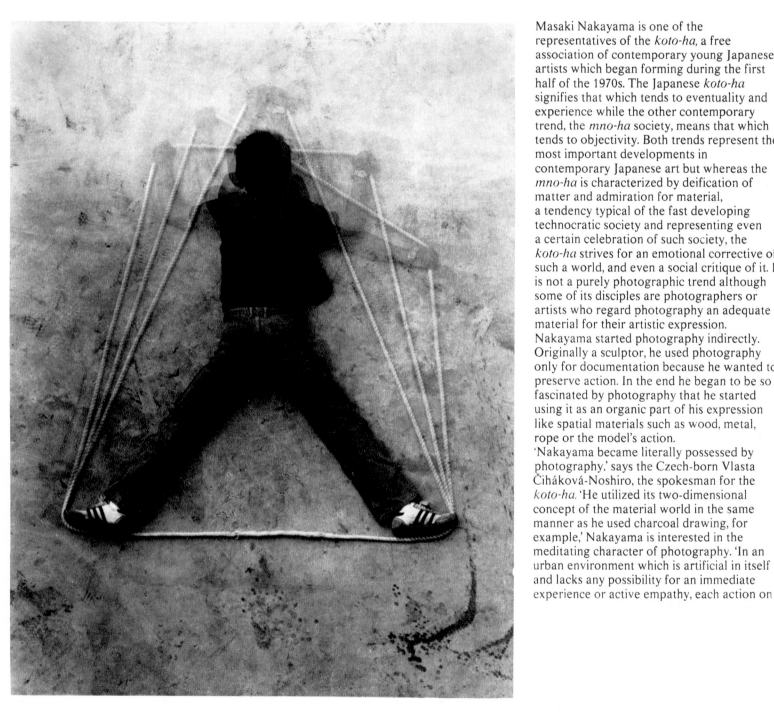

Masaki Nakayama is one of the representatives of the *koto-ha,* a free association of contemporary young Japanese artists which began forming during the first half of the 1970s. The Japanese *koto-ha* signifies that which tends to eventuality and experience while the other contemporary trend, the *mno-ha* society, means that which tends to objectivity. Both trends represent the most important developments in contemporary Japanese art but whereas the *mno-ha* is characterized by deification of matter and admiration for material, a tendency typical of the fast developing technocratic society and representing even a certain celebration of such society, the *koto-ha* strives for an emotional corrective of such a world, and even a social critique of it. It is not a purely photographic trend although some of its disciples are photographers or artists who regard photography an adequate material for their artistic expression. Nakayama started photography indirectly. Originally a sculptor, he used photography only for documentation because he wanted to preserve action. In the end he began to be so fascinated by photography that he started using it as an organic part of his expression like spatial materials such as wood, metal, rope or the model's action.

'Nakayama became literally possessed by photography,' says the Czech-born Vlasta Čiháková-Noshiro, the spokesman for the *koto-ha.* 'He utilized its two-dimensional concept of the material world in the same manner as he used charcoal drawing, for example,' Nakayama is interested in the meditating character of photography. 'In an urban environment which is artificial in itself and lacks any possibility for an immediate experience or active empathy, each action on

the part of the author acquires a great and socially deeply critical significance — notwithstanding the remarkable fact that the use of a material substance in a way materializes the immaterial image while the very existence of photography sort of dematerializes matter itself ... The correlation of reality and illusion, so important for humanity literally smothered daily by a never-ending flow of mediated information so that man ceases to have time or even be interested in corroborating them by his own experience, is a warning which should stir a new sensibility in humanity moulded purposely as a mere passive consumer of the products of its own activity. It should arouse speculation about the sense of a mechanical cycle of an ideally structured society of consumers, producers and producer-consumers.'
Ironically enough, even this tendency, just like any other activity provoking the established order, becomes commercial in the end.

# XI NEW PERSPECTIVES

At the time when J. N. Niepce first made sunlight imprint the image of his house at Gras into a layer of bitumen, hardly anybody realized that a new era in the history of human expression had begun. It was photography and its application to various fields of science and technology that first enabled man to see and understand the phenomena and structures of the invisible world. Invisible radiation penetrates solid and opaque materials and imprints the image on a photosensitive film. Thanks to photography we are now familiar with crystalline structures, the organization of atoms and their nuclei, the inner make-up of organisms as well as inorganic materials. Countless scientists and technicians all over the world employ photography daily in various fields and processes which remain unknown to the general public. Yet these applications of photography concern everyone whether they be in medical radiography, astronomy and meteorology, macrophotography, microphotography, infrared photography and many other fields of application which have helped make life what it is today. In using photography in their quest for knowledge researchers and technicians are often astonished not only by new scientific discoveries but also by the unparalleled beauty of the hitherto invisible world which in many cases equal art in their aesthetic appeal. The authors of these technical or utilitarian photographs usually remain anonymous because their objective is the pursuit of knowledge and their informative value prevails over their purely aesthetic quality, the photograph being merely a tool. In today's world of electronics, the individuality of the author is naturally subdued and empirical scientific and technical knowledge has become as strong an inspiration for contemporary man as aesthetic perception. Thus, although authors of technical photography are only rarely mentioned by name in the history of photography, technical photography has definitely left its imprint on the medium; after all, imagination is no longer the exclusive domain of the creative artist while objectivity has also become at home at the artist's studio. One of the founders of modern art, the sculptor Auguste Rodin, was among the first to realize that 'if we follow nature, we can achieve anything' and that 'a woman, a mountain or a horse are created according to the same principle'. Briefly, works of art are but a myriad of variations and permutations of the essential natural forms of our world.

In 1924 Paul Klee wrote: 'The comparatively simple act of looking through the microscope presents the eye with pictures which we should all declare fantastic and farfetched if we happened upon them by chance.' The affinity of these images to abstract art was formulated in 1931 when *The Illustrated London News* published a series of colour microphotographs by Albine Guillot and M. H. Ragot. The abstractionist artists of the period were fascinated by the world discovered by scholars under their microscopes and the Functionalists of the Bauhaus School of Design became obsessed with the potentials of expression unveiled by scientific and technical photography, discovering in it a new means of imagination and placing in it the hopes of the new age. Radiography, as macrophotography and microphotography, was also found to be an adequate means for the establishment of a new aesthetic imagery and judged to be as important for contemporary life as the strictly representational photographic record of social phenomena which was then finding a wide application in avant-garde architecture, journalism and political practice. Lubomír Linhart, one of the organizers of international exhibitions of social photography in the early 1930s in Prague, even proclaimed — in agreement with László Moholy-Nagy's eight kinds of photographic vision — that 'social photography considers scientific photography (i. e. radiography, microphotography, celestial photography, etc.) to be one of its constituents because scientific photography is aware of its social function and expands human knowledge and vision . . .' Thus galleries which had up to then tried to attract the public interest by artistic creations of amateur photographers and experimenting professionals now started exhibiting photographic magnifications from scientific research of a documentary and reportage character. The practice effectively changed the entire philosophy of photography, breaking down the barriers between artistic and scholarly creativity — it was the message rather than the individuality that became of primary importance. Photography ceased to be an aesthetic fetish and became aware of all its intrinsic values and objective functions. One of the important events that presented photography as an integrated communication system was the exhibition *A Century of Czech Photography* held in Prague in 1939 on the occasion of the hundredth anniversary of the announcement of the invention. Although almost half a century has already passed since this exhibition, the list of the individual sections suggests how complex was the role of photography at the time. Besides a retrospective exhibition summing up the past developments of the medium, there were also twelve special sections dealing with commercial photography, photography in journalism, amateur photography, photography in natural colours, photography in reproduction techniques, research in photography, photography in historical, natural and technical sciences, photogrammetry and aerial photography, photography in school education and photography in popular enlightenment, criminology, industry and trade. For many years all these fields of application (some of which have different names today while others may be classified differently) remained dominated by black-and-white photography. Even the 1939 Prague exhibition restricted colour photography to a single specialized section because colour photography was still quite rare. Photography in natural colours had to be first divorced from older colour or pigment processes. It was only the new Tri-pack film that enabled in 1936 the Kodak and Agfa companies to make the colour process more available. Although some 85 per cent of all camera owners in the world today use predominantly colour films, the mass use of the colour process has been the result of only relatively recent developments. Only since 1962 when Edwin H. Land introduced the Polacolor process for the Polaroid camera which produced colour prints in seconds has the development of colour photography both of the 'instant' and the more conventional forms really taken off and contributed to the aesthetic potential of photography as an art.

Colour photography had been a grail as early as the daguerreotypists who had searched in vain how to make the silvered plate produce a colour image. It had been only the invention of photographic papers that made possible the development of hand coloured prints. Then the Autochrome process invented by the brothers Lumière first showed that colour images could be produced photographically rather than by manual tinting.

Today, photography has reached another milestone in its development and entered the age of spatial, three-dimensional representation. At the beginning, first experiments with laser technology and holography might have seemed as trivial as the one-time experiments of Talbot, Niepce or Daguerre. Today, we know not only how to produce three-dimensional images but are able to do so in colour and have even gone beyond the mere representation of reality into the realm of artistic stylization.

The spiral of development has now completed yet another turn on its upward course to start a new cycle of artistic evolution. It is still difficult to tell what the material and intellectual conditions of the future will be like and what means photography will use to capture it. But research and development is accelerating and what previously took ages can now become a reality almost overnight. The story of photography then is still far from over.

# Forms
of Nature —
Ernst Haas

'However much we try to rebel against nature, we cannot escape being a part of it. The elements that surround us also flow through us; and the cycle of human life bears a close relationship to the span of the four seasons,' says Ernst Haas in the foreword to his book *The Creation,* his photographic tribute to nature. 'Worlds can be seen in many things, for in the smallest cells are reflections of the largest. And in photography through an interplay of scales, a whole universe within a universe can be revealed.' The book took Haas nearly two decades to finish (1952—70); it is divided into three inter-related sections: The Elements, The Seasons and The Creatures. To produce the book, Haas had photographed fire and water, air and earth, the rhythmical pattern of the seasons as well as the countless forms of life on land, in the air and under water and the fascinating forms of the plant kingdom. His large book is a remarkable celebration of birth and death, the endless variations of

natural forms, the eternal cycle of life. Haas was born in 1921. He studied medicine in his native Vienna but his artistic ambitions soon attracted him to photography. He had his first independent exhibition as early as 1947. Three years later *Life* printed twenty-four pages of his colour essay on New York which also included the first of his famous colour studies of the dynamics of motion. Since then Ernst Haas' photography has appeared regularly in picture magazines. For years he was a member of Magnum Photos. He has exhibited in the Museum of Modern Art and the Gallery of Modern Art in New York, at the Photokina World Photographic Expo in Cologne, Germany, and a number of other major exhibitions in various places all over the world. His colour photography became especially famous through two of his major books, *In America* and *The Creation,* genuine photographic bestsellers of the 1970s in which Haas revealed the potentials of colour expression in photography and outlined new directions of the development of colour photography aesthetics.

Haas works with the minimum of equipment. *The Creation* was photographed almost exclusively with Leica cameras, a few pictures taken with Pentax. During the last two years of work on his book, however, Haas preferred a Leicaflex. Even his lenses were quite ordinary: 21, 50, 90, 180 and 400 mm. For close-ups, a Micro-Nikkor 55 mm lens proved best. His colour close-ups of the plant kingdom are an especially instructive example of how an emphasis on the aesthetic function may transform an object of scientific research into an aesthetically effective visual creation. 'If I were asked to offer a piece of advice to amateur photographers,' he said in an interview, 'I'd tell them to learn to work with the minimum hardware because the more oblivious they become of the equipment, the better will they be able to concentrate on the subject and composition of the picture. The camera must be nothing but an extension of the photographer's eye.'

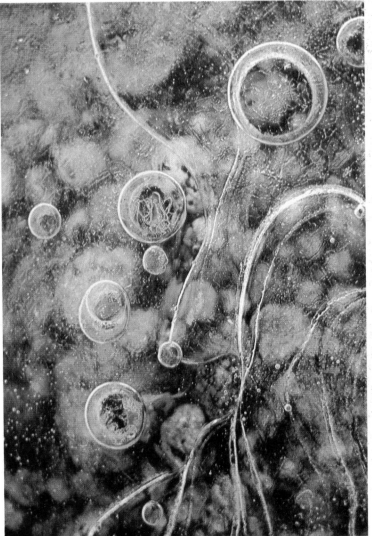

# The Mystery
of Life

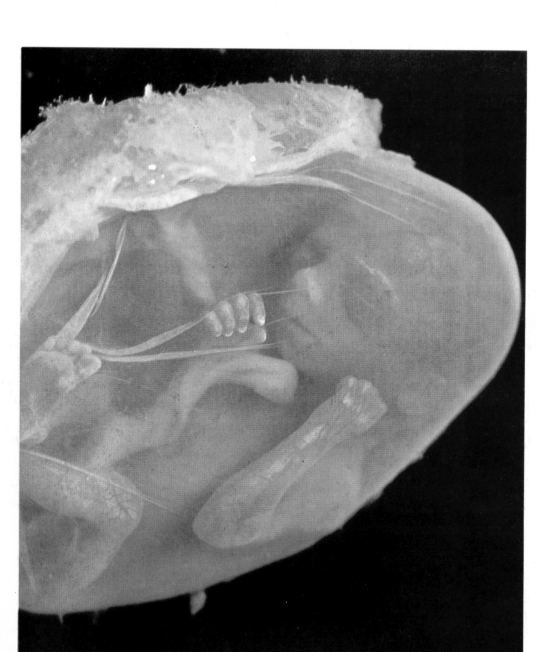

When, in 1965, the ecstatic world press printed photographs of a human embryo captured in various stages of its development inside the womb, the pictures were hailed as a major scientific breakthrough and a great photographic coup, for the pictures were not only revealing to the scientist but also breath-takingly beautiful. This extremely touching record of the start of human life had the force of a poetic simile. The pictures showed a fifteen-week embryo only fourteen centimetres long, yet it had recognizable human features: a beating heart, nerves and muscles. 'It is like the first look at the far side of the Moon,' said a leading Swedish gynaecologist.

It took the Swedish photographer Lennart Nilsson seven years of close cooperation with physicians, of photographing embryos and tissues earmarked for scientific research and solving technical problems associated with photographing living embryos inside the womb from the time of conception until birth. For his portrait of a living fifteen-week embryo Nilsson used a wide-angle (110°) lens and a special light source fixed to the end of a speculum. Five years later, in 1970, Nilsson managed another feat. This time his camera captured the instant of conception when a sperm gamete and an ovum embedded in the silky folds of tissue united their genetic material.

Nobody has done more with a camera to unveil the mysteries of the human body than Nilsson. Not only did he design and make special equipment required to photograph inside the body but his pictures, highly appreciated by scientists for their informative value, are also aesthetically appealing and reveal even a careful photographic composition. One of Nilsson's most remarkable pictures is an upside down image of a girl on the retina of a young man's eye. The picture was made by a special camera used by ophtalmologists for eye examination. Also famous is his picture of the human heart produced with a wide-angle lens as small as a grain of rice and placed in the surgically opened chest cavity some ten centimetres

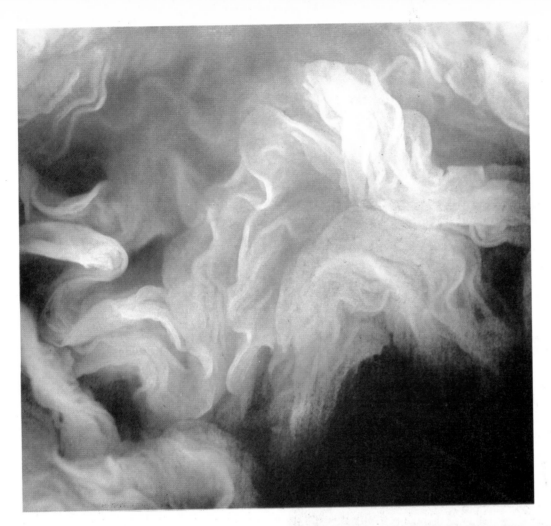

away from the pounding heart. Using two electronic flashes Nilsson made a fish eye shot of the naked beating heart and the surgery team. Another famous picture of his shows the blood pulsating in the aorta.

Then in 1982 another Swede, a physician named Per Sundström, published his pictures of the entire process of conception, extending the work of Lennart Nilsson. Sundström, however, used the standard laboratory technique, photographing the embryo outside the womb. Using a scanning electron microscope, he captured an ovum just delivered from the fallopian tube and the behaviour of the sperms at the moment of contact with the ovum ready to be fertilized. To make visible the movement of the tiny sperms which are a thousand times smaller than the ovum, he stained them gold. Although these purely scientific photographs lack the charm of Nilsson's unique rendition, inventiveness and taste, they are also aesthetically appealing, making the spectator an eywitness to the mysterious, fascinating processes of human reproduction.

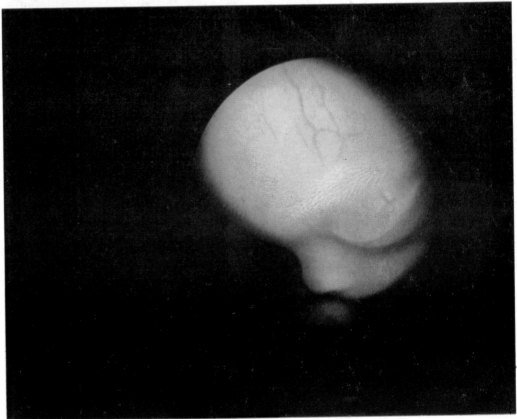

# Photography at Long Distance

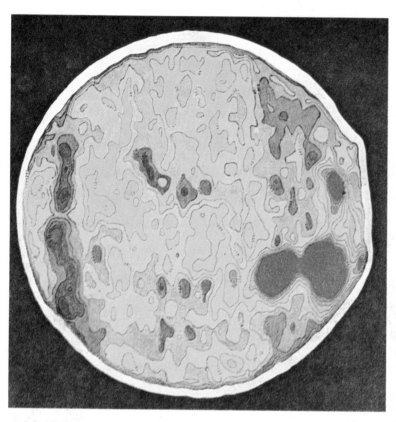

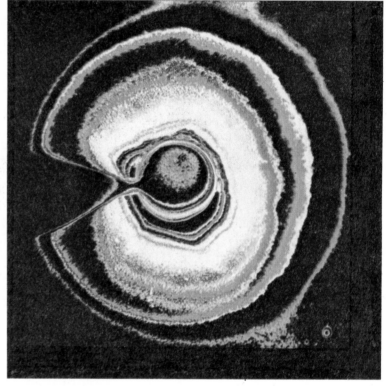

The press release was quite brief: 'On August 25, 1981, after four years of travelling through space and covering almost two billion kilometres, the Voyager 2 space probe came in contact with the second largest planet of our solar system, the fabled, mysterious and menacing Saturn.' With an astonishingly insignificant delay of 3.1 second outside schedule and a deviation of only 66 kilometres off course, the probe travelled for several scores of minutes above the planet, photographing its surface from the distance of 101,000 kilometres. The fascinating pictures of the colourful landscape transmitted back to Earth and supplemented by data obtained by Voyager 1 provided more information about the planet than several centuries of previous terrestrial astronomical observations.

What actually is long distance photography and what has it in common with space flight? Photography entered astronomy at the very moment of its birth through daguerreotypic pictures of the Moon which immediately captured the interest of the entire scientific community. Later a special camera, the astrograph, was designed for celestial photography. A prism with a low refraction angle placed in front of the lense of the astrograph transformed the spot-like image of the stars into a narrow band of their spectrum and photography together with photometry became an important part of astrophysics, a special branch of astronomy, which deals with the physical and chemical properties of stars, planets and interstellar matter.

Colour plays a special role in long distance photography. The wide range of colours, a source of an unusual aesthetic experience even for the layman, is produced by the colour filters of automatic cameras whose function is solely geared to the purposes of scientific research, for colour here helps resolution and identification. In the cascade of colour tones captured by photographs of Saturn, the trained eye of the scientist can recognize, for

photographs as a sort of thick lacework.
Just to make those ten thousand photographs
and to transmit them back to Earth was an
outstanding technical feat: at the velocity of
some 60,000 kilometres per hour it was as if
one took a plane from London to Milan and
tried to capture details of Paris street life on
the way!

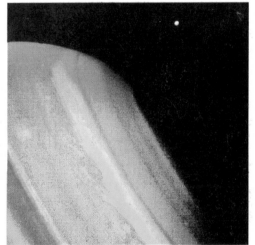

example, vapour clusters, orange cyclones and
the ultramarine blue ice-covered surface of
Enceladus, one of Saturn's ten satellites.
Photographs even revealed that one side of
the satellite Iapetus which is at least ten times
darker than Enceladus could signify the
presence of carbon whereas analytical
equipment on board of the space probe
registered only twenty per cent rock and
eighty per cent ice.
Cameras with high resolution also produced
detailed pictures of the clouds which
impenetrably veil the surface of the
mysterious planet. They corroborated other
data which showed that winds reached
velocities as high as 1,770 kilometres per hour
north of Saturn's equator, and storms formed
which are larger in area than Europe and Asia
put together. A comparison of Voyager 2
pictures with those transmitted by Voyager 1
a year earlier revealed that Saturn's climate
had changed during the period: there were
more storms and a higher cyclonic activity
was observed, but mysterious lightning, much
more powerful than any found on earth,
continued flashing over the surface as wildly
as before.
By photographing Saturn through the
individual rings, scientists obtained a clear
idea about the structure of them. As the planet
disappeared and emerged again in front of the
lenses of the space probe, each ring could be
measured and their size calculated to an
accuracy of 100 metres. Thousands of
necklaces of ice and rock, dark blue, brown or
gold in colour, round or oval in shape or in the
form of regular, irregular and strangely
knotted loops were recorded by the Voyager 2

# Space
# Photography

To the astronauts, the Earth must have seemed as a glistening oasis in the endless wastes of space. 'The Earth looks like a gemstone on dark velvet,' exclaimed Frank Borman during the Apollo 8 flight which helped prepare the way for the first historic landing of man on the Moon. During the six days spent orbiting the only satellite of the Earth, the Apollo 8 crew took many photographs of the Earth which, although intended for purely scientific purposes, were also breathtakingly beautiful.

Ever since the advent of space exploration, photography has played an increasingly important role in space. Whereas for instance Apollo 8 carried only two specially adapted Hasselblad Electric 500EL cameras, with a number of 70 mm casettes each for either 200 black-and-white or 60 colour pictures, Apollo 9 had seven cameras, four of which were mounted on a common controllable frame and precisely synchronized. The range of photographic equipment on the succeeding flights, i.e. Apollo 10 carrying the first lunar module which orbited the Moon, and the historic Apollo 11 mission during which the manned lunar module first landed on the Moon, was even greater. However, of the total number of hours which the Apollo 8 crew spent training for the mission, only eight were devoted to photography because since the first unmanned flights space photographic equipment has been fully automated. In fact even the first photographs of the far side of the Moon and the first close shots of the lunar surface were obtained by automatic equipment.

Photographs from space astonish us not only because we realize that they are a great technical feat but also because they are highly symbolic. When Apollo 9 was passing over America, Russell Schweickart photographed his friend David Scott as he stepped into space while two hundred and fifty kilometres below him the meanders of the Mississippi were clearly visible.

Ironically, unlike the camera, the special Hasselblad which has since achieved fame as a piece of 'lunar' equipment, Neil Armstrong, the first man to land and also to photograph on the Moon on July 20, 1969, has remained unknown as a photographer, although his photographs are indeed historic. 'It's a small step for man,' he said then, 'but a giant step for mankind,' a statement which certainly embraces photography.

# The Earth
# Seen from Above

There is hardly anybody who would not be interested to see the Earth from the bird's eye perspective. A lithograph by Honoré Daumier published in the *Boulevard* magazine in 1862 showed citizen Tournachon, better known as Nadar, who 'raised photography to the heights of art' when he ascended with his camera in a balloon and managed to take a picture of the Arc de Triomphe from the height of five hundred metres above the rooftops of Paris. However, the exhibition *Our Beautiful Earth* held in the NASA Museum in Washington, D.C., in 1979, ascribed the first aerial photograph to James Black who photographed Boston from a balloon in 1860. The idea of using aerial photography for topographical purposes is at least as old as Nadar's photograph of Paris in 1862. Today, man-made satellites, spacecraft and space shuttles perform aerial photography for military, economic and scientific purposes as envisioned once by the practically minded Nadar. Some of the aerial photography projects may be of a highly specialized character as attested for example by an Intercosmos satellite project which in 1981 photographed from the height of eight to nine hundred kilometres a part of Bulgaria where archeologists presumed the existence of a yet undiscovered complex of tombs of Thracians, the ancient inhabitants of the region. Indeed, under later cultural strata and products of natural changes of the landscape, the satellite discovered hitherto unknown burial grounds. Specially designed photographic equipment penetrated some 30 metres below the surface and recorded the presence of masonry, metal and other objects.

392 Cyclone above the Atlantic. A picture made by Cosmonauts P. Klimuk and V. Sevastyanov from the Salyut 4 spacecraft, from the height of 350 kilometres

393 The delta of the Ganges. A satellite photograph, 1977. Programmed colour coding distinguishing vegetation (red) from marshland (blue)

394 Georg Gerster: Artificial mound surrounding an oasis to protect the date palm, representing man's major interference with natural environment, Algeria, 1966

The application of aerial photography is very wide today and a number of fields largely depend on it, e.g. land survey, construction industry, forestry, geology, archaeology, agriculture, meteorology and climatology. Stereoscopic aerial photography can even be used to determine the height of trees in forested areas and thus to control and plan felling and the exploitation of timber. Aerial photography is invaluable for obtaining background information for land reclamation projects, assessment of soil quality and moisture, underground water reserves, etc. In New Guinea it was only aerial photography that made it possible to survey for oil some one hundred thousand square kilometres of swampy land.

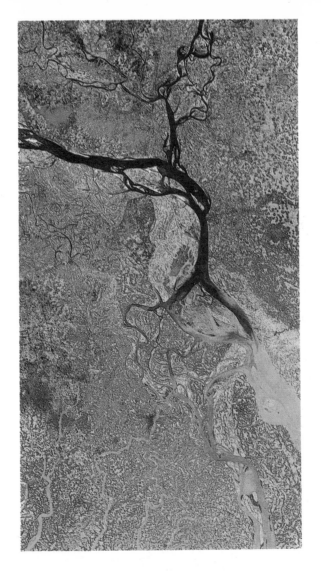

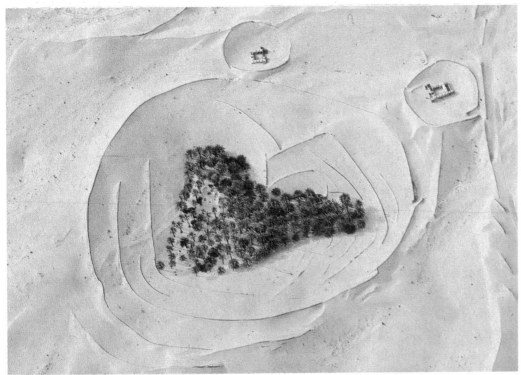

Especially important in this field is colour and infrared photography. Aerial infrared photography registers the heating economy of entire urban areas because the images unmistakably show different rates of heat radiation. It will also identify potential forest fires by sensing dangerous heat even before the flames appear. Aerial colour photography will register different shades of soil hue which reveal the moisture content.
Sometimes all these phenomena which are outside our ordinary experience may constitute an unexpected source of aesthetic appeal. When viewed from the bird's eye perspective, the Earth becomes more colourful, more interesting and beautiful. Details of descriptive character give way to general aesthetic impression transcending the image into a masterpiece of modern art in which the abstract features and structures of the remarkably coloured surface seem to have originated only in the vivid imagination of the artist.

# The Organization and Structure of Matter

facilitated our understanding of atomic structure.

Many important discoveries would not probably have taken place had it not been for photography because the camera can 'see' better than the human eye. Whereas the optical stimulation of the eye nerves must take a certain time and have a certain intensity to permit the image to be registered by the brain, photosensitive materials absorb optical signals until a latent image is produced. Thanks to this essential quality, photography when coupled with other special methods can record phenomena that are invisible to the eye. Apart from microphotography in which optical microscopes have been long replaced by extremely powerful scanning electron microscopes, and macrophotography facilitating detailed study by great magnification, science and technology has been successfully using invisible, especially infrared radiation — electromagnetic radiation beyond the red of the visible spectrum starting at 760 mm wavelength —

The first daguerreotypic microphotographs produced by coupling the camera lens to the microscope eyepiece appeared round 1840, i.e. very soon after the announcement of the invention of the daguerreotype process. European scientists of the period were very eager to apply the invention to natural sciences, especially physics and chemistry which had contributed most decisively to photography's invention.

Since the 1840s, photography has facilitated new methods of recording and registration such as polarography, spectrography and radiography. Some of the most essential contributions photography has made to science are the remarkable discoveries concerning the organization and structure of matter. Thanks to photographic methods, crystallographers and chemists have unveiled the mystery of crystal growth and the crystalline structure of various materials. Physicists owe to photography their understanding of the wavelength character of X-rays. Ever since the discovery of radioactivity photography has been widely used in the study of radiation and has

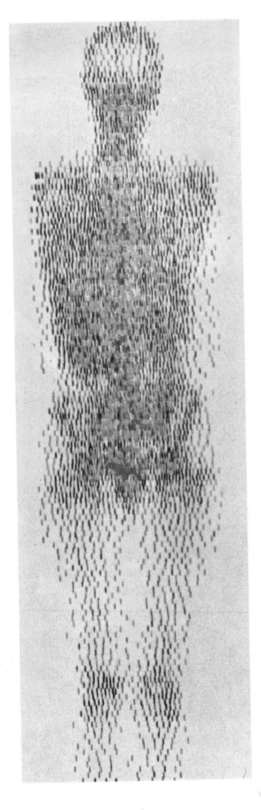

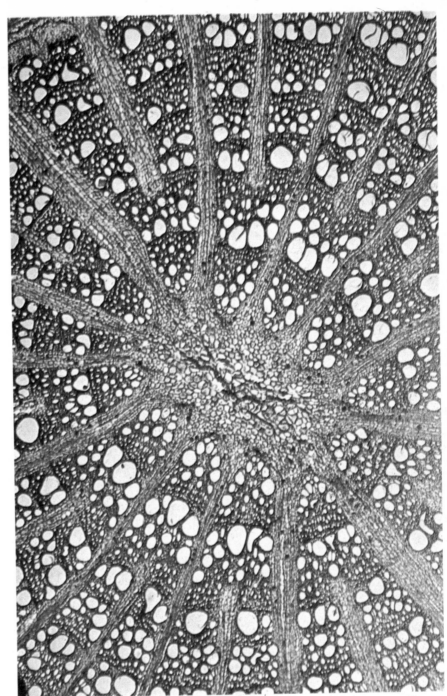

for photography. The infrared band is eleven times as wide as that of visible light and its penetration and reflection properties depend on the chemical composition of individual materials which facilitates not only 'seeing in the dark' but also permits the scientist to record photographically phenomena which cannot be seen in normal conditions. Then there is ultraviolet radiation which lies beyond the violet of the visible spectrum. When coupled with photography it may be utilized in a similar manner to infrared photography. Use is also made of fluorescence, i.e. cold visible light emitted by certain materials when exposed to ultraviolet radiation.

X-rays will penetrate various materials which are impenetrable to normal light, recording the internal structure on sensitized films or plates. Radioactive radiation of the alpha, beta and gamma type also produce a latent image on sensitized materials. Radiography is used mainly in medicine and defectoscopy, i.e. non-destructive testing of materials and products, which helps reveal hidden faults. The ways photography can be used in science and technology are numerous and in each application, photography not only provides man with invaluable information about the organization and structure of organic and inorganic matter but also yields beautiful imagery.

# Photography
# Controlling
# Time

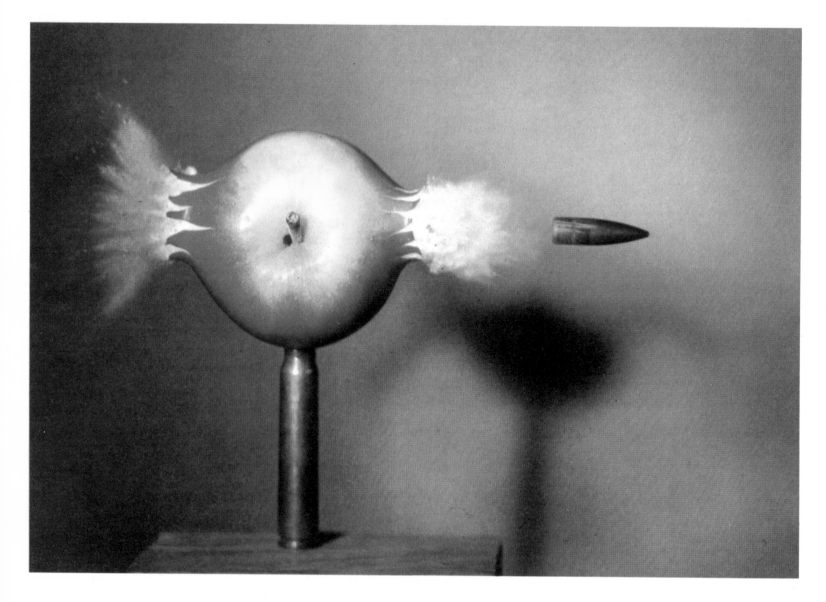

It was photography which first showed ballistics experts exactly what happens during the split second a bullet leaves a gun. Projectiles in flight travelling at a velocity exceeding that of sound were photographed successfully in 1884 when Ernst Mach, professor of physics at Prague University, used an electric spark as a stroboscope. The most difficult part of the project was how to synchronize light with the instant in which the projectile passed by the camera lens. This research done at the dawn of the science

eventually lead to the best known and most popular application of high speed photography — cinematography. The individual images (frames of the film strip) representing phases of the action are perceived as uninterrupted motion when projected continuously. The principle of cinematography utilizes the natural property of the human eye known as 'optical inertia'. It is this property, for instance, which makes a lit cigarette waved in the dark appear as a continuous streak of light and not as a series

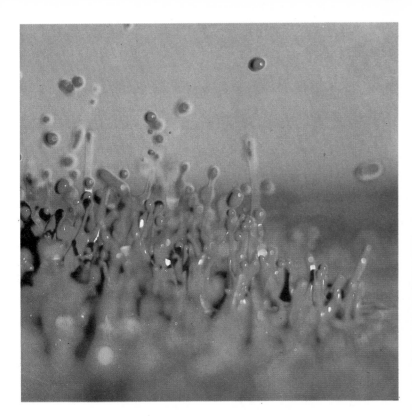

399 Harold E. Edgerton: Penetration of a bullet through an apple at a speed of 2,800 feet per second, 1964
400 Hans Peter Widmer: Eruption, 1961
401 Instant interference photograph of a shock impact wave breaking against a razorblade edge

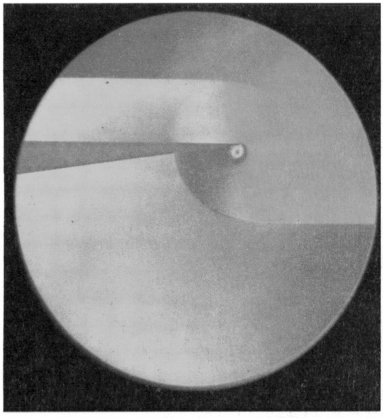

of glowing spots shifting their position. Most phenomena which are too fast or too slow to be perceived by the eye must be registered by high speed and time-lapse photography, respectively. High speed photography, using thousands of exposures per second in fact decomposes the motion to be recorded into the individual phases that appear as stills, while time-lapse photography registers the individual phases of development which in the instant of exposure seem stationary but when projected continuously will appear as uninterrupted motion although in reality the phenomenon observed may take hours, weeks or even months to be completed. The photographic or cinematographic camera in the hands of a researcher has thus become an important source of scientific information. Normally it is possible to 'freeze' motion by using exposures of one thousandth of a second which is the maximum speed attainable by mechanical shutters on most standard cameras. However, high speed photography requires much faster speeds which can be attained by special equipment. For instance, the famous series showing the splash of a drop of milk, made by Dr. Harold E. Edgerton of the Massachusetts Institute of Technology in 1938 used the speed of one six-thousanth of a second. Today sophisticated high speed photographic equipment can even make an exposure in one-billionth of a second. Advanced technology has made it possible for the scientist to study for example birds in flight in astonishing detail. Sport coaches can study athletes' style and performance; physicians can check on the performance of various bodily organs; technicians are able to inspect the operation of various machines and their assemblies and parts as well as record the most complex of experiments. Scientific photography can record things that seem incredible. For instance, there are photographs of the instant band interference of the shock wave reflection from the edge of a razorblade; of the air vortex between electrodes after a spark; of soap bubbles bursting, or of the behaviour of ink residues trapped in the intaglio matrix in rotogravure printing at the speed of nine metres per second.

Unlike regular exposure, high speed photography is always a much more perfect and photographically purer record of the observed phenomenon, a record much richer in detail which would otherwise remain indistinguishable to the eye. Beautiful composition and unexpected associations and accents produced at random often have a strong aesthetic appeal, especially when the photograph in question is in colour. Unlike the expert who uses the colour to read specific information from the picture, for the layman such a photograph is merely a revelation of hidden beauty.

# Images of the Future — Holography

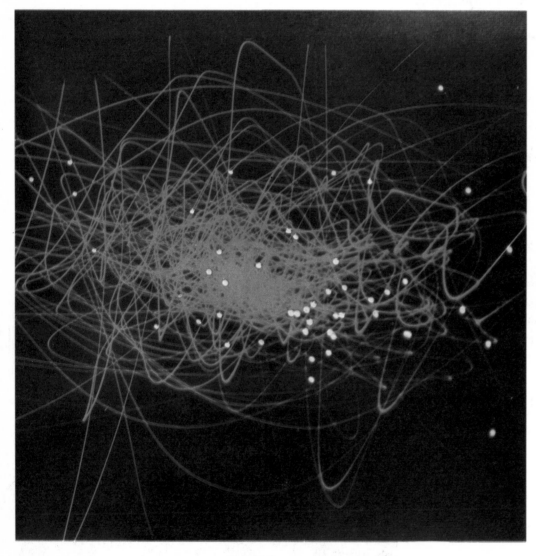

Now that man has mastered the art of colour photography, the next step is to produce three-dimensional images, the ultimate representation of reality. Holography, as the field of three-dimensional representation is known, still remains largely the domain of science but artists are already looking impatiently over the shoulder of the researchers. In fact the artist's contribution to the development of holography is not entirely insignificant. It was an artist named Garry Pethick who in the late 1960s discovered a method of cheap reproduction of holographic pictures so that it could become

widely available. Today, holography has ceased to be an exclusive affair restricted mainly to the exhibition room. Holograms are now becoming part of our everyday life. We have holograms on bank and credit cards, we can buy them as postcards and see them in use as promotional devices. Holograms have even ceased to be unique spatial exhibits dependent on special holographic equipment and projection to be viewed.

Holograms started in 1947 when Dennis Gabor, a Hungarian-born British researcher, stumbled upon the principle of holography when searching for better methods of

reproduction. However, the state of theoretical knowledge and technological knowhow at that time made the invention technically impracticable. It was only much later, in 1971, that Gabor's specific contribution was recognized by the Nobel Prize. At the presentation of the Prize, Dennis Gabor was the first model in history to sit for a holographic picture.

Earlier, in 1964, the Nobel Prize for physics was awarded jointly to A. M. Prokorov and N. Basov of the USSR and F. H. Townes of the United States who had independently of each other formulated the theoretical concepts of the utilization of lasers for holography. The principle was made practical the same year when two US scientists, Emmeth Leith and Yuris Upatnieks, demonstrated at the convention of the Optical Society of America the first transmission hologram of a three-dimensional object; the image was titled *Train and Bird*.

The world immediately became greatly interested in the use of laser technology for the new reproduction technique producing plastic colour images of reality. Besides holograms reconstructed by monochromatic light, there also appeared reflection holograms reconstructed by white light, a process invented by Y. N. Denisyuk of the Soviet Union. His excellent holograms of old paintings were demonstrated in the mid-70s at a symposium in Kiev.

Using pulse laser beams, outstanding results were achieved in 1966 by L. D. Siebert of the now defunct Conductron Corporation whose technology was also used for the holographic portrait of Dennis Gabor at the 1971 Nobel Prize awarding ceremony. Since then, better and better holograms of ever bigger and deeper objects have been made. At exhibitions both pictorial or focused holograms are exhibited where the hologram permeates the image and may be reconstructed by a flat white light source, and cylindrical holograms surrounding or enveloping the object.

Scientists have even developed holography of moving objects as well as full colour holography which now finds practical use in advertising, exhibition display, medicine and making of replicas of rare and valuable artefacts. Since the end of the 1960s there has been a number of schools, often led by

pioneers of holographic representation,
e.g. Lloyd Gross in San Francisco, which are
involved in the advancement of holography.
International shows are held, one of the best
at the International Center of Photography in
New York in 1975. Besides scientists who
exhibit results of their research and
development work, holography is now ever
more becoming the domain of artists who find
it a good means of expression both in
representational and abstract art.

# Bibliography

Aleksandrov, A.—Shaikhet, A.:
Arkadi Shaikhet, *Planeta, Moscow, 1973*
Diane Arbus, *Chêne, Paris, 1973*

Atget, Eugène:
Old France, *Gordon Fraser, London, 1982*

Bailey, David:
Trouble and Strife, *Thames and Hudson, London, 1980*

Ballhause, Walter:
Zwischen Weimar und Hitler, *Schimmer-Mossel, Cologne, 1980*

Benjamin, Walter:
Kleine Geschichte der Photographie, *Suhrkamp Verlag, Frankfurt, 1976*

Brandt, Bill:
Shadow of Light, *Gordon Fraser, London, 1978—81*
Nudes, *Gordon Fraser, London, 1978—81*
Portraits, *Gordon Fraser, London, 1978—81*

Brassaï:
The Secret Paris of 30's, *Thames and Hudson, London, 1976*

Capa, Cornell:
The Concerned Photographer, *Grossman, New York, 1972*

Cartier-Bresson, Henri: Photographer, *Thames and Hudson, London, 1980*

Coke, V. D.:
The Painter and the Photograph, *University of Mexico, 1972*

Contemporary Photographers, *Macmillan, London, 1982*

Czartoryska, Urszula:
Od pop-artu do sztuki konceptualnej *Wydawnictwo Artystyczne i Filmowe, Warsaw, 1973*

Dada 1916—1966, *Goethe Institut, Munich, 1969*

Danziger, James—Conrad, Barnaby:
Interview with Master Photographers, *Paddington Press, London, 1977*

Davidson, Bruce:
East 100th Street, *Harvard University, 1970*

Der Arbeiter-Fotograf, *Prometheus, Cologne, 1977*

Doherty, R. J.:
Sozialdokumentarische Photographie in den USA, *Bucher Verlag, Luzern, 1974*

Dyko, Lidiya:
Boris Kudoyarov, *Planeta, Moscow, 1975*

Eisenstaedt, Alfred:
The Eye of Eisenstaedt, *Thames and Hudson, London, 1966*

Erwitt, Elliott:
Photographs and Antiphotographs, *Thames and Hudson, London, 1972*

Fárová, Anna:
Henri Cartier-Bresson, *SNKLHU, Prague, 1958*
Werner Bischof, *SNKLHU, Prague, 1960*
André Kertész, *Odeon, Prague, 1966*
Robert Capa, *Odeon, Prague, 1973*
Fotograf František Drtikol, *Uměleckoprůmyslové muzeum, Prague, 1973*

Film und Foto der Zwanziger Jahre, *Hatje, Stuttgart, 1979*

Frank, Robert:
The Americans, *Aperture, New York, 1969*

Freund, Gisèle:
Photography and Society, *DRG, Boston, 1980*

Gernsheim, H. and A.:
Concise History of Photography, *Thames and Hudson, 1971*

Gibson, Ralph:
Déjà vu, *Lustrum Press, New York, 1973*

Gidal, Tim:
Deutschland — Beginn des Modernen Photojournalismus, *Bucher Verlag, Luzern, 1972*

Gräff, Werner:
Es kommt der neue Fotograf!, *Reckendorf Verlag, Berlin, 1929*

Harbutt, Charles:
Travelog, *Cambridge Press, 1974*

Haskins, Sam:
Cowboy Kate, *Prisma, Paris, 1968*
Cinq Filles, *Prisma, Paris, 1969*

Haus, Andreas:
Moholy-Nagy, *Chêne, Paris, 1979*

Herzfelde, Wieland:
Photomontages — John Heartfield, *Gordon Fraser, London, 1977*

Hiley, Michael:
Frank Sutcliffe, *Gordon Fraser, London, 1974*

Hill, Paul—Cooper, Thomas:
Dialogue with Photography, *Farrar, Straus and Giroux, New York, 1979*

Hunter, Peter:
Erich Salomon, *Aperture, New York, 1978*

Jammes, André:
William H. F. Talbot, *Bucher Verlag, Luzern, 1972*

Jeffrey, Ian:
Photography: A Concise History, *Thames and Hudson, London, 1981*

Jeníček, Jiří:
D. J. Růžička, *SNKLHU, Prague, 1959*

Kahmen, Volker:
La Photographie est-elle un art?, *Chêne, Paris, 1974*

Karginov, German:
Rodcsenko, *Corvina, Budapest, 1975*

Karmen, Roman:
Max Alpert, *Planeta, Moscow, 1974*

Karsh, Yousuf:
In Search of Greatness, *Knopf, New York, 1962*

Keim, Jean A.:
La Photographie et L'Homme, *Casterman, Paris, 1971*

Kelly, Wise:
The Photographer's Choice, *Addison House, Danbury, 1975*

Kertész, André:
Sixty Years of Photography, *Thames and Hudson, London, 1972*

Killip, Christopher:
Isle of Man, *Art Council of Great Britain, London, 1981*

Lartigue, Jacques-Henri:
Les Femmes, *Chêne, Paris, 1973*
Instant de ma Vie, *Chêne, Paris, 1979*
Les Autos, *Chêne, Paris, 1974*

Linhart Lubomír:
Sociální fotografie, *Levá fronta, Prague, 1934*
Josef Sudek, *SNKLHU, Prague, 1956*
Alexandr Rodčenko, *SNKLHU, Prague, 1964*
Jaromír Funke, *SNKLHU, Prague, 1960*

El Lisitzki, *VEB Verlag der Kunst, Dresden, 1980*

Lyons, Nathan:
Photographers on Photography, *Prentice Hall, New Jersey, 1966*

Man, Felix H.:
Neue Galerie, *Aaachen, 1978*

McCullin, Donald:
Hearts of Darkness, *Secker and Warburg, London, 1980*

McDonnel, Kevin:
Eadweard Muybridge, *Chène, Paris, 1972*

McLuhan, Marshall:
Das magischen Kanäle, *Fischer Verlag, Frankfurt, 1970*

Medium Fotografie, *Fotokinoverlag, Leipzig, 1980*

Mellor, David:
Germany — the New Photography, *Arts Council of Great Britain, London, 1978*

Duane Michals, *Alskog-Crowel, New York, 1973*

Lisette Model, *Aperture, New York, 1979*

Moholy-Nagy, László:
Malerei, Fotografie, Film, *A. Langen Verlag, Munich, 1927*

Morozov, Sergei:
Russkaya khudozhestvennaya fotografiya, *Iskusstvo, Moscow, 1955*
Sovetskaya khudozhestvennaya fotografiya, *Iskusstvo, Moscow, 1958*
Fotograf-khudozhnik Dmitriev, *Iskusstvo, Moscow, 1960*

Mrázková, Daniela—Remeš, Vladimír:
Fotografovali válku, *Odeon, Prague, 1975*
Die Sowjetunion zwischen den Kriegen, *Staling Verlag, Oldenburg, 1981*
Josef Sudek, *Fotokinoverlag, Leipzig, 1982*
Tschechoslowakische Fotografen 1900—1940, *Fotokinoverlag, Leipzig, 1983*
The Russian War, *Dutton, N. H., 1977*

Mukařovský, Jan:
Studie z estetiky, *Odeon, Prague, 1966*

Newhall, Beaumont:
The History of Photography, *Secker and Warburg, London, 1972*

Newman, Arnold:
One Mind's Eye, *Secker and Warburg, London, 1974*

Parekh, Kishor:
Bangladesh, a Brutal Birth, *Image Photo-Service, Hong Kong, 1972*

Plossu, Bernard:
Surbanalisme, *Chène, Paris, 1972*

Pollack, Peter:
The Picture History of Photography, *Harry N. Abrams, New York, 1958*

Man Ray — Photographs, *Dover Publications, New York, 1979*

Renger-Patzsch, Albert:
Die Welt ist schön, *K. Wolff Verlag, Munich, 1928*

Riis, Jacob A.:
How the Other Half Lives, *Dover Books, New York, 1980*

Rinke, Erich:
Fotografie im Klassenkampf, *Fotokinoverlag, Leipzig, 1980*

Rodtschenko, *Wienand, Cologne, 1978*

Roh, Franz:
Fotoauge, *Wasmuth Verlag, Tübingen, 1977*

Řezáč, Jan:
Sudek, *Artia, Prague 1964*

David Seymour, *Grossman, New York, 1974*

Skopec Rudolf:
Dějiny fotografie v obrazech, *Orbis, Prague, 1963*
Nadar, *SNKLHU, Prague, 1960*

Smith, W. E. and A:
Minamata, *Alskog-Sensorium, New York, 1975*

Sontag, Susan:
On Photography, *Penguin Books, London, 1977*

Steinorth, Karl:
Photographen der 20er Jahre, *Laterna Magica, Munich, 1980*

Alfred Stieglitz, *New York Graphic Society, 1905*

Paul Strand, *Aperture, New York, 1971*

Szarkowski, John:
Ansel Adams, *Chène, Paris, 1977*
Looking at Photographs, *Idea Books, Paris, 1976*

Tausk, Peter:
Die Geschichte der Fotografie im 20. Jahrhundert, *Du Mont, Cologne, 1977*

Teige Karel:
Výbor z díla, *Čs. spisovatel, Prague, 1969*

Time-Life Library of Photography, *Amsterdam, 1972*
Documentary Photography
Great Photographers
The Great Themes
Photojournalism
Photography as a Tool
Frontiers of Photography

Volkov-Lannit:
Istoriya pishetsya obektivom, *Planeta, Moscow, 1971*
Boris Ignatovich, *Planeta, Moscow, 1973*

Ward, Patrick:
Wish You Were Here, *Gordon Fraser, London, 1977*

Weegee:
An Autobiography, *Ziff-Davis, New York, 1961*

Weston, Edward:
Daybooks, *Horizon Press, New York, 1966*

Willmann, Heinz:
Geschichte der AIZ, *Dietz Verlag, Berlin, 1974*

Witkin, Lee—London, Barbara:
The Photograph Collector's Guide, *Secker and Warburg, London, 1979*

PERIODICALS:
Camera, *Bucher Verlag, Luzern*
Revue fotografie, *Orbis, Prague*
Creative Camera, *Art Council of Great Britain, London*
European Photography, *Göttingen*

# Photographic Credits

Abbas: *Abbas;* Alpert, Max: *Max Alpert;* Adams.
Ansel: *Ansel Adams;* Arbus, Diane: *Diane Arbus
Estate, New York;* Atget, Eugène: *Museum of
Modern Art, New York;* Bailey, David: *Camera Eye,
Ltd., London;* Ballhause, Walter: *Walter Ballhause;*
Baltermants, Dmitri: *Dmitri Baltermants;* Beaton,
Cecil: *Sotheby and Co., London;* Benedict-Jones,
Linda: *Linda Benedict-Jones;* Bischof, Werner:
*Rosellina Burri-Bischof;* Blossfeldt, Karl: *Galerie
Wilde, Cologne;* Blüh, Irene: *Irene Blüh;* Brandt, Bill:
*Bill Brandt;* Brassaï: *Brassaï;* Cameron, Julia
Margaret: *Victoria and Albert Museum, London;*
Capa, Robert: *Cornell Capa;* Cartier-Bresson, Henri:
*Henri Cartier-Bresson;* Cieslewicz, Roman: *Roman
Cieslewicz;* Clergue, Lucien: *Lucien Clergue;*
Daguerre, Louis Jacques Mandé: *Société Française
de Photographie, Paris;* Davidson, Bruce: *Magnum
Photos, New York;* Demachy, Robert: *Bibliothèque
Nationale, Paris;* Dmitriev, Maxim: *Sergei Morozov;*
Drtikol, František: *Ervína Boková;* Eisenstaedt,
Alfred: *Life, New York;* Emerson, Peter Henry:
*International Museum of Photography, George
Eastman House, Rochester;* Erwitt, Elliott: *Elliott
Erwitt;* Evans, Walker: *Library of Congress,
Washington, D. C.;* Fenton, Roger: *Royal
Photographic Society of Great Britain, London;*
Franck, Martine: *Martine Franck;* Frank, Robert:
*Robert Frank;* Funke, Jaromír: *Anna Funkeová;*
Garanin, Anatoli: *Anatoli Garanin;* Gibson, Ralph:
*Ralph Gibson;* Gnevashev, Igor: *Igor Gnevashev;*
Gnisyuk, Mikola: *Mikola Gnisyuk;* Haas, Ernst:
*Ernst Haas;* Harbutt, Charles: *Charles Harbutt;*
Haskins, Sam: *Sam Haskins;* Heartfield, John: *John
Heartfield Archiv, Deutsche Akademie der Künste,
Berlin;* Hine, Lewis Wickes: *International Museum
of Photography, George Eastman House, Rochester;*
Ignatovich, Boris: *Boris Ignatovich;* Karsh, Yousuf:
*Yousuf Karsh;* Kertész, André: *André Kertész;*
Killip, Chris: *Chris Killip;* Krims, Leslie: *Leslie
Krims;* Kudoyarov, Boris: *Boris Kudoyarov;* Lange,
Dorothea: *Oakland Museum, Oakland, California;*
Lartigue Jacques-Henri: *Association des Amis de
Jacques-Henri Lartigue, Paris;* Lisitzki, El:
*Bauhaus-Archiv, Berlin;* Luskačová, Markéta:
*Markéta Luskačová;* Lutens, Serge: *Christian Dior,
Paris;* Macijauskas, Aleksandras: *Aleksandras
Macijauskas;* Meiselas, Susan: *Susan Meiselas;* Man.
Felix H.: *Felix H. Man;* McCullin, Donald: *Donald
McCullin;* Merlo, Lorenzo: *Lorenzo Merlo;* Michals,
Duane: *Duane Michals;* Mikhailovski, Vilhelm:
*Vilhelm Mikhailovski;* Model, Lisette: *Lisette Model;*
Moholy-Nagy, László: *Bauhaus Archiv, Berlin;*
Mucha, Alphonse: *Jiří Mucha;* Munkácsi, Martin:
*Joan Munkacsi Hammes, New York;* Muybridge,
Eadweard: *International Museum of Photography,
George Eastman House, Rochester;* Nadar:
*Bibliothèque Nationale, Paris;* Nakayama, Masaki:
*Vlasta Čiháková;* Nappelbaum, Moisei: *Moisei
Nappelbaum;* Newman, Arnold: *Arnold Newman;*

Niepce, Joseph Nicéphore: *Gernsheim Collection,
University of Texas, Austin;* Page, Tim: *Tim Page;*
Parekh, Kishor: *Kishor Parekh;* Plossu, Bernard:
*Bernard Plossu;* Ray, Man: *Juliet Man Ray;*
Rejlander, Oscar Gustave: *International Museum of
Photography, George Eastman House, Rochester;*
Renger-Patzsch, Albert: *Albert Renger-Patzsch
Archiv, Galerie Wilde, Cologne;* Riis, Jacob A.:
*Dover Publications, New York;* Robinson, Henry
Peach: *Royal Photographic Society of Great Britain;*
Rodchenko, Alexander: *Varvara Rodchenko;*
Rössler, Jaroslav: *Uměleckoprůmyslové muzeum,
Prague;* Růžička, Drahomír Josef: *Jan Lauschmann;*
Salomon, Erich: *Berlinische Galerie, Berlin;* Sander,
August: *Berlinische Galerie, Berlin;* Saudek, Jan: *Jan
Saudek;* Seymour-Chim, David: *Magnun Photos,
Paris;* Shaikhet, Arkadi: *Anatoli Shaikhet;*
Shterenberg, Abram: *Abram Shterenberg;* Smith,
William Eugene: *Black Star Publ. Co., New York;*
Steichen, Edward: *Museum of Modern Art, New
York;* Stieglitz, Alfred: *National Gallery of Art,
Washington, D. C.;* Strand, Paul: *Aperture, New
York;* Štyrský, Jindřich: *Uměleckoprůmyslové
muzeum, Prague;* Sudek Josef: *Uměleckoprůmyslové.
muzeum, Prague;* Sutcliffe, Frank Meadow: *Sutcliffe
Gallery, Whitby;* Sutkus, Antanas: *Antanas Sutkus;*
Szurkowski, Leszek: *Leszek Szurkowski;* Talbot,
William Henry Fox: *International Museum of
Photography, George Eastman House, Rochester;*
Teige, Karel: *Památník národního písemnictví,
Prague;* Trakhman, Mikhail: *Mikhail Trakhman;*
Umbo: *Rudolf Kicken Galerie, Cologne;* Ward,
Patrick: *Patrick Ward;* Weber, Wolfgang: *Kodak
AG, Stuttgart;* Weegee: *Marcuse Pfeifer Gallery,
New York;* Weston, Edward: *Arizona Board of
Regents, Center for Creative Photography, Tuscon;*
Zelma, Georgi: *Georgi Zelma.*

# Index

# Acknowledgements

I have been lucky to become acquainted with numerous photographers from all parts of the globe. Some I have met personally, others I know from correspondence, phone calls, publications and exhibitions. Many have become my close friends. I have also been lucky to meet many other people involved in photography: editors, historians, publicists, theorists, publishers, collectors and curators, many of whom I am proud to call my friends as well. Without all these people, this story of photography would have never been written because in a sense they all helped me write it. Some of them are mentioned by name in this book, but most are not. Still, I remain greatly indebted to all who have contributed to the photographic image of modern man and his world.

I should also like to express my gratitude to photographers included in this book, or their families, for invaluable information, picture material and the kind permission to use it. For the same reason, my thanks go also to the following museums, galleries and other institutions:

Aperture, New York
Arizona Board of Regents, Center for Creative Photography, Tucson
Association des Amis de Jacques-Henri Lartigue, Paris
Bauhaus-Archiv, Berlin
Berlinische Galerie, Berlin
Bibliothèque Nationale, Paris
Black Star Publications Co., New York
Camera Eye Limited, London
Christian Dior, Paris
Deutsche Akademie der Künste, Berlin
Dover Publications, New York
Galerie Wilde, Cologne
International Center of Photography, New York
International Museum of Photography at George Eastman House, Rochester
Kodak AG, Stuttgart
Library of Congress, Washington, D. C.
Life, New York
Litovskoe obshchestvo khudozhestvennoi fotografii, Vilnius
Magnum Photos, New York and Paris
Marcuse Pfeifer Gallery, New York
Museum of Modern Art, New York
National Gallery of Art, Washington, D. C.
Oakland Museum, Oakland, California
Památník národního písemnictví, Prague
Royal Photographic Society of Great Britain, London
Rudolf Kicken Galerie, Cologne
Société Française de Photographie, Paris
Sotheby and Co., London
Sutcliffe Gallery, Whitby
Uměleckoprůmyslové muzeum, Prague
University of Texas, Austin
Victoria and Albert Museum, London

My special thanks must go namely to the following people for their invaluable help: Cornell Capa, Prof. Ludvík Baran, Prof. Fritz Gruber, Mark Haworth-Booth, Rudolf Kicken, Aleš Krejča, Jean-Claude Lemagny, Jiří Macků, Dr. Jiří Mašín, Sergei Morozov, Colin Osman, Varvara Rodchenko, Robert A. Sobieszek, Dr. Karl Steinorth, John Szarkowski, and Líba Taylor.

Last but not least, I should especially like to thank my husband and collaborator Vladimír Remeš for his critical comments, enthusiastic support and wise guidance.

Daniela Mrázková